Spooks

The Unofficial History of MI5 From the First Atom Spy to 7/7 1945-2009

Thomas Hennessey
& Claire Thomas

AMBERLEY

Acknowledgements

The authors which to thank a number of people without whose assistance this book would have taken considerably longer to complete: in particular the staff of The National Archives of the United Kingdom; the Imperial War Museum; the Northern Ireland Political Collection, the Linen Hall Library, Belfast; and to the Security Service for permission to use material from their website. We would also like to thank Linda Herviel, Elizabeth Cantello, Janet Allen and Su Bradley; particular thanks go to Kate Marsh and Simon Mills; Lesley Clay; Marion and Derek Hall; and Ross Gower of Nineteen80 Design and Illustration. Finally thanks to Emma, Susannah, Sam and John for putting it all in persprective.

This edition first published 2011

Amberley Publishing
Cirencester Road, Chalford,
Stroud, Gloucestershire, GL6 8PE
www.amberleybooks.com

© Thomas Hennessey & Claire Thomas 2009, 2011

The right of Thomas Hennessey & Claire Thomas to be identified as the Author of this work has been asserted in accordance with the Copyrights, Designs and Patents Act 1988.

British Library Cataloguing in Publication Data.
A catalogue record for this book is available from the British Library.

ISBN 978 1 4456 0267 7

Typesetting and Origination by Amberley Publishing.
Printed in Great Britain.

Spooks

To the memory of
Harry George Thomas
1947-1993

omnia vincit amor

Contents

1

SIME

The immediate problem facing Britain after the war was not, it seemed, the threat from a resurgent Soviet Union. It was the internal security of the British Empire. No where was this more apparent than in the Middle East. During the war, MI5's main Middle East interest arose out of the fact that it was an important centre of military operations and that in connection with those operations the Abwehr was concentrating its attention on the Eastern Mediterranean and the Middle East generally. Eventually, after being moved around different Divisions, responsibility for the region fell within B Division under Kellar. On the ground the counter-espionage and security organisations in the Middle East had 'naturally' developed from the small pre-war organisation under which a Defence Security Officer as the representative of the Security Service in Cairo sought to fulfil all the functions of the Security Service in Egypt; and maintained relations with the parent body in London and with the British Embassy in Cairo as well as with the various military, naval and air authorities. While the security organisations in the Middle East had expanded enormously they had to a great extent lost touch with developments in London and during 1940 and 1941 had received little benefit from London's developing experience and knowledge of the Abwehr and its ramifications. There had been no direct personal contact. The general confusion in the Security Service in London during the early stages of the war in part accounted for the failure to provide for close co-operation with Security Intelligence Middle East (SIME) which had developed out of the position of DSO when Brigadier Maunsell, the former DSO, had taken over the position of head of SIME as a section of the Middle East Intelligence (MEIC) in the summer of 1939. Another reason for the failure to keep the security organisations in the Middle East and other important centres abreast of MI5's increasing knowledge was to be found in the fact that no part of the organisation in B Division had been made specifically responsible for doing so. The position inside the Security Service was further complicated by the fact that a section known as Overseas Control in A Division had exercised its normal functions in regard to all overseas security organisations with somewhat loosely defined responsibility mainly concerned with the functions of A Division and D Division, i.e. the organisational and preventive sides of the work.

Various attempts to arrange for Brigadier Maunsell to visit London with a view to associating SIME more closely with the counter-espionage work of B Division failed, owing to the constant need for his presence in the Middle East in connection with developments in the military situation. (Lieutenant Colonel) TAR Robertson visited Cairo during March and April 1942. On his return he made a number of recommendations which closely agreed with similar recommendations made nearly a year later by (Brigadier) Dick White after a visit to Cairo in the beginning of 1943. The difficulties in adopting the recommendations as put forward in 1942 arose largely from the complicated position of SIME as part of the military staff of the command in the Middle East and its relations with naval security officers and with the Egyptian authorities, including the Egyptian police. White, in his report, pointed out that its work was considerably hampered by dependence upon military procedure and, in particular, by War Office establishment committees which prevented developments involving an increase of staff even though that increase appeared essential if certain badly needed improvements were to be made in the scope and quality of their work. So, White recommended that SIME should be amalgamated with the Security Service. Sir David Petrie, however, decided that in view of the difficulties the decision should be postponed until after the end of the war. The difficulties which he foresaw arose out of the assumption of responsibilities outside the three mile territorial limit and outside British territory which would involve adjustment with higher military authorities and with SIS; and out of the fact that amalgamation would involve a substantial addition to the budget of MI5.

In spite of these difficulties, White's visit resulted in substantial improvement as a result of the development inside the SIME organisation, of machinery based on the experience of B Division in the UK. Provision for this machinery was partly made by lending officers from B Division and secretarial and registry staff to work in SIME. White also recommended that an establishment on the lines of Camp 020 should be set up and that all these developments should be centrally co-ordinated by a new group at SIME headquarters to be known as B Division as its work was to follow the lines which experience had led B Division to develop in London. Subsequently visits to Cairo were paid from MI5, by Lord Rothschild (to instruct SIME in counter sabotage technique and recent developments). An important consequence of Robertson's visit was the development of arrangements for double-agent and deception work on the lines practised by B1.A in London. The scope and the extent of major double-agent work in the Middle East was determined by the operational situation in the Mediterranean theatre of war. This most important task, which has involved co-operation between Section V, Kellar's section and SIME, meant developing and maintaining a number of channels for the purpose of deceiving the enemy in conformity with the plans of 'A' Force which was responsible for operational planning to deceive the enemy by a variety of measures, including the notional movement of armoured divisions in the desert war. A number of secondary double-agent channels were also developed with the object of penetrating enemy intelligence organisations operating against the Middle East, including Iraq and Persia from Turkey. Information coming in from all sources was 'canalised' through Kellar's section as an 'area' section of B Division.[1]

CHEESE

The so-called CHEESE (or LAMBERT) case was probably SIME's most important XX. The case may be said to have begun with a letter from the War Office informing Cairo that a man described as a British subject whom the French had used as a 'double-cross agent', was on his way to Egypt. It was suggested that he would need help, but must be carefully watched, as his loyalty to the Allied cause was not above suspicion. On 12 September 1940 and again on 15 October, he visited the British Embassy, Belgrade, which reported that he was about to make his way to Egypt via Istanbul. He returned to Italy before doing so, and did not reach Turkey until 26 December 1940. He reported to the British Embassy there, but his journey was delayed by the fact that the Turks arrested him on a charge of belonging to a gang engaged in passport and currency frauds. Eventually his release was secured and his journey to Egypt facilitated.

Though classed as a British national by the War Office, 'CHEESE might be better described as an international adventurer'. Born in Italy, in 1902, of Italian-Jewish parents, he had spent his life in India (1903–13), Switzerland (1913–18), Italy (1918–26) and Australia (1926–37). In 1937, he returned to Italy. In November 1939 he was living at Genoa (where his mother owned a hotel) when he was approached by Dr Hans Travaglio, a leading member of the German Secret Service in Italy, who asked him to go to France as a spy. He immediately informed the British Consul at Genoa (who encouraged him to accept the German offer), and he reported, later, to British authorities in Paris. He worked for the Germans in France, double-crossing them by contact with the French authorities. The French were said to have mishandled his case, but detailed information was lacking.

After the collapse of France, he returned to Genoa. Here Travaglio approached him again, introducing him to his colleagues Major Helferich and a certain Rossetti, whose Christian name CHEESE gave as Clemans. He was instructed to go to Egypt, taking with him a W/T set, and an operator to work it, and to set up an organisation for collecting military intelligence and transmitting it back to Italy. Messages were to be written in French, and encyphered. The plan was approved by Count Scirombo, head of the Italian Intelligence Service in Italy. A visit was paid to Bari and it was arranged that CHEESE's W/T signals were to be received and answered. The Italians then made one change in the plans: CHEESE was not to take a W/T set with him as one was to be sent to him, perhaps by Hungarian Diplomatic Bag. He was given two questionnaires, one Italian, one German, and Scirombo provided him with the names and addresses of those to whom he could apply for assistance at Budapest, Belgrade and Sofia (a certain Eisentrager). He was told that, in any neutral country except Turkey, he could get help from the German Consul by enquiring for 'Abwehr Abteilung' and saying that he came on behalf of 'Emile of Genoa'; he was warned to avoid the German consulate in Turkey, for fear of drawing on himself the suspicions of the Turks or the British. In Cairo, he was to expect a message at the Carlton Hotel, enabling him to get possession of the promised W/T set. He was also to make contact with two former acquaintances of Scirombo – George Khouri and Madame Lina Vigoretti-Antonida. Acting on Scirombo's instructions, CHEESE travelled to Istanbul on a German passport, made out in the name of Renato Ludovici. At Sofia he interviewed Eisentrager. At Istanbul he visited the British Embassy and volunteered all the information about himself and his mission. He was accompanied by a wireless operator of the name of Fulvio Melcher. This man 'shared CHEESE's ill-luck in being arrested by the Turkish Police. He spent three weeks in gaol and, losing heart, returned to Italy as soon as he was released.'

CHEESE himself, provided with a British passport, finally proceeded to Haifa by sea. He was taken to Jerusalem and there interrogated by a representative of SIME, but no fresh information of any importance was obtained. He was then flown by RAF plane to Cairo, where he arrived on 19 February 1941. On arrival, CHEESE was placed in a hotel, not under surveillance, but in daily contact with an SIME officer, to whom he made his reports. He had brought with him £500, in sterling notes of £100. The promised note from the enemy was not awaiting him, and there was no sign of the W/T set. He was instructed to approach the two people in Cairo whose names had been given him.

He did so unaccompanied. CHEESE reported that Madame Vigoretti-Antonida was of 'no consequence. She was unintelligent and quite unresponsive to his hints and suggestions.' But he described George Khouri as 'more promising'. Khouri, a Syrian-born moneylender, was already known to SIME as having assisted in organising anti-British activities in connection with pre-war troubles in Palestine. He introduced CHEESE to a well-known Egyptian journalist, Habib Jamati, from whom CHEESE obtained a little information about Egyptian politics, which he passed on to SIME. CHEESE stated that he asked for further assistance from Khouri and even paid him money in return for a promise to collect information for transmission to the enemy.

The officer who handled CHEESE at the time was very uncertain how much of CHEESE's accounts of his conversations with Khouri could be believed. Khouri, when arrested in 1943, denied ever having met CHEESE. While this was 'undoubtedly a lie', it was considered possible that CHEESE met Khouri on one or perhaps two occasions, that Khouri refused to have anything to do with him, and that the accounts CHEESE gave of subsequent conversations with Khouri were 'sheer invention' on CHEESE's part. Before leaving Cairo, CHEESE told SIME that he had informed Khouri of the setting up of W/T communication, arranged for him to supply the operator with reports for transmission by means of a post-box, and promised to send him more money. In actual fact, no information was ever supplied through this postbox. But with or without Khouri's co-operation, communication with the enemy had to be set up. The promised W/T set from Italy had never turned up, but an amateur-built one was found, the work of an NCO at GHQ signals. The book-cypher code suggested to CHEESE by the Italians proved clumsy and unsuitable: an SIME officer devised a new substitution cypher. It was arranged that SIME should act as an imaginary spy-ring in Egypt, transmitting false information to Italy, while CHEESE returned to take charge of the reception at Bari. He was to stop *en route* at Istanbul and visit the German Embassy: he was provided with some misleading information on general matters, and a story was concocted about his own mission for the benefit of the enemy. This was, briefly, as follows:

1. that, after great difficulty, he had found an amateur W/T set which an Italian had been hiding in his house, and had bought it for £200.
2. that he had set it up in a flat in Heliopolis.
3. that he had secured the services of a certain (imaginary) PAUL

NICOSSOF as Morse (key) operator. This man was left rather vague. CHEESE subsequently told the Germans 'I believe he is a Syrian, but he told me he was born in Egypt.'

4. that transmissions should begin on 25 May 41 and continue twice weekly.

5. that CHEESE had given to NICOSSOF and his accomplices the balance of his £500 – after deducting expenses, the £200 for the W/T set, the money given to KHOURI, and many incidental items. This balance was reported as no more than £150. It is to be noted that, if the enemy takes the trouble to look back at their records of the case (supposing they have any proper records), he will conclude that he has a spy-ring working for over a year, paying out considerable sums to agents & contacts, with no financial resources beyond this original £150.

CHEESE's passport was 'cooked' to show his entry and exit from Egypt. He was flown back to Palestine, and sailed from Haifa to Turkey on 19 April 1941. As arranged, he visited the German Embassy at Istanbul; it proved necessary to pay a number of visits. CHEESE took with him written statements of his activities since leaving Italy, embodying the concocted story. These were given to Zahringer at the Embassy, but copies were left with SIME's authorities, to whom CHEESE also gave written reports of his interviews with Zahringer. CHEESE reported that Zahringer seemed very pleased with the work done in Egypt, and wanted to send him back there immediately, in spite of his own insistence that he must return to Italy for private reasons; but finally Zahringer received instructions from Berlin to facilitate CHEESE's return to Italy. CHEESE left Istanbul for Rome at the end of May 1941. With the 'doubtful exception' of one telegram no further communication was ever established with him. What hand he had in the W/T messages from Bari, and what his other activities had been were 'matters of guesswork only'. The following comments were made by the officer who handled CHEESE during the two months he was in Egypt, and who was in daily contact with him:

1. CHEESE's motives in working for us are difficult to fathom. He is, of course, a Jew, and says he wants to do something to help the Allied cause because it is fighting on behalf of the Jews. In addition, he obviously has considerable love of adventure, and enjoys the work for its own sake. He is very fond of women, and the work gives him opportunities of travel, and of handling large sums of money,

which he would not otherwise get. He showed no particular dislike for the Germans or the Italians; in fact he often described the good times the Germans had given him, and how friendly he was with TRAVAGLIO.

2. As a result of his successful activities in FRANCE, ITALY, TURKEY and then in EGYPT, he had acquired an amazing self-confidence and complete belief in his own ability to travel anywhere and deceive anybody.

3. He is a natural liar, capable of inventing any story on the spur of the moment to get himself out of a fix. He has very considerable intelligence and an inventive mind. For example, he invented cyphers of his own, but immediately grasped the advantages of the one which was put up to him and mastered it in a very short time.

4. I think there is little doubt that if he turns up after the war, he will ask, as a reward for his services, to be given British citizenship and allowed to go to Australia. As far as we can say at the moment (1.9.42) he has done us well and deserves consideration.

The initial attempts at transmission, beginning, as arranged on 25 May, proved unsuccessful: no reply or acknowledgement was received. After a technical examination, the conclusion was reached that the frequencies agreed upon were unsuitable and would need altering. Arrangements had been made, in case of W/T difficulties, for telegrams to be sent to CHEESE in Rome, via Istanbul, in a simple code, suggesting commercial dealings. By this means, the new frequencies were communicated. Further attempts at transmission were then made, and successful contact was at last established on 14, 17 and 21 July. Since that time, for a little over a year, messages were sent and/or received on most Mondays and Thursdays. Occasionally, by special arrangements, messages were exchanged on other days, and from early July 1942 there had been almost daily communication. The occasional lapses from the twice-weekly standard – particularly in the first three months of 1942 – may have been due to technical difficulties or to enemy slackness and loss of interest. But even in these months, SIME's signals were acknowledged at least once a week.

In the first three months (July–September, 1941), the messages sent out were not of any great importance: the art of deception by W/T agents had not yet been fully developed. During this time the amateur set was found unsatisfactory and abandoned in favour of an ordinary army set. The operator had also to be changed, at least twice, owing to illness. The enemy did not seem to have allowed these changes to arouse their suspicions. The organisation at Bari appeared to be 'very bad'. The encoding was 'particularly careless' and there was much repetition of questions. The 'slipshod methods' suggested that CHEESE himself was handling the job at the other end. By October–November, 1941, the organisation of deception was rapidly developing. Advanced Headquarters, 'A' Force, saw in CHEESE 'a possible opportunity for a decisive stroke'. 'A' Force dealt with purely military information (this included naval and air force items and movements of highly important individuals). The information despatched was gradually put on a far higher level, and close liaison was maintained between 'A' Force, SIME and the Operational authorities.

'One device developed at this period is well worth a mention': as CHEESE's reports to Zahringer had been vague on the subject of the personnel of his spy-ring, 'it was difficult to be precise about the methods supposedly being used to collect information in Cairo without queering his pitch in Italy, where he might have been elaborating stories of which we had no knowledge. It was therefore suggested in our second message (21 July) that we had got into touch with a "good South African contact" from whom information was forthcoming.' He was later (29 September) 'replaced' by a South African NCO, confidential secretary to a general, and in a position to acquire first-class information. Experience showed that the enemy 'is curiously unwary and eager to accept stories of the disloyalty of disgruntled Colonials, Irishmen, etc., and even of the supposed ex-members of the Fascist organisations in England. Our imaginary figure (nicknamed PIET) was however provided with subsidiary motives, and represented as in great difficulties over women and money.'

Owing to the 'extreme meagreness' of the funds that CHEESE had left behind, the imaginary PIET had to act his part on promises rather than cash. But he appeared to have done so convincingly. 'As far as we can judge, the enemy swallowed PIET whole. He certainly proved a useful excuse for transmitting high-grade intelligence which would have been quite beyond the reach of CHEESE's associates.' This intelligence was best summed up in a telegram despatched much later (6 January 1942) to 'Snuffbox, Oxford' from which the following is an extract:

Have been officially informed that LAMBERT [CHEESE] was main source by which successful deception recently achieved, resulting in complete strategic surprise at outset of Western Desert campaign. Without Lambert, main theme of deception plan which was put over on 20/10 & 27/10 could not have reached enemy before 18/11. This very satisfactory and completely justifies care and trouble taken. LAMBERT still in touch but doubt further utility...

During November–December 1941, 'there was no indication in the W/T traffic that the enemy realised how seriously he had been fooled. He still sent promises of money and demands for military information in much the same style as before, and on 1 Jan 42, even sent good wishes for "bonne collaboration dans la nouvelle année".' Information reached SIME from Most Secret Sources that the enemy had lost confidence in CHEESE. From similar sources came the report that CHEESE himself was arrested (SIME subsequently heard that he was released after some two to three months) presumably on suspicion of having had a hand in the deception.

But after the New Year message of good wishes, there was a marked change. The enemy frequently failed to reply to, or even acknowledge, SIME's signals, and contact was seldom established more than once a week. His messages showed far less interest in military matters, and few questions were asked on military subjects. Traffic continued sporadically on the subject of the money which was said to be on its way, but enemy messages were such 'as to lead us to suspect that traps were being set. It was for instance proposed that the enemy should send the money to Istanbul, and that we should send someone to fetch it. This looked very like an attempt to kidnap a British agent... or at least to learn more of our organisation. We toyed with the suggestion over some messages, pleading lack of money for the journey and suggesting that we might find a "neutral merchant" to act as intermediary. A scheme was tentatively laid on for action at Istanbul, but the enemy appeared to lose interest, and it was not thought wise to persevere.' In retrospect, it was perhaps 'not fanciful to describe the enemy's messages as those which might be expected from one who was trying to keep the source still open, for its own sake, with little or no assistance (eg questionnaires) from those who were interested in it as a reliable channel for military information. And in spite of occasional spurts of energy, the business was conducted in a somewhat half-hearted way.'

Between January and July 1942 – that was between the time when SIME received the report 'LAMBERT still in touch but doubt further utility', and the time when SIME began to receive subsequent reports, again from Most Secret Sources, that the enemy was regarding the source as 'credible' (4 July), 'trustworthy' (12 July) and arranging for direct communication of SIME's messages from Cairo to CHEESE in Rome to be sent from Athens to the HQ of the Panzer Armee in Libya – other messages SIME began to receive indicated 'a renewed eagerness on the part of the enemy for military information and the unprecedented request (on 2 Jul 42) for <u>daily</u> transmissions in place of the usual twice-weekly ones'. SIME found it 'impossible to be certain how this re-establishment was effected'. The probable contributory factors, it was thought, apart from the 'general unwariness and inefficiency of the enemy', were: the building-up of a new 'spy-story'; the handling of military information; and W/T procedure.

All 'outside evidence' received by SIME went to show that, since the Italian declaration of war and the prompt internment of Italians suspected of espionage, the enemy had been starved of reliable and up-to-date intelligence from Egypt. He was 'consequently doubly greedy for it, inclined to swallow bad (in the absence of good) information, and careless in his correlation and checking up'. Though CHEESE was originally recruited by a predominantly German organisation, it seemed that the arrangements for his journey, W/T set, etc., were in Italian hands, and he himself complained to Zahringer of the inefficiency of the arrangements. The handling of the CHEESE messages was done at Bari, and linguistic evidence (the Italianate idioms embedded in the French of the messages) seemed to show that the translation, and possibly the writing, of the messages was in Italian hands: 'Perhaps the whole case was being handled by Italians, and handled with a laziness and carelessness that Germans would not have tolerated.'

It had been plausibly suggested by officers within SIME that, some time in the early summer of 1942, a new director of intelligence took over (perhaps in view of Rommel's offensive) and demanded more information from Egypt. Since this demand could not be satisfied from really reliable sources, CHEESE's case was quoted as at least a working proposition. 'Its murky past may have been concealed or minimized: the [British] deception of Nov '41 explained away or ignored.' It was possible that CHEESE, released from prison in Rome 'with a new stock of plausible ingenuities on his tongue, may have had a hand in re-establishing what he had originally foisted on his employers, and found them once more ready to be deceived. All this must naturally remain pure speculation. If true, it leads to the pleasing conclusion that "wishful thinking" is not a monopoly of the democratic peoples.'

As the events of November 1941 had presumably discredited CHEESE's imaginary spy-ring in enemy eyes, 'it was clearly wise to represent it as falling (and finally fallen) to pieces'. The fact that no money had been received for a year made this story plausible – 'indeed somewhat overdue'. The fact that the enemy had never enquired into the membership or circumstances of the ring made it easy to fabricate. Constant 'whines' for money were sent to Italy. The enemy's suggestion that CHEESE himself might return with funds was warmly welcomed. When neither he nor the money appeared, the gang was represented as finally dissipated. While the (true) fact of George Khouri's internment was reported, 'the other absconding members were left in their original anonymity'. But the enemy was encouraged to conclude that the agents who had 'so sadly misled him in November would no longer be sending inaccurate or poisoned intelligence'.

Attention was concentrated on the one name that CHEESE had left SIME – Paul Nicossof, the imaginary W/T operator. It was implied that he was ignorant of military matters and only able to answer such questions as were within the range of the ordinary man in the street. 'Then more difficult matters were broached, he pleaded lack of funds to hire agents. He transmitted "Suis seul" and "Suis à bout". He threatened to sell or pawn the W/T set to pay the debts which he implied he had accumulated. He grew sarcastic and even impudent about the never-ending stream of false promises to which the enemy treated him.' It was possible that, but for an unforeseen event, 'these efforts to keep him "in character" and make his story consistent might have landed him in an <u>impasse</u>. He could hardly carry on indefinitely without money. His patience (like Hitler's) would have had to be exhausted sooner or later. He would have had to close down. Such a closing down would not, at the time, have been regarded as a great loss. The value of the military information sent was negligible: the attempt to use his appeals for money in order to trap other enemy agents (or at least learn more of enemy organisation) seemed quite unsuccessful. The failure to obtain any money meant that "PAUL" could not go on indefinitely: but it also seemed a sign that the enemy had lost interest, and that it was not worth our going on.'

But then the 'unforeseen event occurred, justifying our pertinacity'. The Germans began to advance on the Libyan front. Their intelligence service 'naturally became hungrier than ever' for Egyptian information. At the same time, Nicossof was provided with a new and excellent motive for continuing, and 'feverishly multiplying' his activities. He could now begin to picture himself as 'the man who brought Rommel into Egypt', dream of the entry of the Panzer Armee into Cairo and imagine high German officers hastening to his hotel to thank him, pay all his debts, and load him with money and medals. While 'protesting violently against the inexplicable' inefficiencies of Bari, and the danger into which they put him, Nicossof began to 'show a new energy and enterprise'. Messages were even prepared to indicate that he was beginning to suffer from the 'monomania common among successful spies; it was not thought advisable to send these, and it was clearly becoming unnecessary to do so. CHEESE seemed to be completely re-established, and on the most favourable lines. The enemy had been given every excuse for forgetting the past: new contacts, which PAUL represented himself as making, could be continued or dropped at will: mistakes and deceptions could be explained away on the plea of lack of funds, or of PAUL's unfamiliarity with the business of collecting military information. Prospects were good either for a renewed course of misleading and fogging enemy intelligence, or, with good luck, for a large and more decisive stroke.'

The W/T messages sent over between January and June 1942, contained the minimum of military information. Few questions and no formal questionnaires were received from the enemy. Doubts as to whether or not 'he was trusting us made it dangerous to answer what was sent, or to volunteer information. And the particular spy-story which was being "put across" naturally confined military intelligence to the lowest grade and the meagrest proportions.' Between 1 January and 25 June 1942, only three items of military intelligence were sent:

1. Planning of an American Aircraft factory near Cairo. (Enemy enquiries about site, capacity, etc., were first evaded, then answered with the excuse that the agent who supplied the original information had disappeared.)

2. American Officers and Soldiers seen in streets. (Enemy enquiries for further details were met with a brief reply giving three shoulder-badges noticed).

3. The address of GHQ in Cairo was correctly given. (This had been asked for, and correctly answered, nearly a year before. The address is such common knowledge throughout the M[idle]E[ast] that a trap was suspected. But it is possible that the enemy is even more ignorant of conditions in Egypt than we suspect. His second enquiry may imply that he had lost record of the first, or that he thought there had been a move).

This was the sum total of military information transmitted. The enemy's questions on other points (location of 23rd Infantry Division, location of Polish, Free French and Colonial Units, and shipping intelligence from the Canal zone) were either ignored or answered with the plea 'No money. No agents to collect information'. It was not till the latter half of June that anything further was transmitted. Even then, the matter supplied was at first of low grade, though, in order to build up confidence, it had to contain a high proportion of truth. Advanced HQ, 'A' Force was fortunately able to supply the enemy with information that he already possessed, new items that were unlikely to be of use to him, or truth that would probably confuse him more than a deliberate lie.

It had been arranged with CHEESE that, while the actual messages were to be put into the newly-devised cypher, discussion over the air of such things as frequencies, times of contact, requests for repetitions and so on, should be carried on in what was called the Amateur Code, an international convention established among W/T amateurs before the war: 'It is safe to say that, had this arrangement not been made, and had all traffic been restricted to cyphered messages, communication would have repeatedly broken down altogether.' It was discovered that this Amateur Code gave scope, not only for technicalities, but for 'a quite surprising range of familiarities' – apologies, greetings, confidences, and even such messages as 'Hope to meet you after the War!' It was occasionally so used by the 'extremely intelligent Sergeant of Signals (an ex-amateur) who has represented PAUL NICOSSOF in his capacity of W/T operator during the last nine months. Latterly, he was taken into confidence about the particular mood in which PAUL would be transmitting. It is believed that much verisimilitude was added to the encyphered messages by timely suggestions of danger and urgency and, on other occasions, of ease and good-fellowship. It is certain that something was learnt of the enemy's W/T operators and of how best to deal with their vagaries.'

An officer familiar with the whole background of the case was present at each transmission, giving the Sergeant a rough outline of what was required and dictating such things as promptness or delay in replying, courtesy, irritation or warnings. The enemy's requests for fuller and more frequent information increased, his mistakes in cyphering, failure to keep appointments and general inefficiency of W/T procedure, 'increased to such an alarming extent that it was at one time feared we were going to lose contact altogether'. The W/T experts called in to advise on this 'curious aberration came to the conclusion that the fault lay almost entirely with the enemy'. This 'greatly strengthened' the impression that there was extremely imperfect co-operation at

Bari between the Directors of Intelligence, eager for information from Egypt, and the staff at their disposal, 'disinclined to take much trouble or ensure its proper reception'. The imaginary PAUL was made to send protests and pathetic appeals, but it was thought inadvisable to make them too emphatic, 'in case the culprits should begin suppressing his messages to conceal their own inadequacies, from their superiors'. All of this meant that, in 1942, CHEESE was 'still in action, and it is hoped that he will long remain so, to the better confusion of His Majesty's enemies'.[2] The Germans considered the intelligence so valuable that they established a special wireless to Rommel's HQ Panzer Armee Afrika to pass on CHEESE's reports.[3]

With Axis faith re-established in CHEESE, he was sent back to Cairo to continue transmitting intelligence to Italy. SIME retired the real CHEESE and, instead, completely took over sending the messages themselves. As Captain C.H. Roberts recalled, CHEESE's background as far as the Italians and the Germans were concerned in the middle of 1942 was thus:

His '*crise de nerfs*' in mid-July 1942 indicated that his mode of living wasn't normal.

A man of mixed Caucasian and Syrian parentage – temperamental – shrewd – not without considerable courage – a skilled W/T operator and mechanic – living in hourly danger of detection and death yet proud of his ability to elude the attention of the British Intelligence Service – he lived on his wits – awaiting the reward for his services to the Axis.

In July he found an 'amie' – a Greek girl animated by hatred of the British – well-educated – intelligent witty and courageous sustaining him when discouraged or disgruntled – she aided and abetted him by forming a series of friendships – and possibly 'alliances' – with British and American officers – military and Air Force.

From these she extracted information of varying degrees of reliability and importance. This enabled CHEESE to supplement information gleaned from his Greek military friends – and other acquaintances.

Without funds – he could no longer employ reliable agents. All information – whether high level or low – true or false – he passed on to his Axis friends – leaving them to sift the chaff from the wheat.

Those sources that misinformed him he discarded, and thus always had the requisite retort if and when accused of passing on false information.

For instance – On August 17th 1942 he said that he was sorry for having given false information but without money he had to collect such information as his friends told him and report what he saw himself.

He chose a flat in HELIOPOLIS from which to work; because its proximity to military W/T installations guaranteed his transmitting set from detection.

He was suspicious of his neighbours and said so on September 23rd 1942. On several occasions he has declined to transmit over extended periods because of the danger in which his prolonged use of direct current from 'mains' might involve him.

Uncertainty of livelihood – curtailment of his Black Bourse activities and the non-arrival of funds from his Axis partners finally forced him to find regular employment.

After trying from December 7th 1942 until December 25th he secured a post as an interpreter… commencing his duties on January 1st 1943.

His amie continues to collaborate. He mentioned her first to the Germans on July 24th – and on July 27th he said that she could decode already and was learning to transmit.

At the moment she is the active intermediary for collecting the money due to him – and both are anxiously awaiting its arrival.

Between 1 August 1942 to 16 February 1943 an informal committee – which (under the direction of the Commander, Advanced HQ 'A' Force really constituted CHEESE) – had built up, and passed over successfully, no less than six major items. These, Roberts and SIME believed, 'engendered six serious headaches!' Despite these items, Most Secret Sources informed SIME that CHEESE was still quoted as 'reliable' and 'authentic. 'In addition CHEESE maintained a steady stream of low-level information, of which a high proportion was true.

A number of messages sent by the imaginary CHEESE included a good number of complaints about money while some embodied details of plans to get money to him. These messages gave 'a good picture of CHEESE's temperament. They run the gamut of his emotions; rising from pathetic whines to a crescendo of angry – not to say violent – accusations of hypocrisy and deliberate deceit; then dying down to a disgruntled "no money – no information".' In response to the enemy's 'provocative replies' to his complaints in August 1942, he had evolved, and the enemy had accepted, a plan by mid September, whereby a Greek merchant friend went (27 September) to Aleppo to collect CHEESE's money. The friend, scared by the execution of five Axis spies at Aleppo a few days previously – returned 4 October and CHEESE abandoned this plan. 'He was very discouraged.'

During October a plan – complete in detail to dates, time, place, recognition and passwords – was evolved. The money was to be expected between 10–15 November. This plan fell through also (possibly because of the 8th Army's activities at this time). On 21 November, CHEESE 'blows up', and, as a result received, on 7 December the news 'that the money is already in his town'. This 'electrifies' CHEESE. He finds a friend's flat ('amie' having given up hers through lack of funds) where 'amie' could receive the money. This was to be delivered by a 'hamel' (porter or native labourer) in either a bottle of milk or in 'a packet'. But the flat was (factually) raided by the Egyptian police. This gave CHEESE 'a severe attack of the "jitters"'. He passed on this news on 17 December, and said his 'amie' was looking for another and safer place. On 20 December 'he tells the enemy that the police raid was a domestic affair; but he is badly frightened'. However, 'he borrows the money for and finds another (quite safe) flat – installing "amie" by 15 January 1943. He asks the enemy to divert the courier to the new address. They reply that they will try their best, but doubt whether it will be possible to do so. On 6 February the enemy confirms that it is impossible to effect the desired change, and filled with an increasing anxiety, CHEESE now awaits the courier's arrival at the former address.'

During this period CHEESE – in reality the person of Sergeant Shears – faced and overcame numerous technical difficulties. Of the 163 occasions when he was on the air as many as 24 transmissions were unsuccessful, due to four causes: 1. Bad atmospheric conditions – (particularly October – November); 2. Heavy interference; 3. Incompetence or laziness of enemy operator; 4. Enemy 'not on the air'. The third cause became so bad that on 21 October that CHEESE (Shears) registered a complaint 'in no mean terms. This had the effect of bringing new operators into action.' The enemy now used 6 operators whom SIME called:

1. The 'original' for whom CHEESE has a high regard.
2. The 'goon' – a dull-witted and lazy operator.
3. 'Curt' – so called from his style.
4. 'Good' – an expert 'Ham' operator.
5. 'New Good' – first appeared late in Dec. 1942.
6. 'Square Morse' – a good operator who sends in Continental style.

The code used was 'somewhat cumbersome' although SIME evolved a style – over a period of several months – that was distinctive, and which could be picked up in a day by a new cipher officer – if need be. This style used 16 variants for each letter – before any one was repeated. SIME believed that to break down this code – so used – would entail 'very considerable trouble' over a prolonged period. The shortest message sent contained 15 groups – and the longest 270. The enemy used two encoders – 'one of whom is lazy and careless – sometimes shockingly so. He causes endless trouble when we have to decode his "messages". Neither displays any desire to use more than a minimum of variants for any given letter, and from a Security "intercept" point of view – both are criminally careless.' The cypher devised for CHEESE was an extension of the familiar PLAYFAIR system. The keyword was written down (omitting any repeated letters) as the beginning of a square of 5 letters by 5. This square was then filled by writing down the rest of the alphabet omitting all letters already used. In order to reduce the alphabet from 26 letters to 25, it was also necessary to omit 'K'. Thus, if the keyword was ELEMENTS the square would be:

```
E L M N T
S A B C D
F G H I J
O P Q R U
V W X Y Z
```

Each letter of the 'clear' was represented by a pair of cypher letters. The first letter of the pair might be *any* letter in the same vertical line as the letter to be enciphered: the second was any letter in the same horizontal line. Thus LD represented A, UM represents T, etc. The cypher differed from PLAYFAIR, in that there were 16 alternative ways of enciphering any given letter. E can be enciphered as SL, SM, SN, ST, FL, FM, FN, FT, OL, OM, ON, OT, VL, VM, VN or VT. 'K' being omitted from the square, was the signal for numerals. The first two lines of the square, following 'K', became the figures 1 (E), 2 (L) etc., up to 0. The signal for 'numbers off' was the letter G *encoded*, i.e. AH, WJ or the equivalent. The letters standing for numerals had also to be encoded: 1 was not represented by E but by SL, OT or its equivalent. It was arranged that the third word of each message should be the keyword for the next. Thus if a message (say on Monday) began with the words 'Argent pas encore arrive' the square for Thursday's message would be as follows:

```
E N C O R
A B D F G
H I J L M
P Q S T U
V W X Y Z
```

In case of emergency or doubt, a standard keyword was arranged. If it was not known whether the cypher side had or had not received the last message or was likely to make any mistake about it, the square was to be constructed on the keyword EQUINOX. To indicate that this was being done, the first group of the message was to be SCOOI. 'This precaution proved a wise one. Owing partly to the incompetence of the enemy, partly to technical troubles, the emergency codeword has had to be used over and over again.' It would be 'clear to the expert that, in spite of the alternatives, the cypher does not present any very grave difficulties to the "cracker". This did not matter, so far as we were concerned, though it should have caused the enemy some anxiety, had he been alive to our W/T security precautions. Meanwhile it was easy and quick to work, and (with a little care) free from possible ambiguities.'[4]

For SIME the benefits of the case began to dry up in 1944 when it tried to 'export' CHEESE to Greece, leaving behind his girlfriend – MISANTHROPE – to continue operating the W/T in Cairo. The Germans provided CHEESE with elaborate instructions as to where to find a W/T and money which they said they had buried in an Athens suburb. When British troops occupied Athens an SIME officer searched for the W/T but could not find any trace of it. Consequently it was impossible to establish contact with the enemy from Athens. MISANTHROPE informed the Germans of the W/T's absence. The Germans proposed alternative arrangements, instructing MISANTHROPE that CHEESE should contact a certain Greek whose address they provided. Discreet enquiries were made by SIME in Athens but no trace of this person was found; later SIME found that the individual had been arrested by the Greek Deuxième Bureau in January 1945 together with his W/T. After this, SIME decided to wind down the CHEESE – MISANTHROPE deception so that no suspicion that might fall on the case had an impact on other XX cases still be exploited.[5]

2

God's Chosen Terrorists: Palestine

The threat to British national security from religious
fundamentalists is not something that the Security Service has
had to contend with only at the beginning of the twentieth
first century: in the immediate aftermath of the Second World
War, MI5 – both at home and in Palestine through SIME
– was drawn into the militant desire to create an independent
Jewish state in the Middle East. The immediate threat to British
interests appeared to be not from an expansionist Soviet Union
in Europe but from internal threats to the British Empire.

The growth of Zionism presented the British with problems before
and during the Second World War. An SIME paper, prepared in 1943, to
answer a request for a statement of the Zionist problem would serve as
a background for Defence Security Officers in the Middle East, 'exposed
to Zionist political influences'. SIME reported that it had become
evident in the last ten years that Zionism could be treated as a single
phenomenon, either chronologically or psychologically, but that it had a
number of aspects:

1. The age-old desire, inspired by religious sentiment, of the Jews
scattered through the world (the 'Diaspora') to return to the Land of
Israel (Eretz Israel). It is difficult for a non-Jew to assess the depth or
extent of this desire; it may be broadly said however that, throughout
the centuries that have passed since the destruction of Jerusalem in
70 AD and the collapse of the Jewish national spirit, it has been
felt intensely only by a small minority, but that in ever-decreasing
intensity it has always been present in the minds of ever-widening
circles of those who share the Jewish faith, so that only in those
who have completely allowed their religion to lapse has it ceased to
strike a chord of home-sickness. Although some Jews have returned
to their Promised Land, especially in the last hundred years, the
concrete expression of this religious Zionism remained until recently
nebulous, owing to the seeming impossibility of its realisation.

2. (a) During the 19th century however, Zionism began to take on
a more practical shape; wealthy Jews in Western Europe, such as

Moses Montefiore and Baron Edmond de Rothschild, took an interest and lent their support in establishing settlements of their poorer co-religionaries in Palestine; and there were not a few Anglo-Saxon Protestant visionaries who, schooled from their childhood in the Old Testament, dreamed that the scriptures might be fulfilled and that a Jewish Kingdom might again be established in the Holy Land.

2. (b) From 1880 onwards the practical settlement of Jews in Palestine, with the approval of the Ottoman Sultans who still ruled the land, began to outstrip theorizing about political Zionism; but in 1896 a young Viennese Jewish press-correspondent named Theodore Herzl… was moved by the disgust inspired in him by the <u>affaire Dreyfus</u> to write a book called 'The Jewish State', in which he declared that the only escape for the Jews from Gentile oppression was for them to have a national state of their own… The publication of Herzl's book marks the beginning of <u>political Zionism,</u> or in other words of Jewish nationalism… attention must here be directed to the fact, so unfortunate for the peace of the Middle East, that the growth of Zionist nationalism has coincided in time almost exactly with the 'Arab Awakening'… The war of 1914–18, by bringing about the ruin of the Ottoman Empire, greatly accelerated the pace both of Zionism and of Arab nationalism… and early in 1917 the Balfour Declaration was… published:

'His Majesty's Government view with favour the establishment in Palestine of <u>a national home for </u>the Jewish people, and will use their best endeavours to facilitate the achievement of this object, it being clearly understood that nothing shall be done which may prejudice the civil and religious rights of existing non-Jewish communities in Palestine, or the rights and political status enjoyed by Jews in any other country.'

But no official clarification of the vague term 'national home' was ever made. Nor do the statesmen responsible for the Declaration and its implementation seem to have appreciated that the 'existing non-Jewish communities in Palestine', whose civil and religious rights were to be safeguarded, actually numbered more than 90 per cent of the total population, and that a few at least of their natural leaders had taken part before and during the war in the Arab nationalist movement. The Churchill White Paper of 1922 affirmed that the Balfour Declaration 'did not contemplate that Palestine as a whole should be converted into a Jewish National Home'. Article 4 of the Mandate for Palestine had laid down that 'An appropriate Jewish agency shall be recognized as a public body for the purpose of advising and cooperating with the Administration of Palestine in such economic, social and other matters as may affect the establishment of the Jewish national home and the interests of the Jewish population in Palestine and, subject always to the control of the Administration, to assist and take part in the development of the country.'

The Zionist Organisation, so long as its organisation and constitution were in the opinion of the Mandatory Power appropriate, 'shall be recognized as such an agency'. The effect of this article was to confer on the Jewish community in Palestine (the Yishuv) a considerable measure of self-government, 'and to transform the Zionist Organisation into something like a department of state, responsible however primarily to the Jewish community and only indirectly to the Mandatory Administration'. No provision had been made in the Mandate for any comparable body representing the Arabic-speaking majority, which might advise and cooperate with the Administration on its behalf.

Thus, Article 4 of the Mandate had handed to the Zionist Organisation the official representation of the interests of the Jewish population in Palestine, even though by no means all of the Jews in Palestine were political Zionists. The Jewish population, which had been estimated at about 66,000 in 1920, had more than doubled itself by 1929; by the middle of the Second World War it had risen to about the half million mark, and its proportion of the total population had increased from less than 10 per cent in 1919 to more than 35 per cent. And, on to the original claims of the political Zionists, there had been grafted a Jewish refugee problem, 'which, it is safe to say, was never contemplated by the British Government that approved the Balfour Declaration and obtained for itself the Mandate for Palestine. This problem, which with the rise of the Nazi terror and its extension over Europe has come to involve potentially millions of Jews, has in its essence no connection with either Palestine or Zionism. It is clear that the question of finding a home for hundreds of thousands or millions of people has to be answered practically, not by ideological or sentimental solutions. But the Zionists, by steadily insisting on a Zionist solution of the problem, have consistently sought to involve it with Zionism and Palestine.'[1]

Broadly, as a later appreciation put it, 'there are two main currents in political Zionism to-day'. Firstly there were those Zionists – commonly referred to as 'Old Zionists' – who in the main followed in the wake of the Jewish Agency, the body established in Palestine under the terms of the Mandate for the purpose of representing the interests of the Jewish population vis-à-vis the British administration. 'Many Jews of this particular political persuasion would have been satisfied before the war with the establishment of a Jewish National Home according' to the terms of the Balfour Declaration. 'To-day however they are mostly unanimous in demanding a Jewish state, though there are divisions in their ranks, and there have lately been signs of a cleavage between the more moderate elements' typified by Dr Weizmam, the elderly Zionist leader, and those who followed the leadership of younger and more violent exponents of Zionism, such as Ben Gurion, a prominent representative of Jewish Labour and Chairman of the Zionist Executive. Closely associated with Gurion were Moshe Shertok, Head of the Jewish Agency's Political Department in Jerusalem, and Berl Locker, Secretary of the Agency in London, while David Linton, Assistant Secretary, 'had hitherto steered a middle course.'

The extremist wing in Zionist politics had been represented since 1923 by the 'New' Zionist organisation and whose members called themselves 'Revisionists', which was founded in that year by the late Vladimir Jabotinsky, a Jew of Russian origin 'who had had a not undistinguished service' during the 1914–18 war, 'and who for many years was an idol' second only to Weizmann in Zionist eyes, particularly among the extremists. Since its foundation, the Revisionist aim had been the immediate establishment of a Jewish State comprising both Palestine and Transjordan, and it had fought a continuous battle for ascendancy over the Jewish Agency.[2] The wartime SIME report noted how a large party among the Zionists had by now become convinced that a show of strength was sufficient to force the hand of the irresolute British Government. As Jabotinsky put it in 1932: 'A declaration of a Minister or a High Commissioner does not mean a firm decision of the Government, and a firm decision by Government does not mean that it will insist on it after a year. Furthermore, even if Government insists on its decision after the lapse of a year, it does not mean that it would be able to execute it. There is always a great distance between the intention and the possibility of carrying it out.'

By 1935 there had been sporadic Arab terrorism against Jewish settlements, and in April 1936, 'one or two trivial acts of violence, of a kind to which the country had become inured, provided the spark from which the Arab Rebellion blazed forth'. In the countryside the disorders soon crystallised into organised Arab guerrilla warfare directed against the Jewish settlements and the British troops who were hastily brought into Palestine to suppress the Rebellion. 'For the Army and Police, the Arab guerrillas were the enemy, and they naturally therefore welcomed the Jews as allies. A corps of Jewish Settlement Police was formed and armed and urban Jews recruited as auxiliary policemen. Throughout the three years of the Rebellion the alliance between the Jews and the British forces of order was close.' A British Commission, set up to inquire into the causes of the Rebellion, came to the conclusion that there was no hope of lasting peace in Palestine under the existing Mandate and recommended, broadly speaking, the partition of Palestine into a Jewish and an Arab state, the latter to be united with Transjordan.

During the first four years of the World War, observed the SIME appreciation of 1943, the half-million Jews of Palestine 'have insisted on taking their place as one of the Allied Nations in the struggle against the Axis. There can be no doubt of their passionate sincerity in this, or of the largeness of their contribution to the war-effort in proportion to their numbers. They have raised thousands of volunteers, men and women, for the forces, and have increased their numbers by methods of compulsion inside their community which amount to conscription. But they have continued to insist on their national identity as Jews, have protested against their inclusion in the Palestine Regiment, and have demanded through their spokesmen in Britain and the USA the formation of a Jewish Army, to take its place alongside the other Allied armies.' Since this would have meant the tacit recognition of a Jewish National State, 'at any rate potentially', the British Government had resisted it, but had conceded the formation of Jewish units inside the Palestine Regiment. These units had assumed the right to wear the Jewish colours and to play the Jewish national anthem.

But though the Zionists were virtually unanimous that the first aim of their disciplined men and women was the defeat of the Axis, 'they are no less unanimous that their immediate postwar aim is the attainment of the Jewish National State'. To this end they demanded the immigration of vast numbers of Jews in the immediate postwar period in order to present the Arab world with a fait accompli; Zionist politicians had spoken semi-officially of 'three million Jewish immigrants in the first two years'. They were actively making propaganda in Britain and the USA, and with the government of the USSR, and were seeking to strike a bargain with the Polish Government in exile, by which that Government should assist the Zionists to attain the transfer to Palestine of the millions of Jews who lived in Poland before the war. They were also exploiting the Allied conquest of North Africa to create a Zionist 'outlook' and recruit potential immigrants among the assimilated Jews of those countries.

British security forces and intelligence were faced with a new threat, in 1937, when Jabotinsky had founded the Irgun Zvai Leumi (National Military Organisation in the Land of Israel), an illegal paramilitary organisation although his sudden death meant that the Revisionists lacked effective leadership. More frank and outspoken than the Zionists proper they made no secret of the fact that they were ready to resort to force to overcome the resistance of the Arabs and, if necessary, the British Administration. 'However, as the pendulum of British policy had tended to swing away from the Zionist pole since 1937, the Zionist demands and intentions had steadily become more extreme until there was now virtually nothing to distinguish them from those of the Revisionists; and overtures for their reunion, which had been made from time to time, had apparently broken down only because of the clash of personalities.' Early in the war another small Revisionist gang, which had played an important part in reprisals against the Arabs in the later stages of the Rebellion, broke with the Revisionists over the question of continuing a policy of terrorism and reconstituted itself round a leader named Abraham Stern. 'Its methods were frankly terrorist', directed apparently chiefly against the police and Administration, and it also raided Jewish banks and held up rich Jews to provide itself with funds. SIME believed that it may have been the Stern Gang (which called itself Irgun Zvi Le-umi b Israel) that in Haifa harbour, early in 1941, blew up a shipload of Jewish refugees from Europe, whom the administration would not accept as immigrants into Palestine. Several hundred Jews were drowned; the intention of the outrage 'was presumably to create a major political issue and stampede the government into accepting further refugee ships'.[3]

In January 1942, the Stern Gang used a bomb at Tel Aviv to kill Deputy Superintendent Schiff, the local police chief, and Inspector Goldman; four other policemen were injured. Less than a month later the police gained their revenge when, on 12 February, Abraham Stern was traced by police in Tel Aviv and shot dead 'while attempting to escape'. Information leading to the tracking down of Stern was obtained by police through the secret censorship of notes smuggled out of Jaffa Hospital by two wounded members of the gang recently apprehended. Since the assassination of DSP Schiff, police investigations had led to the arrest of fifteen important members of Stern's gang while three others 'no less important' had surrendered themselves unconditionally. Within the short space of three weeks since the Schiff murder it was reported to the War Office that 'the untiring efforts of the police have resulted in practically the entire destruction of the brains of the gang including its leader'.[4]

So, SIME could, with some confidence, state, by 1943 that as the Stern Gang was never more than a few hundred strong and its active membership probably numbered under a hundred, it was 'thus a nuisance to the police and public and a danger to individual notabilities rather than a major threat to security' and declare that the chief significance of the Stern Gang 'is perhaps to the historian: they are the modern counterpart of the Jewish sicarii who, in the first century AD when Rome had annexed the Jewish Kingdom, carried on the struggle against Roman officials and their Jewish collaborators by assassination and were the militant nucleus round which the Jewish Revolt formed.'[5] Despite this success, it was not the Stern Gang that worried the DSO Palestine so much:

> It must be realised that while the great majority of the Jewish community in Palestine is law-abiding, there is a large paramilitary organisation of the General Zioniste, called the Hagan[a], which number many thousands of young men trained and disciplined on fascist lines, who would obey the order to rebel against the mandatory Government, if it were ever given by their political leaders... the Irgun... and the Stern Group... with their hold-ups and assassinations, are an immediate nuisance to the Palestine Police, but if after the war high policy should decide against the fulfilling of Zionist battalions of the Hagans, now quiet but united in their demand for as Eretz Israel large enough to contain several million Jewish inhabitants, might constitute a graver danger to Security than the small Jewish extremist groups or even the Arab Rebellion of 1936–1939.[6]

In March 1942, Jewish sources informed British Intelligence that the Hagana ('Defence') was not at the moment active to any appreciable extent, because the majority of its members were serving in one or other of the Forces. At that time there were approximately 10,000 Jews serving in His Majesty's Forces, 5,800 in regular police units, and 15,400 special policemen, all of whom had received training in arms. 'This gives a total of 13,200; to which had been added a number of boys and girls between the ages of thirteen and seventeen, who had been given an elementary training without the use of arms. There might be as many as 10,000 in this category.' A Jewish Agency official had recently remarked that there were approximately 30,000 men in the Hagana armed with 5,000 rifles, in addition to an unknown quantity of revolvers and machine guns.

Generally speaking, the Hagana and the Irgun Zevai Leumi – which the Jewish Agency estimated as having a membership of 1,000 although SIME thought 2,000 to 3,000 a more likely estimate – were inactive at this time, mainly because 'they are ostensibly defence organisations and are therefore only mobilised when the Arab bands are active. The danger of these two illegal organisations may only become apparent should Palestine Jewry receive a political setback after the war.' The Stern Group, while not completely destroyed, appeared to have produced a wave of revulsion amongst Palestine Jewry, and public bodies (such as the Tel Aviv Municipal Council) had issued proclamations urging the public to assist the authorities in tracing those responsible for the bomb outrages, murders and robberies. The Irgun Zevai had also issued statement dissociating itself from the Stern Group.[7]

Periodic outrages continued, however: in April 1942, just after an Assistant Inspector-General of Police had backed his car out from a garage and had driven off, an Arab servant picked up in the driveway two sticks of gelignite bound up with a detonator. These exploded in his hands and killed him. The subsequent investigation showed that the bomb had been attached to the underside of the car and connected in such a way as to explode when the electric current of the car was turned on, but the bomb had fallen off. Earlier in the day, children reported to the police that they had seen a suspicious looking object in the road near the house of the Inspector-General of Police and the British community school in the German colony. The police found a huge bomb filed with seventy sticks of gelignite and 6 lb of rivets attached to a long wire by means of which they could be actuated in an open field behind the adjacent Jewish suburb of Rehavia. The bomb was found to be of the same type as that found unexploded on the scene of the murder of the Deputy Superintendent Schiff at Tel Aviv in January, and of other similar attempts by the Stern Gang.[8] This, and further incidents, would confirm that the remnants of the Stern Group had rallied to new supporters – 'the ultra nationalistic, hysterically blood thirsty morbidly idealistic school of thought which was typified by Stern himself'.[9] But on 20 February 1944 a pamphlet was issued by the HQ of the Irgun Zvai Leumi addressed to the Jewish Nation. It stated:

> The IZL in Palestine who have taken it upon themselves the duty of realising the dream of Israel's awakening, have declared war on British political policy in Palestine, through which millions of Jews have been exterminated. British policy in general has placed all

Europe on the verge of destruction. The IZL has declared war. The IZL is active and will be active. Mischief makers are hereby warned that they must not turn the indignation of the masses of the Yishuv against the political policy of the Palestine Government into an internal struggle between ourselves. If you try to wipe out a Jewish fighting group, we will protect them. That group is mistaken. It tries to create an entirely new Zionism, and it has abandoned the ideas of HERZL… AND JABOTINSKY, but it is solitary and has no supporters. The members of the group are persecuted by the Police and their Jewish assistants… Today we have begun a holy battle. We shall fill the prisons again and we shall mount the scaffold. Even if we are persecuted and beaten, we shall not complain. We shall not give up… Our war is a sacred war, and GOD will help us. Amen.

The first indication of collaboration between the Stern Group and the Irgun was suggested when the IZL publication Hazit ceased attacks on the Stern Group. This was followed by a declaration on the part of the IZL that they would afford protection to Sternists.

Towards the end of May 1944, Zvi Ben Shaul Tabori, who had been arrested in a police roundup on 2 March, was tried by a Military Court for illegal possession of a pistol and ammunition. He refused counsel and made a statement in court in which he refused to acknowledge the court, stated that he derived his authority to posses the pistol from the Fighters for Freedom of Israel, the only authority he recognised in Palestine, and demanded the status of a prisoner of war. He was sentenced to seven years' imprisonment which was reduced by the General Officer Commanding to five years. On 19 June, Anchel Spiflmann (alias Israel Kauffman) and Malka Lerner (alias Chisia Shapira), arrested on 10 March in Tel Aviv, were sentenced by the Military Court to ten and four years respectively for illegal possession of arms and ammunition. These sentences were confirmed by the GOC. Both accused refused to plead or to recognise the court, both refused legal aid, and both demanded the status of prisoners of war. On 27 June sentence of death under the amended Emergency Regulations was passed by the Military Court on Rafael Barnebaum for illegally carrying a pistol, twenty-six rounds of ammunition, a hand grenade and a bomb, and discharging a revolver at a police constable. Like the persons previously tried, he refused counsel, and would not recognise the court, made a long statement and demanded treatment as a prisoner of war. The death sentence was commuted by the GOC to imprisonment for life. The Defence Security Office assessment of recent events was that:

> From the behaviour of these members of the Stern Group and the IZL it is clear that they regard themselves as martyrs; and it would appear that this attitude is being deliberately encouraged by the leaders of the organisation as a means of propaganda. Certainly they have succeeded in gaining the sympathy of an appreciable portion of the Jewish public, particularly the young, who are moved by such gestures as BIRENBAUM's singing of Hatikvah after the death sentence had been passed on him …Many of the members of these underground groups have suffered under Nazi persecution in Poland and elsewhere; this fact too induces a sympathetic understanding of their attitude in the public. There is also a strong tendency to compare these organisations to the resistance groups of occupied Europe.
>
> At first the attitude of both press and public was, superficially at least, one of strong condemnation. A campaign of unorganised violence was considered as most harmful to the Zionist cause. From about the middle of June, however, this attitude underwent a change. Although the terrorist were still condemned as acting against the interests of Zionism, stress was laid on their determination, courage and even heroism. After the death sentence had been passed on BIRENBAUM, this tone became more strongly marked.
>
> Petitions for BIRENBAUM's reprieve were submitted by persons representative of all shades of Jewish opinion; their reasons were in most cases vague even if sincere. Some pleaded that the offender was a misguided youth, whose crimes were comprehensible in view of the tragic circumstances in which he personally and Jewry as a whole at present found themselves; others claimed that the execution of a Jew would be unfitting in these days of wholesale persecution. Behind all these arguments lay the unspoken feeling among the mass of the Yishuv... of condemnation for the organisation and its methods, but of the sympathy and understanding for the individual. Elishu GOLOMB, the Hagana leader, is reported to have called a meeting of Jewish journalists and instructed them to plead for BRENBAUM's reprieve in their newspapers.

There was no doubt that had the sentence not been reduced both the Stern Group and the IZL 'would have made some attempt at revenge.

Even now further acts of terrorism are not unlikely, having regard to the avowed policy of the groups and the chagrin which the Sternists are probably feeling at having been cheated of an addition to their list of martyrs.' Though the police had made several successful hauls in recent weeks, it did not seem likely that they had succeeded in crippling the groups' resources either in material or in manpower; while the morale of the organisation has certainly not been broken. There had been a report of negotiations between the Hagana and the Stern Group, 'in which the latter were said to be prepared to promise to refrain from acts of violence provided that none of their members were sentenced to death, and that the police did not shoot and kill to prevent their escape. In return for this promise the Hagana were to provide funds and protection for the group.'

Reports also indicated that both the IZL and the Stern Group had in recent months received numbers of new recruits, many of whom were 'young people impatient of the apparent moderation and inactivity of the Agency and the more reputable Zionist institutions'. As police seizures showed, they possessed considerable quantities of explosives and equipment, in the use of which they had 'shown some proficiency', as well as arms and ammunition. Though they were not as well trained as a rule in the use of the latter as the Hagana, 'they are much less chary of using them'. In considering the 'fanaticism and reckless bravery' of these two groups, as well as the sympathy shown them by some portions of the public, 'it is interesting to see that most... Leaders of the Stern Group are Poles, many of whom have left Poland since the German occupation.' Nathan Friedman-Yellin, the present leader reached Palestine from Warsaw in 1941. In the IZL too, another leader Menahem Beigin, was a member of the Polish Forces.[10]

There were clearly divisions within the Jewish Agency between those sympathetic to the extremists and those wary of them. During April 1944, the Agency proposed to the British Palestine HQ conditions on which they were prepared to co-operate in the rounding up of Jewish terrorists. They would select twenty-five to fifty men to carry out the physical arrest of terrorists, and asked that these men be issued with firearms and blank permits, so that the police would not learn their names. The Agency would detain any terrorists so captured in various settlements and would inform HQ Palestine of their names, but not the place of detention. In return they asked for assurance that no Jewish settlement found to be harbouring a wanted person should be punished, and that if the police learnt the whereabouts of a fugitive they would not, while looking for him, search for arms at the same time. The proposals were not accepted by HQ Palestine.[11]

On the night of 22/23 August, attacks with bombs and firearms were made on District Police HQ and three police stations in Jaffa and Tel Aviv. A police vehicle was also ambushed on the Jaffa-Tel Aviv road. At one police station personnel were held up and fourteen rifles were stolen. Posters made of cloth bearing the badge of the Irgun Zvai Leumi and inscribed 'Danger – Mines' in three languages were placed at various places where mines had been laid in the road. A company of Royal Engineers assisted the police in carrying out searches and patrols. The police carried out intensive searches 'and checked with great success.' Several wanted men were apprehended including a member of the Stern Group who had escaped from Latrun Detention Camp and also the man who printed Stern Group pamphlets. Intelligence suggested that the affair at Tel Aviv was in the nature of a tryout against the strength of the police. If this were found to be successful attacks would be staged on police stations, among other targets, simultaneously, in Tel Aviv and Jerusalem. There was little doubt, according to the Defence Security Officer, that the Stern Group and the Irgun Zvai Leumi were obtaining considerable sums of money by threat from the Jewish population. In Tel Aviv, café owners and proprietors of restaurants seemed to be the 'most faithful field'. A report was received that the Irgun carried on 'negotiations' lasting seven days with the director of a bank in Tel Aviv: 'Since these outlaws have in the past proved that they have no scruples in carrying out their threats (which in most cases are death) one can appreciate the feelings of those threatened but on the other hand it could be a serious blow to the Extremist element should the source of financial supply be cut.'[12]

By January 1945 it had been learned 'through a tried Jewish source' what the views of 'responsible persons', within the Jewish Agency, on the position of the Stern Gang and the Irgun Zvai Leumi were. They were believed to represent the 'official' views of this body, 'but it does not necessarily follow that they correspond with the true facts':

1. As a result of the recent arrests, the effective strength of the Stern Gang has been reduced to about 80 members. The Irgun Zvai Leumi is believed still to have about 2,500 adherents.
2. Both terrorist organisations are thought to be short of money. Encouraged by assurances of Government protection, the attitudes of the Yishuv towards extortioners has stiffened very considerably and successful cases of blackmail are believed lately to have been few in numbers and not very productive.
The arms at present held by the organisations are not considered

sufficient to enable any large-scale attacks to be made against barracks or defended buildings; they are still adequate, however, for continuing attacks on selected persons.

3. Dissension is believed to have occurred in the ranks of the Irgun Zvai Leumi with the result that some of its leading members, followed by others of less importance, have now resigned. Most of these dissidents claim that they joined the organisation in the belief that it was composed of a body of idealists, but experience had convinced them that it had degenerated into a gang of racketeers. The threat, however, of reprisals from their brethren among the Yishuv has probably also been a deterring influence.

4. It is thought not unlikely that the two organisations may attempt some dramatic coup – particularly if the murderers of Lord Moyne are condemned to death. But it would be an act of desperation and not a sign of renewed strength.

The same members of the Jewish Agency claimed for the Yishuv, acting under the direction of the Agency, a considerable share of the credit for the alleged weakened state of the terrorist organisations. Arms captured by the police could have been replaced if the Agency had not backed the Yishuv in resisting demands for money. The 'moral outlawing' of the terrorists was also regarded as being the result of the Agency's influence on public opinion.[13] Perhaps as a sign of the pressure that the terrorists were under in Palestine, it was in the first quarter of 1945 that disturbing intelligence emanated from SIME: the subject was the possibility of terrorist attacks by members of the Stern Gang on 'certain high personages' in Cairo and London. Colonel Kellar of MI5 HQ had already been despatched from London to SIME in December 1944, returning early in 1945. In the report he submitted to Sir David Petrie he described:

one very disturbing report on the possible future activities of the Jewish terrorist organisation was submitted by the [Jewish]Agency Security Officers at a meeting which Colonel Hunlake [DSO Palestine] and I had with them shortly before I left Jerusalem. This was that the Agency had reason to believe – although they were without as yet any positive evidence – that the Irgun and /or Stern Group were now planting their agents abroad under cover such as that of merchant seamen and [British]Army personnel in units which were likely to take them out of the Middle Eastern area. This is a threat which we are bound to take seriously at home since some confirmation that this report has substance may be found in the fact that last summer pamphlets were discovered on the doors of certain Whitehall Departments criticising the British Government for its refusal to form a Jewish Army and signed 'National Military Organisation', the English name for the Irgun. We are not, however able to trace the matter further; it has only to be remembered that the Colonial Secretary [in London] is viewed in Palestine as strongly anti Zionist to appreciate that an attempt on his life and on those of other Colonial Office officials may well be made at home by the same type of fanatical member of one or other of these terrorist organisations as was responsible for the death of Lord Moyne... The Agency have undertaken to provide Hunloke with any convincing evidence they may receive on the matter and he will signal this to MI5 immediately. It is, however, for consideration whether, without awaiting for this latter information from Palestine, we should warn the Police here without delay of the facts as we know them at present.

At MI5, Petrie was in two minds about sending this material to Sir Alexander Maxwell at the Home Office, 'as it is very desirable to avoid starting a scare by circulating information of an alarmist character so long as it has not been reasonably well substantiated'. Concern in the Colonial Office, about the possibility of such attacks, however, put 'a somewhat different complexion on the matter and so I think you may be interested to have the more detailed story told by Kellar'. MI5 cabled to Hunloke whose reply, received on 30 March, was to the effect that he could add nothing to the following extract from a letter addressed by him to Colonel Kellar on St Patrick's Day:

> The I[nspector]G[eneral of Police] has, from what he quotes 'a source that in the past has proved reliable', information that among others listed for the attention of the STERN Group [is]... my poor old friend Eddie WINTERTON. We have been told by the Agency that the STERN Group have been endeavouring to get into any of the 3 services in the hope that this will facilitate travel abroad in order to keep an eye on leading English personalities. I naturally do not know, nor have I asked who this reliable police source is, but I feel it is not the Jewish Agency. It does sound probably rather far fetched, but on the other hand nothing is too far fetched for these fanatical assassins.

Hunloke had no indication of the cover to be used, but entry into Britain might well be obtained in any Service uniform. This, Petrie informed

Maxwell, 'is all I know on the subject, and although the information is still rather vague, it is nevertheless deserving of serious consideration. There is no doubt whatever of the desperate nature of the members of the STERN Group and that their... reach far is shown by the still recent murder of Lord Moyne. Cases of murder in this country at the hands of the instruments of terrorist gangs with headquarters far distant from it are the assassination of Sir William Curzon-Wyllie in 1910 (or 1911) and of Sir Michael O'Dwyer in 1939... I shall let you know if we hear anything further of substance.'[14]

In February 1946 MI5 received a telegram from Hunloke, informing them that the Palestine CID had learned from a good source that the Stern Group were likely to attempt the assassination of the High Commissioner and the GOC Palestine, following on these attacks with attempts on the lives of various Palestine police and Government officials. The DSO drew attention to a Stern Group broadcast on 31 January in which the High Commissioner was advised to prepare graves for his police and soldiers rather than to transfer their corpses to England. The broadcast concluded with the words 'his fate has also been doomed'.[15] Intelligence indicated that the Stern Group had recovered from its earlier setbacks and was becoming more ambitious and daring in its planning: in January 1946, MI5 had received a report from Palestine, indicating that the Foreign Secretary, Ernest Bevin, was being considered as a possible victim for assassination. In February, Hunloke informed London that a similar report had been received by the Palestine CID, from sources described as 'reliable'. According to this report, the Stern Group were training members for the purpose of sending them to the United Kingdom to assassinate members of His Majesty's Government, 'Mr Bevin especially mentioned.' The DSO Palestine considered that a recently reported presence of leaders of the Stern Group in Jerusalem might add some support to this account of special training activities. He added that the Group was receiving a steady flow of recruits, its present strength being estimated by CID at 500.[16]

Meanwhile, the clear and present danger to British assets remained in Palestine. On 25 April 1946, at approximately 8.45 p.m., some twenty to thirty Jewish terrorists commenced an attack on the Airborne Division's car park in Tel Aviv. Seven British soldiers were killed. The attack began with the throwing of an anti-personnel bomb into the car park, followed by heavy bursts of fire from adjoining houses. Under cover of this fire, the guard tent was rushed and two soldiers inside were killed in cold blood. Twelve rifles were stolen. Four other soldiers were shot and killed by fire directed at the car park. One Lance Corporal was fatally wounded and died in hospital. Police personnel in adjoining station opened fire on the attackers while retreating. Bloodstains indicated that casualties were inflicted. All approaches to the car park were mined prior to the attack. This seriously hampered the bringing of medical assistance to the casualties. The attack was carried out 'apparently with the object of causing maximum bloodshed'.[17]

Attacks such as these appeared to involve some degree of co-operation between the Hagana and the IZL and Stern Gang. But it also produced tensions within the Hagana. As SIME monitored tensions within that organisation, the DSO Palestine was able to report how influential members of the Jewish Agency had warned, in April 1946, that continued collaboration with the IZL and Stern Gang would force a split that could see a breakaway Hagana formed. The result was that the Hagana Command 'now finds itself in rather an awkward position. On the one hand it cannot sever relations with the extreme Right organisations, and on the other hand, it can't foresee what will happen if it fails to comply' with the demands of the moderates.[18] As far back as 1943, SIME had identified the 'extremist David Ben Gurion', and chairman of the Agency, as the real danger man within it. The democracies, he had said, Britain and the USA, aimed not at Zionism, but at assimilating the Jews in their own countries to their own cultures. 'The Nazis, by persecuting and expelling the Jews of Europe, have done more for Zionism than the democracies have... Our public enemy No. 1 is Hitler; but enemy No. 2 is the British government...' All differences within the Zionist framework were to be subordinated to the attainment of the fundamental goal, the Jewish State. SIME pointed out that the 'totalitarian tendency of all this is unmistakable'.[19]

From late 1946 to early 1947 the situation in Palestine had been characterised by a deterioration in public order arising from an extension in the scope and number of terrorist outrages and from the Jewish Agency's political frustration after the failure of negotiations in London. As a result of this frustration, and for fear that because of its apparent inaction the Jewish community should slip into the hands of the extremists, the Agency had shown even greater reluctance than formerly to co-operate with the British Administration against the terrorists, unless such co-operation were accompanied by increased Jewish immigration. 'Consequently, British forces have been deprived of vital assistance in their operations against the terrorist, and the Agency's feverish insistence of increased immigration as a means of self-justification continues to involve HMG in the distasteful and purely negative interception and detention of immigrants arriving clandestinely in Palestine waters.' The immediate tasks were, therefore:

1. To induce the Jewish Agency to co-operate against the terrorists. Co-operation with individual sections of the Jewish community may be effective in isolated instances, but the Agency alone has sufficient information and personnel trained in counter-terrorism to deal effectively and speedily with terrorist organisations.
2. To limit Jewish illegal immigration which leads to estrangement between the Jewish community and the Palestine Government and has frequently provided the occasion for terrorist outrages.

Although conclusive evidence was lacking, the accepted figures, which were supported by Jewish Agency estimates, for 1945–1946 membership of the Irgun and Stern Group, were respectively 5,000 and 400 members. Terrorist operations were then comparatively spasmodic, aimed at individual targets, and demanded relatively few trained saboteurs or assassins. The scale of recent outrages, such as sustained attacks on security posts and vehicles in and around Martial Law areas, indicated that the terrorists now commanded not only an effective popular support, but also a larger membership. This larger membership arose from:

1. Success in recruiting among demobilised soldiers and recent immigrants, 600 of whom arrived in a ship sponsored by the Revisionist Party from which most of the terrorists are drawn. A large majority of both soldiers and immigrants have experience in underground work in Europe, which, together with the bitterness caused by close acquaintance with the fate of European Jewry, provides the emotional background of terrorism.
2. Desertions from Hagana and Palmach ['strike force' of the Hagana] by reason of the Jewish Agency's inaction and lack of success in negotiations with HMG.
3. Growing self-confidence within the terrorist organisations arising from successful operations; political and probably financial support from American Jewry, and the Jewish community's dissatisfaction with the Agency.

There had been no weakening in the Agency's public denunciation of terrorism; symptomatic of its attitude was a recent naming of an illegal immigrant ship after Haim Arlossoroff, a prominent left-wing member of the Jewish Agency who was murdered by the terrorists in 1940. In November 1946, the Agency, claiming for political reasons to be unable to co-operate with the Palestine Government against other sections of the Jewish community, opened an 'Educational Campaign' to wean Jewish public opinion from the terrorists. The partial success of the campaign could be seen in recent public co-operation with the Government, although it was of no importance in comparison with the extended scope of terrorist outrages. Nevertheless, during a recent Zionist conference in Switzerland, and again in early January 1947, the Agency was reported to have caused the terrorists to desist from outrages. It was not known whether this was achieved by threat of reprisals or, as in 1945–1946, by some form of operational agreement. The Agency had maintained its own Hagana counter-terrorist service. This had thwarted at least certain terrorist attempts to penetrate and recruit members from Hagana and Palmach formations; had impounded terrorist vehicles and arms caches, and, as in early 1945, on occasion had privately detained suspected terrorists for interrogation. There had been no evidence of operational liaison in Palestine.

On the European continent, however, the situation was different. An agreement concluded in 1946, for co-operation between Jewish Agency and Revisionist illegal immigration services, had seen fruition in the recent arrival in Palestine of the Revisionist ship *Abril*. As the Irgun was the only executive arm on which the Revisionists could depend, and co-operation in Europe presupposed at least relations and means of communication within Palestine, it was reasonable to deduce that even if operational liaison did not obtain at present, the Agency had the means of contacting Irgun leaders at will. SIME found it impossible to establish accurately the success of Hagana operations against the terrorists. The Agency, at variance on the one hand with the Government, and on the other, at least temporarily with large sections of the Jewish community, could not hope for a success comparable with that of its 1945 operations, when a measure of co-operation with the Administration obtained and the Jewish community was largely in support. As a recent example, in one area certain Hagana settlements objected to a general mobilisation for counter-terrorist purposes after the sentencing of one terrorist, Dov Gruner: 'Yet it is certain that the Agency has still both a sufficient following in the country, and is sufficiently well informed on terrorist matters to neutralise both the Irgun and the Stern Group. However, as public order deteriorates and the terrorist organisations become stronger, so the task becomes more difficult; but the same argument applies even more forcibly to Government attempts unaided by the Jewish community's support and by Agency information.'[20]

Blowback

It seemed that, with the announcement that Britain would quit Palestine in 1948, handing the Mandate over the United Nations Organisation, the Security Service would be relieved of its obligation to counter Jewish terrorism. But, as an MI5 officer explained to Special Branch officers, this was not necessarily so:

> I should like to begin by reminding you that the subject upon which I am proposing to talk is that of 'Zionist subversive activities'.
>
> This title has been chosen with some care, and I would emphasise the words 'Zionist' and 'subversive'. MI5 are not of course concerned with the activities of Jews as such. Nor does MI5 devote time to studying Zionist activities as a whole, except where these are definitely of a subversive nature or prejudicial to the defence plans of the British Empire. There is nothing illegal in Zionism as a political creed. It only comes within our province when the activities of some of its extremist supporters qualify beyond doubt to be described as secret, subversive or illegal, and thus a danger to the security of the Empire and of this country.

Counter-terrorism was 'of course properly speaking no part of the work of the Security Services'. The detection and prevention of terrorist acts fell to the Home Office and to the police, and this question of policy was formally agreed in 1947 as between the Security Service and Scotland Yard. MI5 had, nevertheless, been 'able to assist the Police to some effect in carrying out their responsibilities in this direction, by passing on information obtained from secret sources, usually in the course of enquiries into the activities of individuals or organisations not themselves known to have terrorist intentions, but whose subversive political tendencies have caused them to be a fit subject of study by the Security Service'.

Once the Government announced its intention of surrendering the Palestine Mandate on 15 May 1948, and of withdrawing all British troops from the country by 1 August, MI5's first feeling 'was to some extent one of relief, in that it seemed that there would shortly cease to be a reason for Great Britain continuing to be a target for terrorist activities'. It had long been the object of the terrorists to remove the

British Government and forces from Palestine, and with this object in sight, it seemed reasonable to expect that 'we would no longer be regarded' by the IZL and the Stern Group as 'Public Enemy No. 1'. Now MI5 thought that events seemed 'likely to prove this assumption wrong. However logical it might have been, the Jewish terrorists are unfortunately not logical people. There has not in the past been much evidence of reason in their selection of persons or buildings as symbols of British rule and as therefore qualified for attack. Their conception of the British as their primary enemy is deep-rooted and will not be so easily eliminated. There are signs, moreover, that the political situation will not be lacking in what they themselves may choose to regard as grounds for continued grievances against this country.' For example, the United Nations Palestine Commission, in its report to the United Nations Organisation, had recommended that a free port should be granted to the Jews by 1 February in order to assist immigration. From the British point of view, there were obvious difficulties in acceding to this request, since port facilities in Palestine were bound to be needed for the evacuation of British troops and stores, which in any event could only be complete with difficulty by the time of Britain's final departure. Accordingly, Sir Alexander Cadogan, of the Foreign Office, made it known that His Majesty's Government was unable to comply with this request, and that no free Jewish port would therefore be granted:

> This... is bound to be regarded by the Jews as provocative step on our part. More important, it will give a reason for the continuation of illegal immigration at least until the time when British rule in Palestine ceases. Continued illegal immigration will mean a continued necessity for Naval and Military plans to intercept and dispose of Jews attempting to reach Palestine by sea, and thus entail a prolonged danger of clashes with the terrorists and with the HAGANA, the defence force of the Jewish Agency. Immigration has always been the sore spot of the Zionist, and as long as it is British policy to restrict it, so long will they continue to regard the British as their enemies. Nor is this question of immigration likely to be the only Jewish grievance against us.

Already, Zionist propaganda was active in accusations against the Government of partiality in permitting the supply of arms to the Arabs, while an embargo was placed upon the export of weapons and military supplies to the Jewish forces. In particular, the American ban on the export of arms to the Jews was pointed out as being unfair, it being also hinted that this policy had been developed as the result of British pressure. The fact that the Arab Legion was led and staffed by British officers was singled out as an example of a general British policy of secretly supporting the Arabs to the detriment of the Jews. In general, Great Britain was accused of a 'perfidious' desire to see the UNO plan frustrated and the Arabs emerge the dominant power in the Middle East.

These, considered MI5, were 'reasons enough' – at least in the eyes of the Jewish extremists – for the terrorists to continue to direct their activities against Britain at least until 1 August, the date upon which, 'in theory', British troops were to be finally withdrawn. But, in the report submitted to the Security Council by the United Nations Palestine Commission on 16 February, the Commission pointed out that they could not assume responsibility for enforcement of the partition plan without some impartial military force to keep the Jews and Arabs apart. As the Mandate would have ended on 15 May, such a force must obviously be international in character. 'It would be impossible for it to bear any national label; least of all could it be an official British force. The fact however remains that the British have had thirty years' experience of rule in Palestine, and have been responsible up till now for the whole of the development of the governmental system of that country. British troops and British police alone possess the experience necessary for keeping order in the supremely difficult conditions which apply there… therefore… it seems inevitable that a part of its make-up must be British. And even if the Government has no official responsibility for the policy under which that force will operate – for the policy will, of course, be a UNO policy – the continued presence of British troops, police or administrators in Palestine, though only so to speak on loan to UNO, is more than likely to be regarded by the terrorists as sufficient reason for continued attacks against us.' As in the past, such attacks might not be confined to Palestine itself. In this connection it was 'perhaps significant that there has been as yet no sign of any disbandment of those terrorist organisations which are known to us to be operating in Europe, including this country.'

There was also admiration and approval of the terrorists in the United States. Particularly vociferous in this connection has been the so-called Bergson Group which included, at various times, a number of organisations, of which the most prominent had been the Hebrew Committee of National Liberation and the American League for a Free Palestine under the general leadership of Peter Bergson, a Lithuanian

Jew, who was originally a member of the Revisionist organisation proper, and who first went to America from Britain in 1941. The Bergson Group was represented in Europe by its organisation in Paris, which was brought into being largely by the efforts of Bergson's second-in-command, Samuel Merlin.

By January of 1947, it was clear to MI5 that the headquarters of the Revisionist organisation in Europe was in Paris, where they had by then established a World Secretariat. It was noticeable that two of the leading members of this Secretariat had already been reported as active supporters of the Irgun Zvali Leumi, and possibly actual members of that organisation. Also from that time onwards, MI5 received from several sources reports of increased activity on the part of the Revisionist Youth Organisation, known as Betar, in Europe, and on the part of both the Irgun and the Stern Gang among the Betar. Parallel with this development of activities by the Revisionist organisation itself, MI5 were also watching the French Branch of the Bergson Group, who showed signs of being more open in their activities, and who, as in the United States, were publicly advertising their intention of placing their resources at the disposal of the terrorist organisations. Reports from the French police stated at that time that the Bergson Group were fostering the development of terrorist organisations in France itself. Although MI5's information on this subject was not entirely clear, it seemed on the whole probable that, at least in Paris, the Bergson Group and the Revisionists had forgotten their political differences and were collaborating in assisting Continental terrorist activities. The Security Service believed that France 'is still the principal centre in Europe from which Revisionist extremist activities, including terrorism, are directed. Subsidiary organisations have been developed in a number of other European countries, including Italy, Germany, Austria, France and last but not least the United Kingdom.'

Italy, for example, had for a long time been known to MI5 as an important centre of Zionist activity, 'a reason for this being that the heel of Italy has been the most frequently used point of embarkation for Jewish illegal immigrants on their way by sea to Palestine'. Refugee camps throughout Italy had been kept continuously filled with Jews who had been assisted from Central Europe across the Austrian frontier by the illegal immigration organisers. While these organisers had, MI5 believed, been mainly Hagana representatives, the Revisionists also had played their part in this traffic, and proof of the presence of the Irgun was sufficiently provided in November 1946, when they struck their first blow in Europe by exploding a bomb in the

British Embassy in Rome. There were strong indications at that time that the United Zionist Revisionist Organisation and the Betar were both collaborating with the Irgun in terrorist plans. Since then there had been less evidence of the active planning of terrorist outrages in Italy itself, but the Revisionists were known to be strongly represented there, one of their most prominent figures being Leon Carpi, a lawyer in Genoa, who had been known since before the war to be involved in illegal immigration.

In Germany, there was ample evidence of the existence of Revisionist and Irgun cells in Displaced Persons camps in both the British and American Zones. 'Perhaps the most interesting case in Germany', however, was that which involved the placing of explosive charges on the main railway line between Berlin and Hanover in May and June 1947. The discovery that this attempted outrage was the responsibility of the Irgun was mainly the result of good work on the part of the German police. The charges consisted of gelignite, as used for quarrying, placed between the lines and attached electrically to a detonator on the line itself. In the case of the charge placed on the line at the end of June, the total quantity of explosive material was about 30 kg. When the police first examined it, they discovered that part of the wrapping of the explosive consisted of a sheet of newspaper printed in Hebrew. This proved to be a piece of the paper *Unsere Stimme* known to be published in Belsen camp. The wire connecting the explosive material with the detonator was covered with a yellow insulating material later. From certain other pieces of paper wrapping, it was possible to trace the explosives back to a quarry at Bochum in the Ruhr, where examination of the foreman's explosive book showed that the particular package of explosives had been issued to Rudolf Merten. The questioning of Merten elicited the fact that he had on three occasions supplied gelignite to a second person named Theodor Heinemann, who had himself acquired it at the instigation of a former criminal. Further interrogation established that 'this criminal' was in turn in close touch with a Jew named Hubert Abraham of Munich.

Meanwhile, the German police had been making separate enquiries in Hanover itself, based on little more than witnesses' descriptions of 'certain persons of Jewish appearance' who had been seen near the place where the explosives were found. As a result of these enquiries, two Jews named Jacob Redlich and Jacob Kryszek were arrested on suspicion. Attached to Redlich's bicycle was found a piece of yellow wire identical in every respect with that which had earlier been found connected to the explosives on the railway line. In the interval before these arrests took place the police found that Redlich and Kryszek had been in communication with a Jew named Orlinski in Munich. Orlinski was watched and arrested, together with Hubert Abraham. Subsequent enquiries showed that the arrests were fully justified, and although the terrorists were reluctant to give information when questioned, Orlinski later supplied information confirming that the headquarters of the Irgun in Europe was in Paris, with a subordinate headquarters in Munich, the 'whole being supported by the United Zionist Revisionist Organisation'.

The activity of the terrorists in Austria had been even greater than in the case of Germany, though here MI5 were not in possession of the full information. For example, on 12 August a British leave train carrying 175 members of the Forces and other officials was derailed three miles from Malnitz, which was at the end of a long tunnel on the border of the American Zone of Austria, on the main line connecting Munich and Salzburg with the south. The line had been used for the last two years mainly for the transport of British troops. The derailment was caused by the placing of two bombs on the line, of which only one exploded. If the second bomb had exploded, the train would have left the rails and gone over the embankment. A Jewish refugee was arrested shortly afterwards, after he had used a pistol to resist arrest. Handbills, which were distributed later in Jewish detention camps in the Salzburg area, claimed on behalf of the 'High Command of the IRGUN ZVAI LEUMI' that the attack on the train had been the work of the Irgun. On 3 August two explosions occurred in the cellar of the Hotel Sacher in Vienna, used as quarters for British officers. Subsequent examination of the remains of the bombs showed them to be primarily of an incendiary type, connected to clockwork fuses. This outrage was later claimed to be the work of the Irgun. Threatening letters had also been as common in Germany and Austria as elsewhere, and the attacks at Malnitz and in the Sacher Hotel were followed by a series of anonymous bombing threats, one of which – 'surprisingly enough' – involved the American Legation in Vienna.

In the meantime, MI5 had numerous reports on terrorist activities and of the concealment of arms and explosives in France; but despite liaison between Scotland Yard and the French police, it had not always been easy to obtain much information from that country. It had, though, 'been somewhat noticeable' that Jewish terrorists apprehended in France tended not to receive considerate sentences. As an example on the scale on which the terrorists had been endeavouring to collect weapons, was the discovery by the French police, in July 1947, in an empty house at Nanterre, near Paris, of five heavy machine-guns, one light machine-gun, seven rifles, 600 kg of cartridges for various arms of various calibres and 150 kg of explosives. Seventeen persons were subsequently arrested, but of these only two were convicted, and they received only four months and two months imprisonment respectively, with fines of 2,000 and 1,200 francs. One of the arrested men was Jerzy Moskowitz, possibly connected with Amnon Moskowitz, whose name appeared in MI5's first Terrorist Index as a member of one of the terrorist organisations.

'More spectacular' was the Rabbi Korff affair of September 1947, which involved a project for an air-raid on London, in the course of which leaflets were to be dropped in the name of the Stern Gang, together with high explosive bombs. The prime mover was Rabbi Baruch Korff, an American citizen born in Russia, who had already come to MI5's notice as co-chairman of an organisation in the United States known as the Political Action Committee for Palestine. In the previous July, Korff had reached the headlines in the USA by introducing at a press conference a man reputed to be a leading member of the Stern Gang, travelling incognito in the name of Hiljel. The pressmen who attended the conference were not permitted to see Hiljel, who was hidden behind a half-open door. In the following month, Korff was announcing his intention of parachuting illegal immigrants into Palestine and claimed that millions of dollars had been subscribed by private American sources, American and Canadian planes having been purchased from surplus war stocks. It was with this project in mind that he went to Paris. Here he substituted for the parachute project an air-raid on London.

In all ten persons were arrested, of whom two at least were strongly suspected members of the Stern Gang. One of these was Jacques Martinski, who had already come to attention in Britain, when he landed at London Airport on 6 March 1947. After an explosion took place in the Colonial Club in Trafalgar Square he was refused leave to land because of his inability to substantiate the reasons which he gave for his visit to the UK. It was deemed significant by MI5 that when the French police searched his room in Paris after the Korff affair, they found wrappings for packets of explosives. These explosives, from the description on the wrappers, were exactly similar to those used in the bomb planted at Dover House in London on 15 April 1947. All the persons detained in Paris after the Korff adventure were later released on indefinite bail. One of them was reported to have escaped police surveillance and to have disappeared. Although Korff 'and his friends seem to have really meant business, the whole episode in the outcome proved something of a farce'.

Of more serious interest from MI5's own point of view was the presence in Paris of Monia Bella, a Jew of Russian origin, whom the Security Service's sources reported to be in fact the principal Irgun representative in the French capital. He was certainly the principal contact there of his brother Leo Bella, 'the central figure of the group of suspected terrorists in London who have been occupying our attention and that of Special Branch for some time past'. The Security Service believed that Leo Bella, in particular, had been planning terrorist outrages in Britain. MI5's information about 'these people' had been obtained gradually over the course of the past three and a half years, beginning with investigations which were made towards the end of the war into the activities of the Revisionist organisation in London, of whom the principal figure was Abraham Abrahams, editor of the Revisionist paper *Jewish Struggle*. This paper 'consistently put forward the extreme Revisionist case for the establishment of a Jewish state in the whole of Palestine and Transjordan. Although it stopped short of open support of terrorist methods, it went as far as it possibly could in acting as apologist for the terrorists, and in giving prominence to the terrorists' claim to be members of a patriotic "resistance movement" struggling to free Palestine from the foreign invader.'

'Even less restrained' in its propaganda was the Revisionist youth group, or Betar, for which at one time MI5 believed Abrahams also to be responsible. In December 1945 the Betar, whose headquarters were in a Jewish Club in Stoke Newington in North London, began publication of the *Jewish Struggle*, recommending the use of violence and condemning the British as Nazis. This paper reproduced in facsimile and in translation pamphlets known to have been issued by the Irgun in Palestine. In December 1946, by which time investigations by Special Branch and MI5 had resulted in the identification of the young Jews mainly responsible for the publication of this paper, 'these people' were officially warned that if further issues were published, prosecution would follow. This effectively put an end to the *Jewish Struggle*.

It was at this stage that Leo Bella, who was a stateless person of Russian origin, 'first really began to interest us'. He had been a member of the Revisionist head office since his arrival in the UK in 1936, 'but a successful under-cover technique' had so far concealed the extent of his association with Abrahams and the other more open political leaders of the organisation in London. When, however, MI5 began to examine the methods whereby the editors of the *Jewish Struggle* obtained propaganda material direct from Palestine, it became clear that the main channel of communication for this purpose was through Leo Bella. Since then it had been established from 'secret sources' that Bella was the controlling figure behind a group of conspirators whose aim – hitherto unsuccessful – had been to organise acts of terrorism in Britain. His principal associates were Chanel Poniemunski, a twenty-six year-old Pole who joined the Revisionist organisation in London in 1938 and who served during the war; Paul Homesky, a Palestinian aged twenty-two, formerly in the RAF and now a student in London; Erich Prinz, a German of Polish origin who entered the country illegally in 1946; a twenty-three year-old South African named Boris Senior, who, like Homesky served in the RAF during the war as a pilot; Mojzess Kaplan, formerly member of the Polish Medical Corps; Theodor Preschel, a Pole aged twenty-five, who was studying at a Rabbinical College in London; Isaac Pressman, a naturalised British subject of Russian origin, forty-five years of age and a director of a firm of chemical manufacturers in Stoke Newington; and a certain Schapiro, whose identity was uncertain, but who may have been a Polish member of the London Betar who formerly served in the Pioneer Corps. Also relevant was Robert Briscoe, a member of the Irish Dail, who had long been an active Revisionist in Dublin and in contact with Bella and other Revisionist leaders in London.

Erick Prinz was arrested on 26 August 1947, when he was sentenced to one month's imprisonment on charges under the Aliens' Order and recommended to be deported. It was in Isaac Pressman's garage in London that CID discovered twenty-seven hand-grenades and a number of detonators on 19 July. Unfortunately, there was insufficient evidence against Pressman to justify a prosecution, 'but it may be noted that a considerable quantity of terrorist literature was found in his flat at the time'. MI5 had gathered the intelligence on these terrorists and passed it on to Special Branch but: 'the greater part of this information was obtained from secret sources, and had therefore to be used with the greatest care. It was of course impossible to use any of it as evidence for prosecution purposes.' As MI5 acknowledged, so 'slender is the information' upon which they often had to go, that until Prinz's actual arrest, the Service did not even know him by this name. It was the regular habit of Bella and his friends to refer to each other by cover names, and MI5 'knew practically nothing' about Prinz except under one of these cover names.

Throughout the summer of 1947, MI5's sources reported that Bella and his associates were anxious to collect explosive material for some unspecified purpose. Among the persons whom Bella hoped to use for this was Mojzess Kaplan, 'almost certainly identical' with a member of the Polish Forces who was known to have played a leading part in organising a Betar or youth group in Glasgow. The man whom the Security Service later knew as Prinz was also concerned with Bella in the plans to make use of Kaplan's services. At the end of April another former member of the Polish Forces in Scotland 'came into the picture.' This was a certain Szafran in Falkirk, thought to be identical with Feiwel or Nahum Szafran, formerly in the Polish Air Force. MI5 'were never very clear' about Bella's plans in connection with this man, but they knew that it was agreed between him and Prinz that Szafran should be contacted in Scotland. Although MI5 thought that a definite attempt was made to carry out this arrangement, and although Prinz actually travelled to Falkirk in May to meet Szafran, the whole thing came to nothing. This information about Kaplan was confirmed in a Special Branch report of 29 May, according to which Kaplan had in fact been attempting to obtain arms and explosives. MI5 'learned simultaneously' from its own sources that Prinz had again been in contact with Bella and had been urging the necessity to make further progress in the plan in which Kaplan was involved. It became clear from the Special Branch information that the aim of this plan was undoubtedly to collect weapons and explosives material, an aim in which Bella and his friends were believed to have been unsuccessful, except to the limited extent later shown in the Pressman case.

Prinz again came to MI5's attention in July, when he and Homesky were known to have left London in a hired car for the purpose of collecting certain unspecified material in the Marlborough district. The Security Service were able to pass information to Special Branch about this trip, the result of which the car was intercepted on the return journey. Nothing of interest was found in the car, but Homesky's companion – who was not yet known to MI5 as Prinz – produced an identity card in the name of Julius Ballon. This card proved not to be his own, Julius Ballon being another Jew, who, 'by an interesting coincidence', was employed as works foreman to Isaac Pressman. Ballon claimed that he had lost his identity card, but it seemed more than possible that he had knowingly allowed Homesky's companion, later identified as Prinz, to use it.

From this time onwards, Special Branch, acting mainly on MI5 information, undertook intensified measures to locate Homesky's companion, who since the interception in July, had disappeared and remained unidentified. At last, on 26 August, the Security Service obtained information about an intended meeting between this man and Bella and Homesky. As a result Special Branch was able to arrest him, and in the proceedings which followed, he was identified as Erich Prinz. In the statement which he made to police officers he gave a 'most unsatisfactory' account of his arrival in Britain, and claimed that he had been brought there by Polish soldiers in 1946 wearing Polish uniform. He also stated that he had been given civilian clothes in Portsmouth Dockyard and picked up outside the dockyard by a man unknown to him, who was waiting with a car. He was sentenced to one month's imprisonment on charges under the Aliens Order with a recommendation for deportation.

The case of Isaac Pressman was the only one in which MI5 had definite knowledge of the acquisition of explosive materials by Bella and his friends, though this knowledge was obtained only from secret sources and none of it could be used in evidence. Pressman, who, was a British subject by naturalisation (formerly Russian) and director of a firm of chemical manufacturers in Stoke Newington in North London, was detained by the Metropolitan Police in July 1947, following upon information given to the police by a chauffeur, which led to the finding of the twenty-seven hand-grenades and a number of detonators in his garage. Otherwise, however, there was nothing from sources which could be used which in any way indicated that Pressman was a member of the Bella Group. From MI5's own sources, however, his association with Bella was clear enough.

The Security Service never succeeded in establishing where the grenades found in Pressman's garage were originally obtained, although there was some reason to suspect that they had been pilfered from an RAF airfield in the vicinity of Marlborough in Wiltshire. From the time, however, of the breakdown in Bella's arrangements to make use of the Pole, Szafran, in Falkirk, MI5 had reason to suspect that Pressman and Bella were both concerned in a scheme to obtain explosive material from somewhere in the west of England, and reports suggested that Pressman paid a visit to Somerset at the end of June in order to examine the possibility of obtaining such material from quarries in that area.

The Pressman story was carried a stage further at the beginning of July, when Bella and his group made elaborate and secret arrangements to meet Homesky at Paddington Station on 6 July, when he was to bring a package from the West Country, arrangements being made for it to be housed in Pressman's garage. One report showed that, by 6 July, Bella and Pressman had completed arrangements for the use of the garage for this purpose. At that time, 'although it became abundantly clear after the event', MI5 had no reason to suspect the real purpose for which the garage was being made available. When, however, the chauffeur informed the police on 19 July about the presence there of the hand-grenades, 'it was safe to infer' that these grenades were in the package which Homesky had brought to Paddington from the West Country on 6 July and that Pressman, moreover, had had full knowledge of the undertaking and had lent his garage for the purpose.

Since that time MI5 had heard little of Pressman, and 'until quite lately' the Bella group as a whole had been relatively quiescent, 'no doubt deterred from activity' by the arrest of Prinz and the close investigation into the activities of Pressman. Good intelligence had thwarted the extreme Zionists from initiating a terrorist campaign in the United Kingdom. At the heart of it was the central direction of intelligence by one organisation – MI5. It was a lesson that MI5 and British Intelligence, generally, was to forget.[21]

3

PRIMROSE
The First Atom Spy 1945–1946

The end of the Second World War meant a considerable change for the Security Service. Many of the talented individuals drawn into the Service upped stumps to resume their pre-war careers or set off for new adventures. Dick White was tempted to follow them but, at the age of forty, he was unsure of what he could do beyond the intelligence field. With minimal savings and no pension, it was, he confessed, 'an awful anticlimax'. TAR Robertson welcomed him back to London with the words, 'It's just ticking over'.[1] Physically too there was a change for MI5 in terms of bricks and mortar as the Service moved to Leconfield House, its new headquarters in Curzon Street. Perhaps the biggest change, though, was the appointment, by the Prime Minister, Clement Attlee, of Sir Percy Sillitoe as the new Director General. Many thought Guy Liddell was the natural choice for the top job, after Sir David Petrie retired in 1946. But Attlee appeared to be distrustful of the shadowy men of the Security Service. Liddell, instead, became Deputy Director General.

Sillitoe did not have a background in intelligence – he was a policeman. Born in London, in 1888, he had, by 1908, became a trooper in the British South Africa police. He transferred to the Northern Rhodesia police in 1911, was commissioned, and took part in the German East Africa campaign during the war, afterwards serving as a political officer in Tanganyika from 1916 to 1920. He and his family returned to Britain where, in 1923, he was appointed Chief Constable of Chesterfield and he stayed two years. After a year as Chief Constable of the East Riding of Yorkshire, Sillitoe was appointed Chief Constable of Sheffield in 1926 where he revitalised the force and restored law and order to a city which had been in the grip of criminal gangs. He broke the power of the gangs by the use of plain-clothes police patrols. Sillitoe's five years in Sheffield made his reputation and saw him appointed as Chief Constable of Glasgow in 1931. He repeated his earlier success there too, taking command of a force of 2,500 men, second in size only to the Metropolitan Police. He was appointed CBE in 1936 and knighted in 1942. In 1943, Sillitoe received his last police appointment, as Chief Constable of Kent, before taking over on 1 May 1946, in succession to Sir David Petrie.[2] His appointment was received with dismay inside MI5. Dick White's comment was: 'He didn't understand intelligence.' And he added: 'One did not need to know Sillitoe well to dislike him.'[3] White found Sillitoe 'vapid and shallow and frequently wrong. I was close to leaving to try my hand at something else… I swallowed my justified anger.'[4] Class seems to have a been a factor in some of the antagonism towards Sillitoe. Some of the MI5 officers spoke Latin in his presence 'to emphasise their superiority'.[5] Sillitoe realised that 'I was now among men of a type different from those who had previously worked under me.' He 'found it so extremely difficult to precisely find out what everyone was doing' and was angered that he could not command 'unquestioning obedience to rules and a scrupulous respect for discipline'. His subordinates did not volunteer their secrets and wondered 'uneasily what precisely my role was to be'.[6] Sillitoe was reduced to installing a glass partition in the door of Guy Liddell's office to enable him to identify his deputy's visitors – although it has to be said that he established a good working relationship with that particular officer[7] – perhaps due to the Deputy Director's previous – although untypical – career as a police officer. Sillitoe's background – social and professional – was bound to lead to tensions (as was his tendency for self-publicity). He had 'a commanding presence' known by his policemen as the 'Captain' or the 'Big Fellow', autocratic and a disciplinarian in his leadership. He had little time for the 'book-learned intellectuals' he found in MI5.[8] Neither side was to earn much respect from the other as Sillitoe's tenure saw MI5 rocked by the first of a serious of spy scandals that would cast a long shadow over the efficiency – indeed loyalty – of the Service.

The threat came from the Soviet Union. But the British Government was slow to pick up on this – Churchill had, once Russia had entered the war in 1941, discouraged counter-espionage activities against his new ally. The Soviets, however, did not play by Queensbury rules. Dick White later claimed that he was concerned by Soviet intentions while others in Whitehall took a more relaxed view. But he was, at least, reassured by Roger Hollis – whom he respected – that MI5's penetration of the CPGB had remained effective throughout the war. White claimed to be less sanguine about the Government's reluctance to deal with Communists in the Civil Service. Furthermore, in 1946, White was acutely aware that neither he, nor Liddell, had any idea about Soviet Intelligence activities *outside* the CPGB: 'No one had sufficiently thought about the communist threat, and the moment I thought about the Russians… I realised it was a completely new and uncharted quantity.' MI5, 'needed real knowledge on how the

Russians were working', and this meant that case-work was required to 'build up the picture'.[9] It was at this point that evidence of Soviet shenanigans came in the form of a Russian defector – Igor Gouzenko – who walked in, off the street, in Canada and offered his services to Western intelligence.

In 1943, Colonel Zabotin the Soviet Military Attache in Ottawa, and Colonel Ramonoff, were sent to Canada to organise the staff of the Military Attache in Ottawa. Accompanying them was Gouzenko. It was the first time any of them had visited Canada. Zabotin set up the office of Military Attaché as an office distinct from the Soviet Embassy. In Gouzenko's words: 'Some work was official, and some unofficial' – by which he really meant that 'it was a centre of the Soviet intelligence system in Canada'. The aim was to obtain, through agents, information valuable to the Soviet Union. Gouzenko worked in a 'secret room'. Code books and copies of all messages were kept in a sealed bag which was delivered each evening to the chief of the secret coding division. The bag held all original and coded messages given to Gouzenko by Zabotin. These were burned in a special incinerator every three months. The list of documents burned was signed by Zabotin, and forwarded to Moscow by mail. Mail packages, enclosed in three wrappings and sealed, contained letters and information from agents. They were not sent through the post office but by a pair of diplomatic couriers who travelled to Russia by ship. There were two such deliveries a month. The basis of this network was the Communist Party in Canada. Fred Rose, a Montreal MP of the Canadian House of Commons and Sam Carr, national organiser of the Labour Progressive Party, were, according to Gouzenko, 'recruiting agents' for the Soviet organisation of agents in Canada.[10]

One of the many objectives of the Russian organisation in Ottawa was the Atomic Bomb. In July, 1944, Dr John Cockcroft, who held the chair of Jacksonian Professor of Natural Philosophy at Cambridge, had been made Director of the Canadian Atomic Energy Project, Montreal and Chalk River, and worked in collaboration with Canadian scientists at the Montreal Laboratory of the National Research Council. Dr Allan Nunn May, a British temporary civil servant, formed part of the research group that came over to Canada, and was at the Montreal Laboratory as a group leader under Dr Cockcroft. In the performance of his duties, May had access to a substantial amount of knowledge of the work that was being done in connection with the Atomic Energy Project. May 'was an ardent but secret Communist' and already known to the authorities in Moscow. Not long after his arrival in Canada he was contacted on instructions from 'The Director' in Moscow Centre, and given the cover name ALEX by the Soviet espionage organisation now in the Dominion and directed from the Embassy by Colonel Zabotin.[11] At the beginning of 1945, Moscow Centre sent a telegram to Zabotin instructing:

> Establish contact with ALLAN NUN MAY who works in a scientific laboratory in Montreal. ALLAN NUN MAY is a very valuable source, therefore you will establish contact with him with as much caution as possible. ALLAN NUN MAY's nickname is ALEK. ALEK is a corporant. For various reasons contact with him was discontinued. It is necessary now to re-establish this contact. Before the beginning of the business conversation with him our man must speak the following phrase: 'Best regards from Michael.' We consider that this contact should be established through SAM. Telegraph your opinions.

On receipt of this telegram Zabotin replied to Moscow that he considered it somewhat risky to establish contact with ALEK through SAM (Sam Carr), and believed that it would be more expedient to establish contact with ALEK through Lieutenant Angelov (codename BAXTER). Moscow approved the decision of Zabotin and in this way Angelov established contact with ALEK. As Angelov met with ALEK and gave him the password, ALEK asked what they wanted from him. On receipt of the tasks he promised to fulfil them. ALEK prepared a typed report on scientific work connected with atomic energy for his next meeting with Angelov.[12] By telegram, dated 28 July 1945, The Director at Moscow Centre sent a telegram to Zabotin (codename GRANT) with reference to ALEX, reading, in part, as follows:

> To Grant
> Reference No. 218.
> Try to get from him before departure detailed information on the progress of the work on uranium. Discuss with him: does he think it expedient for our undertaking to stay on the spot; will he be able to do that or is it more useful for him and necessary to depart for London?
> Director.   28.7.45

These instructions were promptly followed in Ottawa, a few days later, on 9 August 1945, by a telegram to Moscow from Zabotin:

To the Director,
Facts given by Alek: (1) The test of the atomic bomb was conducted in
New Mexico... The bomb dropped on Japan was made of uranium 235.
It is known that the output of uranium 235 amounts to 400 grams daily
at the magnetic separation plant at Clinton... The scientific research
work in this field is scheduled to be published, but without the technical
details. The Americans already have a published book on this subject.
(2) Alec [sic] handed over to us a platinum with 162 micrograms of
uranium 233 in the form of oxide in a thin lamina...
9.7.45 Grant.

This telegram confirmed that May had handed over material to the
Russians. On the same date, another telegram was forwarded by
Zabotin giving information obtained from May on a man by the name
of Norman Veal. This telegram disclosed that May advised against
accepting any information about the atomic bomb from Veal.

To the Director,
Alek reported to us that he has met Norman Veal (he was at his
home). Veal works in the laboratory of the Montreal branch of the
Scientific Research Council... He asked the opinion of Alek: Is it
worth while for him (Veal) to hand over information on the atomic
bomb. Alek expressed himself in the negative. Alek stated that Veal
occupies a fairly low position and knows very little...
9.8.45
Grant.

A few days after May had handed over to the Russians information
concerning the Atomic Bomb, and the above-mentioned quantity
of Uranium 233, Zabotin paid a social visit to a friend living in the
vicinity of Chalk River. He then had the opportunity of seeing the
plant from the river during a motor-boat cruise, and reported to The
Director what he had seen. May made two visits to the same plant: the
first on 16 August 1945, and the second on 3 September. He also went
on several occasions to an American atomic plant in Chicago, doing
experiments in collaboration with American scientists. On 22 August
The Director telegraphed Zabotin:

To Grant
Take measures to organize acquisition of documentary materials on
the atomic bomb!

The technical process, drawings, calculations.
Director,
22.8.45.

On 31 August, Zabotin, not having received any reply from Moscow as to the value of the information on the atomic bomb which he had sent, telegraphed to The Director:

To the Director
I beg you to inform me to what extent have Alek's materials on the question of uranium satisfied you and our scientists (his reports on production etc).
This is necessary for us to know in order that we may be able to set forth a number of tasks on this question to other clients. Have you received all NN mail up to July of this year?
Grant
31.8.45

The evidence showed that May provided the Soviet espionage leaders with information on other subjects as well as on the atomic bomb. In a telegram from Zabotin to Moscow he stated:

To the Director
On our task Alek has reported brief data concerning electronic shells. In particular these are being used by the American Navy against Japanese suicide-fliers. There is in the shell a small radio-transmitter with one electronic tube and it is fed by dry batteries. The body of the shell is the antenna. The bomb explodes in the proximity of an aeroplane from the action of the reflected waves from the aeroplane on the transmitter. The basic difficulties were: the preparation of a tube and batteries which could withstand the discharge of the shell and the determination of a rotation speed of the shell which would not require special adaptation in the preparation of the shell. The Americans have achieved this result, but apparently have not handed this over to the English. The Americans have used a plastic covering for the battery which withstands the force of pressure during the motion of the shell.
Grant.
9.7.45

After his second visit to the Chalk River plant on 3 September, May departed for the UK. The telegrams revealed that Colonel Zabotin's organisation was aware of this departure and that May was instructed to contact a person in London. This contact was being organised between Moscow, London and Ottawa. The following telegrams were exchanged between Zabotin and The Director on this matter:

> To Grant
> Reference No. 218.
> Work out and telegraph arrangements for the meeting and the password of Alek with our man in London.
> Director. 28.7.45

> Grant.
> 31.7.45
> 244
> To the Director,
> We have worked out the conditions of a meeting with Alek in London. Alek will work in King's College, Strand. It will be possible to find him there through the telephone book.
> Meetings: October 7.17.27 on the street in front of the British Museum. The time, 11 o'clock in the evening. Identification sign:– A newspaper under the left arm. Password:– Best regards to Mikel (Maikl). He cannot remain in Canada. At the beginning of September he must fly to London. Before his departure he will go to the Uranimum Plant in the Petawawa district where he will be for about two weeks. He promised, if possible, to meet us before his departure. He said that he must come next year for a month to Canada. We handed over 500 dollars to him.
> Grant.

> 11955
> 22.8.45
> To Grant
> Reference No. 244.
> The arrangements worked out for the meeting are not satisfactory. I am informing you of new ones.
> 1. Place:
> In front of the British Museum in London, on Great Russell Street, at the opposite side of the street, about Museum Street, from the side of Tottenham Court Road repeat Tottenham Court Road, Alek walks

from Tottenham Court Road, the contact man from the opposite side – Southampton Row.

2. Time:

As indicated by you, however, it would be more expedient to carry out the meeting at 20 o'clock, if it should be convenient to Alek, as at 23 o'clock it is too dark. As for the time, agree about it with Alek and communicate the decision to me. In case the meeting should not take place in October, the time and D-Day will be repeated in the following months.

3. Identification signs:

Alek will have under his left arm the newspaper 'Times', the contact man will have in his left hand the magazine 'Picture Post'.

4. The Password:

The contact man: 'What is the shortest way to the Strand?'

Alek: 'Well, come along. I am going that way.'

In the beginning of the business conversation Alek says:

'Best regards from Mikel'.

Report on transmitting the conditions to Alek.

Director.

22.8.45 Grant.[13]

As Igor Gouzenko admitted: 'The telegrams mentioned above were deciphered by me.'[14] And it was he, as a defector, who gave them to the Royal Mounted Canadian Police (RMCP) – who, in turn, passed them on to British Intelligence in London. On 10 September 1945, Malcolm MacDonald, Britain's High Commissioner to Canada, telegraphed Sir Alexander Cadogan at the Foreign Office:

Information so far obtained (including copies of Intelligence despatches from Moscow) comprises large volume of undigested material. Two matters, however, are of immediate significance.

1(a) Agent of Soviet Intelligence Service at present in Canada is A.L. MAY repeat A.L. MAY, Doctor of Physics from Cambridge University, cover name ALEC repeat ALEC. He was sent out from United Kingdom approximately two years ago to work under National Research Council as top flight physicist on ATOMIC mission.

1(b) According to source MAY repeat MAY has for past four years provided ZUBOTIN with 'useful and valuable information' in research developments.

1(c) According to source, he provided two samples of Uranium 235 (presumably in inert form) which were flown by high official to Moscow. Origin of samples not known. National Research Council question whether material actually flown to Moscow was actually U.235.

1(d) MAY repeat MAY is due leave here by Royal Air Force Ferry Command for United Kingdom on September 15th repeat 15th. Telegram from Moscow gives detailed instructions for MAY to contact agent in London. Place of contact, pass words, etc. will be subject of later message as soon as translated.

1(e)... RCMP., external and ourselves, agree he should be allowed proceed on off chance that he makes contact.

1(f) So far we have no scientific opinion as to value of information passed by MAY. He was in a position to pass most valuable information.

1(g)... vetting of United Kingdom's scientist sent to Canada on project was responsibility of British Government and if these leakages on further investigation prove as serious as they appear at moment then HMG will be liable to criticism by United States Government.[15]

Cadogan was also informed, by MacDonald, of John Cockcroft's estimate of the knowledge which May had and which May could have passed to others:

Access to information

1. Complete knowledge design of Canadian Heavy Water pile. I do not consider this to be of major importance.

2. Knowledge construction of US Graphite pile at X.

3. Working experience with Chicago Graphite and Heavy Water pile.

4. No official knowledge of workings of Hanford piles, but likely to have a pretty fair idea of working power, dimensions, major difficulties experienced, etc. Much of this can be obtained by any intelligent physicist from Smythe Report.

5. Knowledge of methods of separating Plutonium and U.233 now favoured by the Montreal chemists.

6. Working knowledge of properties of Uranium 233 – obtained by experiments in Chicago. Appreciation of its probable importance in future in relation to the use of Thorium.

7. Would probably guess the relative role of 235 and 239 in US bombs.

Access to materials

1. Has had access to small samples of U.233 – about 1 Milligram –

and 1 (Micro-Milligram) might have been removed without notice.

2. May have obtained access unofficially to Uranium metal irradiated in the X pile and containing Plutonium in quantities of a Milligram. Such samples would be of great value in starting up chemical separation work.[16]

This information was passed on to MI5 who learnt from the RCMP that Gouzenko – codename CORBY – had confirmed the identification of May as a Soviet agent. May was given the codename PRIMROSE. According to CORBY, PRIMROSE had been in the pay of the Soviet Intelligence Service for many years, and was a secret party member in England. CORBY also claimed that this latter fact was known to some of PRIMROSE's co-workers, but that they did not consider that his political opinions should interfere with his work. Although the telegrams suggested that Uranium 233 had been passed over by PRIMROSE, CORBY believed that Uranium 235 – essential for the production of an Atomic Bomb – was involved, though he had no actual knowledge of the facts. The RCMP ascertained that PRIMROSE did have access to small quantities of U.233. He did not have access to U.235 in Canada, but it was believed that he might have been able to obtain some in Chicago, and it therefore remained possible that the first sample was actually 235. As PRIMROSE also provided information on an electronic device used by the US Navy against Japanese suicide planes, two things appeared significant in this connection:

1. Primrose is not concerned with electronic research, but with the atomic project. Yet Grant asked for information on this topic. While it is possible that he could obtain such data from a colleague, it may also be that Primrose was operating one or more sub-agents in fields where he did not have direct access.

2. The telegram states that this is an American development, information on which had not been passed to the British. Inferentially, therefore, the information may have been obtained from an American contact.[17]

News of Gouzenko's defection was, naturally enough, circulated elsewhere in the intelligence community in London, where it was handed to Kim Philby, then the head of SIS's Section IX, the Soviet department. Philby sought out Guy Liddell to discuss Gouzenko's debriefing. They agreed that Roger Hollis – MI5's Communism expert – should question the defector. Hollis flew across the Atlantic to Canada and met with Gouzenko and questioned him about Nunn May – for one hour. He then flew straight back to the UK presumably confident that the RCMP would extract all other relevant information.[18]

There was still the question of what to do about Nunn May. The view from SIS was that May should be allowed to travel in the hope of giving British Intelligence the opportunity of identifying his London contact and possibly others; Sir Stewart Menzies considered that efforts in this direction would be 'very considerably assisted if RCMP could be induced to suspend direct action against other members of this network at least until after his rendezvous [in London] on October 7th'. If the RCMP were 'unable to give us a guarantee on these lines I must urge that no repeat no direct action should be taken until May has left Canada'.[19] C followed this up with an impassioned plea to British representatives in North America:

> Please do everything in your power to persuade all concerned that best course is to let May travel.
>
> Risk of further disclosure of important information through May is small since it is extremely improbable that he will carry anything of value and what he carries in his head has presumably been passed on already.
>
> It is vitally important to take chance offered of uncovering parallel organisation in this country.[20]

The Canadians agreed and made preparations to shadow PRIMROSE (Nunn May) as he travelled to the UK. Accompanying PRIMROSE on the aircraft leaving 16 September was to be Detective Sergeant Bayfield of the RCMP travelling under cover as Mr Bayfield, special courier for United Kingdom High Commissioner in Canada. London was told it was essential that Bayfield be contacted by the Security Service while going through passport controls in Britain, when he would assist in identifying PRIMROSE if required:

> Contact should say quote How do you like our low lands weather? Unquote repeat quote How do you like our low lands weather? Unquote. Bayfield will reply quote I have not seen much of it yet but it's rather like our maritime provinces unquote repeat quote I have not seen much of it yet but its rather like our maritime provinces unquote.[21]

After PRIMROSE had arrived in Britain, a decision had to be taken on what to do about his proposed rendezvous with the Soviet Intelligence Officer – referred to, by MI5, as 'Agent X'. On 1 October a meeting was held between Dick White and the Assistant Director of Hollis's F Section, together with Colonel Cussen formerly of MI5's Legal Section, Major Leonard Burt, another former MI5 officer and now Head of Special Branch and John Marriott, to discuss what action to take with regard to PRIMROSE. The following was agreed:

> 1. That... no arrest of PRIMROSE should take place at the meeting on October 7th...
> 2. That consequent on the foregoing decision, no attempt should be made to impersonate the Agent X.
> 3. That Special Branch should be informed of the position...
> 4. That no Special Branch officers should cover the 7th October meeting but that Major Burt should be present so as, if necessary, at a later stage to be able to give evidence as to PRIMROSE's presence at the rendezvous.
> 5. That Major Burt should work out with [MI5 Section] B6 the details of their observation on the rendezvous.
> 6. That PRIMROSE should be kept under continuous observation from the morning of October 6th onwards.

There were a number of reasons for these decisions. First of all, except in the most favourable possible circumstances, the case against PRIMROSE at the moment of arrest would not be very strong and, on the assumption that he was both a determined and an intelligent man, his arrest could only be followed by a straightforward interrogation. Furthermore, the interval between the arrest and the interrogation was deemed to be sufficiently long enough to enable PRIMROSE to prepare himself for questioning. It was agreed that, on MI5's present information, the best chance of extracting from PRIMROSE an incriminating admission would be produced by a carefully staged interview at which he would start by being quite unsuspicious of any trouble. An impersonation of Agent X would be pointless in the light of this decision and would have the additional disadvantage of very likely prejudicing operations at a subsequent rendezvous.

If at any later stage there was to be an arrest, it was more than likely that Special Branch would be asked to assist and at any point the case might develop in such a way as to necessitate asking for Special Branch's assistance. It was agreed that the longer 'we delay telling Special Branch, the less likely they are to help us when we really want help'. The alternative of only keeping the rendezvous under observation was discussed, but it was eventually decided that, if PRIMROSE failed to turn up at the rendezvous, it would be useful to know where he had been instead 'since we should then be in a better position to assess why he had not kept the rendezvous'. The one qualification to the decision was this: if PRIMROSE were plainly seen on 7 October to pass a document to Agent X, and that document was positively known to be Top Secret, then PRIMROSE should be arrested. It was, however, agreed that the 'foregoing contingency is very improbable'.[22]

These decisions were refined, somewhat, when it was then decided that PRIMROSE 'is not to be kept under continuous observation from the morning of the 6th October onwards, nor is he to be followed to the Rendezvous. Instead, observations will be kept on the Rendezvous itself and if a) PRIMROSE turns up but no contact is made, then PRIMROSE will be followed away from the meeting-place, but if b) contact is made, Agent X will be followed away from the meeting-place and housed.' It was thought that to keep PRIMROSE under continuous observation for two whole days would obviously involve great risk, particularly at the weekend, and that the only object of such observation 'would be to let us know where he had got to if he did not attend the meeting. This information is likely to be provided in due course from other sources.'

White, together with the Assistant Director of F Section, Burt, and Marriott, visited the scene of the rendezvous, and discovered not only that Great Russell Street was 'much less quiet than we had supposed', but that on the corner of Museum Street and exactly opposite the rendezvous, there was a public house, with an upper room which commanded a view both of Great Russell Street and Museum Street. Major Burt 'stated that relations between Publicans and the police are always such that he would not have the slightest difficulty in arranging to have the use of the upper room on the pretext that he was conducting a criminal investigation. Major Burt, therefore, will be well-placed himself to observe contact, and consideration is being given to attempting also to take photographs.' MI5's Watchers would be in the bar downstairs, which also commanded the appropriate view, and it was decided that it would be unnecessary for any other observation to be kept. Consideration was to be given to arranging for a motor car to drive once or twice along Great Russell Street for the purpose of checking whether the Russians, themselves, were observing events.[23]

As events in London might, naturally, have repercussions thousands of miles away, the Canadians were worried that the arrest of PRIMROSE would force them to act, prematurely, against Soviet agents in their territory. And MI5 had decided that an arrest might occur. Hollis telegraphed this decision to the RMCP but reassured them that the matter would be further discussed with the Canadian Prime Minister, Mackenzie King, upon his imminent arrival in the UK and the instructions might be countermanded. But Hollis telegraphed 'that you make your preparations in the light of the remote possibility that the arrest may take place';[24] if that occurred then:

Limited publicity could not be avoided. Bearing in mind the necessity of preventing a top secret document passing out of the country and the fact that we shall have a clear cut prosecution under the Official Secrets Acts which may not otherwise materialise do you not think it advisable to take this remote chance if it occurs? Would you not in these circumstances be able to adjust your plans and search and interrogate the agents who are mentioned in the documents? In our opinion such circumstances would in this country justify interrogation of the suspects and application to a magistrate for search warrants.

We feel that the focal point of the case now is in Canada but this will shift here if an Official Secrets Acts' prosecution can be brought against PRIMROSE. We repeat that this possibility is remote but we wish to be prepared to take advantage of it.[25]

If we do not arrest on 7th October we suggest you should fix D-Day for such searches and interrogations as you can carry out. We will synchronise the questioning of PRIMROSE from which our experts have reasonable hopes of success. We suggest 18th October repeat 18th October as D-Day but await your decision. This date will give us the opportunity to cover the second meeting without postponing action too long. We believe that undue delay may imperil the success of the operation.[26]

After another meeting in London, this time between White and Major Burt, it was decided that the question of taking a photograph of the rendezvous appeared to be unrealistic and it seemed that unless there was any sort of chance of getting a reasonable photograph, this part of the operation should be abandoned. It was only realised now – on Saturday 6 October – that the vagaries of British Summer Time meant that, in order to take care of the possibility that the change from

Summer Time to Winter Time might alter the meeting arrangements of the Soviet agents, the whole plan for covering the rendezvous should deal with the hours of both seven and eight on 7 October rather than just eight. It was also agreed that Burt should ring White at MI5 at 6.45 p.m. and 7.45 p.m. on 7 October, to enquire whether any alteration had been made to the arrangements; in these circumstances White would reply either 'No change' or 'You may (not) use your discretion'.

Section B6, of MI5, were to stand by a convenient call-box at which Major Burt could telephone them any instructions with regard to covering the rendezvous. At 6.50 p.m. and 7.50 p.m., Tommy Harris was to drive through the vicinity of the rendezvous to ascertain whether any individuals standing there looked as though they might be attempting to cover the rendezvous. If he thought there were any such individuals, he would telephone Major Burt at the Museum Tavern to inform him. Head of the Watchers, Harry Hunter, was to be in the Museum Tavern with Burt, and should from there direct the transfer to the rendezvous of the Watchers standing by in readiness. In the unlikely event of its being necessary for anybody, at the last moment, to call at the Museum Tavern, the entrance on Sunday would be in Museum Street, and entrance was to be effected by ringing the bell marked 'Saloon Bar'. The telephone was in the room in which Major Burt himself would be.[27]

On 7 October, at 6.30 p.m., a man was posted at the junction of Tottenham Court Road and Great Russell Street, to look out for May. Burt, Hunter and a B6 assistant kept watch from inside the Museum Tavern until 7.20 p.m., when watch was transferred to the street by Burt and Hunter, until 8.30 p.m., with the B6 assistant remaining under cover in the Tavern. Another B6 assistant with a car kept watch by the telephone kiosk in Montague Street; Hunter was in telephone communication with him. But nothing 'was seen of May up to 8.30 p.m., neither was any person observed who might be keeping observation at the meeting place'.[28] After all the preparation for the meet neither May nor his Soviet contact appeared.

No further action was taken against Nunn May until the New Year, when it was decided to arrest him. On Thursday 14 February 1946, a search warrant under Section 9 of the Official Secrets Act 1911, was granted by Mr L.R. Dunne, Magistrate, at Bow Street Magistrate's Court, authorising Special Branch to search rooms at King's College, London, and any other rooms which were or might have been occupied by Allan Nunn May. On Friday 15 February, Nunn May was arrested by Special Branch at Shell-Mex House, The Strand. Burt and Major

Spooner from MI5 were already with May when he was arrested for he had already confessed his guilt to them.[29] His written statement, signed by him, read as follows:

About a year ago while in Canada, I was contacted by an individual whose identity I decline to divulge. He called on me at my private apartment in Swail Avenue, Montreal. He apparently knew I was employed by the Montreal laboratory and he sought information from me concerning atomic research.

I gave and had given very careful consideration to [the] correctness of making sure that development of atomic energy was not confined to USA. I took the very painful decision that it was necessary to convey general information on atomic energy and make sure it was taken seriously. For this reason I decided to entertain proposition made to me by the individual who called on me.

After this preliminary meeting I met the individual on several subsequent occasions while in Canada. He made specific requests for information, which were just nonsense to me – I mean by this that they were difficult for me to comprehend. But he did request samples of uranium from me and information generally on atomic energy.

At one meeting I gave the man microscopic amounts of U.233 and U.235 (one of each). The U.235 was a slightly enriched sample and was in a small glass tube and consisted of about a milliogram of oxide. The U.233 was about a tenth of a milligram and was a very thin deposit on a platinum foil and was wrapped in a piece of paper. I also gave the man a written report on atomic research as known to me. This information was mostly of a character which has since been published or is about to be published.

The man also asked me for information about the US electronically controlled AA shells. I knew very little about these and so could give only very little information.

He also asked me for introductions to people employed in the laboratory including a man named Veale but I advised him against contacting him.

The man gave me some dollars (I forget how many) in a bottle of whisky and I accepted these against my will.

Before I left Canada it was arranged that on my return to London I was to keep an appointment with somebody I did not know. I was given precise details as to making contact but I forget them now. I did not keep the appointment because I had decided that this clandestine procedure was no longer appropriate in view of the official release of information and the possibility of satisfactory international control of atomic energy.

The whole affair was extremely painful to me and I only embarked on it because I felt this was a contribution I could make to the safety of mankind. I certainly did not do it for gain.

After having elected to be tried by a jury in London, May, on the day set for his trial, pleaded guilty. In passing sentence Mr Justice Oliver said:

Allan Nunn May, I have listened with some slight surprise to some of the things which your learned counsel has said he is entitled to put before me: the picture of you as a man of honour who had only done what you believed to be right. I do not take that view of you at all. How any man in your position could have had the crass conceit, let alone the wickedness, to arrogate to himself the decision of a matter of this sort, when you yourself had given your written undertaking not to do it, and knew it was one of the country's most precious secrets, when you yourself had drawn and were drawing pay for years to keep your own bargain with your country – that you could have done this is a dreadful thing. I think that you acted not as an honourable but a dishonourable man. I think you acted with degradation. Whether money was the object of what you did, in fact you did get money for what you did. It is a very bad case indeed. The sentence upon you is one of ten years' penal servitude.[30]

In early 1947, further evidence of Soviet espionage was revealed when Alexander Foote, a Soviet Intelligence Officer, was posted from Moscow to Washington. *En route* through Berlin, he defected. Foote was a Briton who had been recruited by Soviet Intelligence in Spain in 1937. He revealed the identity of a Soviet intelligence officer codenamed SONIA working in Britain. MI5 identified the woman as Ursula (Ruth) Kuczynski, living in Chipping Norton, near Harwell, the atomic research centre. Dick White ruled out surveillance. From MI5, Michael Suppell and William 'Jim' Skardon, a former Special Branch officer, questioned her. Kuczynski admitted that, in being married to a Communist, she had been aware of the Soviet intelligence services in Britain – but that was ten years before and since her divorce she had no political involvement with Communists. Skardon believed her. Two days later she disappeared. White was 'puzzled' by her flight considering that Foote's claims could not be substantiated any further.

He later conceded that MI5 was complacent: after the successes of British codebreakers during the war British Intelligence had become 'flabby. We thought we could get by without going back to basics.' It was only with the Berlin airlift that White realised the magnitude of the threat facing Britain: 'It was only in 1948, at the outbreak of the Cold War, that we were aware that we'd been well and truly let down all the way through the Second World War.' White ordered the recruiting of agents into subversive movements.[31] But the damage had been already been done. This was a case of shutting the stable door after the horse had bolted.

On 15 March 1948, the Prime Minister, Mr Attlee, informed the House of Commons that:

> The only prudent course to adopt is to ensure that no one who is known to be a member of the Communist Party, or to be associated with it in such a way as to raise legitimate doubts about his or her reliability, is employed in connection with work the nature of which is vital to the security of the State. The same rule will govern the employment of those who are known to be actively associated with Fascist organisations.

The procedure to be followed involved individual Ministers deciding what, under their control, should be designated 'secret'. A board of three advisors – retired civil servants of 'distinction and proved discretion' – was established to advise Ministers whether the case against civil servants alleged to be untrustworthy was substantiated. It would be for the Minister to decide whether there was a *prima facie* case of untrustworthiness against a civil servant. The civil servant, if he rejected the accusation, could make representation to the Board of Advisors. MI5 would have a private session with the Advisors to present any evidence in their possession against the civil servant. The Advisors had the right and duty to examine the evidence in detail and satisfy themselves whether the facts alleged against the civil servant 'logically follow from the nature of the evidence'. The Security Service were relieved that the ability and discretion of the Board of Advisors meant that their concerns over compromising secret sources were allayed somewhat.[32]

Within MI5, H.I. Lea, tried, for Roger Hollis, to put some rough ideas on how to justify the inclusion of Fascists within the Prime Minister's statement; for to justify the application of the Prime Minister's ruling on the employment of Communists in secret Government work was 'in essence no very difficult task. To justify the same ruling vis-à-vis the Fascists is by no means so easy.' In the case of the former the one obvious and overwhelming reason for control was to be found in the subservience of the Communist Party to the policy of a foreign power. Fascists, however, owed no allegiance to a foreign power now and in the event of a future war with Russia 'it must be assumed that they give their enthusiastic support to the prosecution of the war'. Communists in Britain were subject to the central direction from one source only – the British Communist Party; but so far as the Fascists were concerned no such central authority existed. It was true that the followers of Sir Oswald Mosley formed the only effective and organised Fascist party in Britain but it was also true that there were a number of Fascists 'who would on no account associate themselves with him, politically or otherwise'. For these reasons alone 'it is impossible to apply to British Fascists the same arguments that can be applied to members of the British Communist Party'. The reasons, 'apart from purely political considerations', which could be advanced to back up the statement that Fascists might, under certain circumstances, prove a danger to the security of the State could 'perhaps' be summarised as follows:

1. It is almost certainly MOSLEY's intention in the course of the early years to come to create a Fascist International... It is difficult not to believe that in the event of the formation of such an international the loyalty of the Fascists supporting it would be divided between Britain and the International.

2. It is MOSLEY's publicly announced policy that, with a view to combating Communism wherever and whenever possible, members of the Union Movement should permeate and infiltrate all walks of life in which Communist influence is to be found... It can be assumed, therefore, that a Fascist employed in a branch of the Civil Service, in which he found himself in a position to gather information about a colleague known to him as a Communist or a Communist sympathiser would in all probability go to a good deal of trouble to discover everything he could about his colleague. The risks dependent upon this are obvious.

3. The Communist Party is on the whole well-informed about the activities of the Fascists and is believed to employ a number of agents to obtain its information. Equally it is, I believe, a fact that the Russians find right-wing sources both in this country and elsewhere a fruitful source of information. It is a possibility therefore, that a Fascist engaged upon secret work for a Government Department

might well become a definite target for the Communist or Russian agent.

4. In the event of a state of war existing between Britain and Russia it is probable that British war aims would receive Fascist support. It may well, be, however, that the Fascists would wish for a more vigorous policy towards Russia in the years preceding such a declaration of war than any British Government would be prepared to follow. In this event and also in the event of a further swing to the Right at the American Presidential elections it is possible that attempts might be made by Fascist interests in this country to join forces with extreme right-wing elements in America in an effort to force the British Government's hand.

5. It is a fact that many adherents of Fascism are individuals who are for one reason or another misfits in public and political life. Many suffer from some particular obsession, be it anti-semitism, an irrational desire for monetary reform or a blind-belief in the leadership principle. Others are individuals who have run the gamut of political emotions and have finally come to rest after stormy political careers in the pen. Yet others become Fascists because they have found it easier to be told what to do and what to think without the necessity of having to make any personal effort. Again, many become Fascists because it is surprisingly easy to obtain local prominence in the organisation and because by doing so their ego is easily satisfied. Emotionally unstable as many of these individuals inevitably are, it would be rash to place too great confidence in their discretion.

The truth, as Lea pointed out, was that 'none of the reasons set out… could in my view by themselves justify reasonable grounds for including Fascists within the ruling, but if it is remembered that the real consideration was one of political expediency they may go some way towards providing a basis for cases which may arise'.[33]

Just who were a continuing threat to British national security became clearer when, in January 1949, Percy Sillitoe returned from the United States. There the DG had been informed, by J. Edgar Hoover, the FBI director, that the Armed Forces Security Agency, had in 1948, using NKVD codebooks discovered by Finnish Intelligence in 1939, decrypted a handful of Soviet messages between the States and Moscow Centre. The operation was codenamed VENONA. One group of messages that had been deciphered, in 1945, contained verbatim extracts of telegrams from Churchill to President Truman about the status of the Polish Government-in-exile and negotiations between Stalin and Harry Hopkins, the U.S. special envoy to Moscow. Sillitoe agreed to co-operate, totally, with the FBI. Hoover believed that over 200 officials would have had access to this material. The British and Americans had already agreed, under the BRUSA Agreement of 1943 to unify the decrypting machinery of Britain, America, Canada and Australia. A new treaty, the UKUSA Security Agreement, was signed, in 1947, built on this by dividing the world geographically between the two powers. Under a further agreement an American liaison office for the FBI and CIA was established in London, while SIS and MI5 posted liaison officers at the British Embassy in Washington. The core of the 'Special Relationship' between Britain and the United States, since the end of the Second World War, has been this intelligence co-operation of a quite unparalleled nature between two countries.

In Washington, MI5's first Liaison Officer was Dick Thistlethwaite; his successor was Geoffrey Patterson. They worked with Sir Robert Mackenzie, the Foreign Office's Security Officer in the British Embassy, analysing lists of British officials, trying to identify those with access to the documents decrypted by VENONA. In London the investigation was handled by the (non-public school but grammar school educated) Arthur Martin.[34] In the meantime, the Foreign Office appointed its first-ever Chief of Security: he was George Carey Foster, a distinguished wartime officer in Bomber Command. He had been appointed in September 1946. He found a Foreign Office that had no security to speak of, with files scattered all over the place, unlocked lockers for files and no security checks on officials entering or leaving the building – to see if they had removed files. At first Carey Foster: 'sat there not knowing what to do… For centuries the Office had operated upon trust… and in that family atmosphere they couldn't conceive that there was a wrong 'un among them.'[35] But there was. The question was: who was it? From the intercepts, the Security Service only knew their prey's Russian codename: HOMER.

4

Klaus Fuchs:
The Greatest Spy in History

In August 1949 the Security Service received further information from VENONA, through the FBI, which indicated in some detail that, during the war, there had been another leakage to the Russians relating to the work of a British Atomic Energy Mission in the United States. Research into British files of that period showed that Dr Emil Julius Klaus Fuchs fitted such facts as were known. An intensive investigation into Fuchs's career and current activities began at once while research into wartime records was continued in order to establish that no other person also fitted the known facts.

Klaus Fuchs was born in Germany in 1911, the younger son of Emil Fuchs, a pastor and member of the Society of Friends who, in 1931, became Professor of Theology at the University of Kiel. Klaus studied at Kiel University and it was there that, in 1933, he aroused the suspicions of the Gestapo for his anti-Nazi and alleged Communist activities. In March of that year he fled to Berlin and four months later left Germany for the UK where he was granted a conditional landing permit to continue his studies.[1] Fuchs first came to the attention of MI5 in November 1934 when the Chief Constable responsible for Bristol wrote to Sir Vernon Kell informing the Director of MI5 that the German now resided in the city and that information had been given to the police by the German Consul that Fuchs 'is a notorious communist'. Having said this, the Chief Constable pointed out that during his stay in Bristol, Fuchs was not known to have engaged in any Communist activities.[2]

Between 1933 and May 1940, Fuchs won 'brilliant academic honours' first at Bristol and later at Edinburgh Universities. Under the General Order of May 1940 he was interned and sent to Canada, but in response to recommendations from his University, he was released six months later and allowed to resume his research work at Edinburgh. In mid-1941 an application was made for him to join a research team at Birmingham University on work connected with the Atomic Energy project.[3] This led to MI5 taking a closer look at Fuchs. A contact of Mr Robson-Scott, from Section E1.a, had a KASPAR, who reported that Fuchs was 'very well-known in Communist circles', but he was as yet unable to find out whether he was a Party member, or any details of his activities. With nothing else to go on, an officer in Section F2.b concluded: 'In the circumstances, I do not feel we can hold the case up any longer, as there is no knowing when KASPAR's further information will be obtained.' But if anything very serious against Fuchs should come to light later, 'we could then consider the cancellation of his permit'.[4] In response, Section E4.2 stated: 'We have no objection to issue of a... Permit to Dr FUCHS.'[5]

By now Fuchs had applied to become a naturalised British subject. In May 1942, Section C3b asked F2.b: 'May I have your remarks, please, on the desirability or otherwise of the grant of a certificate of Naturalisation to this man in the "National Interest"?'[6] A report from the Chief Constable of Birmingham reported that 'nothing was known to the detriment' of Fuchs's character. Fuchs was claiming that he no longer possessed German nationality. Discreet enquiries had been made regarding Fuchs's activities and the Chief Constable was 'assured that if he still has any interest in politics it is not an active one and he has not been known to associate with Communists in this District'.[7] F2, after seeing this report, concluded that, since Fuchs 'has taken no part in politics in this country... from the Communist point of view we see no reason to object to the grant of a Certificate of Naturalisation'.[8] Fuchs became a naturalised British subject on 7 August, 1942.

From 1942 to the end of 1943, Fuchs worked at Birmingham University for the wartime Directorate of Tube Alloys. The 'Directorate of Tube Alloys' was a cover for the predecessors of the Atomic Energy Division of the Ministry of Supply.[9] In 1943 an opportunity arose for Fuchs to go to the United States as part of the British contribution to work on atomic energy. Once again, MI5 were called upon to assess Fuchs's suitability. F2.b took out a Return of Correspondence on Fuchs to see whether he was getting any letters of interest. The Return, taken out for a fortnight, showed that he did not get a single letter, and it therefore 'seems unlikely that he is in close touch with anyone of interest. Do you agree, please, that, in the circumstances, there is nothing more that can be done at present?' The question was addressed to another section in MI5. A police report also appeared to be favourable.[10] Once again the Chief Constable of Birmingham informed Sir David Petrie that since Fuchs had become resident in Birmingham 'he has not come adversely under notice'. His only known associate was Rudolf Ernst Peierls, with whom he was living at 38 Calthorpe Road, Edgbaston. Peierls, 'who was formerly German', had been granted a Certificate of Naturalisation on 12 April, 1940, and was Professor of Applied Mathematics at Birmingham University. 'He is said to be a brilliant mathematician and was given excellent testimonials by men of standing in the academic world when he applied for naturalization.' Peierls had visited several European countries and he was married in Leningrad in March, 1931, to Eugenia, a Russian subject. Peierls, whose *bona-fides* 'have never been questioned', had vouched for the trustworthiness of Fuchs.[11] It came as a surprise to F2b that Fuchs was now a British subject; Miss Bagot, from the Section, commented: 'We knew that his naturalisation was under consideration... but the report... did not state that it was a *fait accomplis*.'[12] But she agreed that there was not much else to be done in assessing Fuchs.[13]

So, in December 1943, after given his clearance from MI5, Klaus Fuchs was one of seventeen British scientists sent on a government mission to the United States for the purpose of exchanging technical atomic energy information. The majority of this team returned to the UK early the following year but, so valuable was Fuchs, it was decided he should remain and in August 1944 he was posted to the US research station at Los Alamos working on the Atomic Bomb. He stayed there until the beginning of 1946 when he was appointed to a senior post, by the Ministry of Supply, at the British Atomic Energy Research Establishment (AERE), Harwell, later becoming head of the Theoretical Division there. An MI5 assessment noted how: 'To all who had known him since 1933 Klaus FUCHS was quiet, reserved and wholly absorbed in his work. To his fellow scientists he had become one of the world's leading mathematical physicists.'[14]

On 10 October 1946, Section C2 of MI5 thought that B Division might be interested to know that Fuchs was back in Britain and engaged on 'Atomic Energy work of extreme importance'.[15] The information had come from Henry Arnold, a retired RAF Wing Commander, who was now employed as the Security Officer at AERE since August, 1946. Arnold was responsible to the Director, Sir John Cockcroft, for all matters relating to the security of information, equipment and personnel at Harwell. Fuchs had joined Harwell soon after Arnold's arrival.[16]

Wing Commander Arnold informed MI5 that he had gained the confidence of Fuchs, among other key scientists at Harwell, and had evolved a scheme whereby they were to report their movements to him so that Arnold should know where they went and what company they kept outside Harwell. From the time Fuchs joined the Department, Arnold frequently saw him and at all times endeavoured to impress upon him the necessity for safeguarding official information and documents, and to educate his mind along these lines. 'This I did with all scientists of similar standing at the Establishment.' Fuchs reacted 'most favourably to these discussions and gave the appearance of being a most security-minded scientist, and came to regard me as his friend'.[17]

Meanwhile, an officer in B Division had discovered that at the time they were discussing the case with Arnold neither Harwell nor MI5 knew that there already was a Security Service file on Fuchs 'but I assumed that he had been vetted and that he was regarded by us as being all right. Now, I gather, Arnold realises from some quarter' that Fuchs 'has or had a Communist background.' In view of this Communist background it was necessary 'to assess the value of the information' against Fuchs and, if thought fit, to have further enquiries made about him and his activities in the UK. 'It is, of course, possible that Arnold is having his leg pulled' but Fuchs might 'be passing vitally important information, which he has in his possession by virtue of his work, through various channels to the Russians'. It would undoubtedly be said, if Fuchs 'proves to be a dangerous customer, that his technical ability is such that Atomic Energy Research would suffer very considerably if he were removed from his present employment'.[18]

Within MI5 it was Michael Serpell who was insistent that the Security Service should take more of an interest in the case of Fuchs. Serpell recalled that, when the Nunn May case first broke, an attempt was made to recollect a number of cases of Communists or Communist suspects employed on the Tube Alloy project. The case of Karl Fuchs, he noted, 'escaped our attention at that time but I suggest that it is one of considerable importance'. In 1943 this case 'was dealt with on the rather unsatisfactory basis that he would be of less danger to security on the other side of the Atlantic. I am afraid the Canadian case has shown this argument (which was applied in other cases) to be quite unsound.' There had, however, been some difficulty in 1943 in persuading others of the dangers inherent in the employment of 'such people' as Fuchs. Serpell presumed that 'the position is now considerably altered and that whatever the value of a refugee scientist's work may be to atomic research, his possible danger to security will be considered as a prime issue'.

Serpell noted that the facts of this case seemed to be that Fuchs in his youth 'acted as a communist penetration agent in the NSDAP. That he should have begun his political career in this undercover style seems to me to be of considerable significance at the present time.' It was also apparent that as late as 1943 he was engaged in some Communist activities in a refugee group at Birmingham. What did not seem to be conclusively established was that he was the 'Claus' Fuchs mentioned in a report, as having been a close friend of the veteran Communist, Hans Kahle, in a Canadian internment camp. Although the subject of this file was interned, it was only for a short time (May 1940 to January 1941) and there did not seem to be any direct statement that his internment was in Canada. However, the identification was probable and, if it was correct, the association with Kahle 'may be regarded as particularly dangerous', since Kahle was known to have acted as an OGPU representative in the UK. The quietness of Fuchs's political behaviour did not in the least 'alleviate the danger to security inherent in this communist background'. Except as 'cover' for serious security investigation, Serpell found it difficult to see what useful purpose could be served by Wing Commander Arnold's arrangements with Fuchs and others. He suggested that 'leg-pulling' should go no further. 'The present arrangement may already have made proper investigation difficult since' it must be supposed that Fuchs, 'if he is at the least a secret communist, regards Wing Commander Arnold's request as a warning'.

Serpell pointed out that Fuchs was also a close friend of Peierls and while Fuchs himself was highly placed in atomic research work, Serpell gathered that Peierls 'may be even more important'. In view of their association, Serpell noted that Peierls himself had a Russian wife and was known to have visited Russia in 1937. If proper investigation was to be made of Fuchs's activities and contacts, Serpell suggested that action should be taken at the same time with regard to Peierls. 'In my opinion the present evidence shows' Fuchs to be 'rather more of a liability than an asset but this cannot be said' about Peierls without further examination of his case.[19]

B Division, though, were reluctant to pursue the case and considered that any present action should be limited to warning Wing Commander Arnold about the background of Fuchs and Peierls: 'We should ask him for a report in due course.'[20] But C2 were becoming more and more concerned about the situation. Serpell's concerns had been passed on, verbally, to Arnold who warned that his arrangement with Fuchs was already beginning to lapse, but that he would report anything of interest to MI5. He had recently invited Fuchs to his house, 'but had found him extremely difficult to talk to!' Peierls, meanwhile, was not at Harwell, but at Birmingham University where his work was not the subject of any contract with the Department of Atomic Energy, however, he occasionally visited Harwell and was used in a consultative capacity.[21]

These facts led to a discussion, within C2, as to what course of action to take. An analysis of potential danger points in long term secret munitions led one officer to argue: 'I cannot agree that this case should be dealt with by the traditional method of leaving the suspect alone and hoping to catch him red handed unless we have informed the Atomic Energy Directorate of the facts set out by Serpell, and that FUCHS is a possible (I would prefer to say probable) Russian agent, and obtained their consent to his remaining where he is.' He considered that MI5's recommendations should be that Fuchs 'be divorced from all contact with atomic energy'; and that Peierls should not be used any longer as a consultant. To allow these men to continue working on atomic energy 'may compromise the future of atomic energy secrecy, which is a great deal more important than the fact that such secrecy must be considered compromised up to date'.[22]

Roger Hollis was asked for his opinion. As he saw it, the two points for consideration in the case of Fuchs were that he worked with the German Communists in 1933 as a penetration agent in the NSDAP, and was reported as a close friend of Hans Kahle, a Communist in the detention camp in Canada in 1940. As regarded the second point, Hollis thought it should be borne in mind that detainees sent to Canada in 1940 were supposed to be ardent Nazis. It was known that some mistakes were made and that anti-Nazis were sent amongst the Nazis. This clearly occurred in the case of Kahle and Fuchs 'and it is not altogether surprising that the two should have become friendly, surrounded as they must have been by Nazis who would have been uncongenial to them. I myself can see nothing on this file which persuades me' that Fuchs 'is in any way likely to be engaged in espionage or that he is any more than anti-Nazi.' As for Peierls, the only significant point Hollis could see in his case was that he married a Russian wife. If Lord Portal, in charge of atomic research, wished to exclude people with records such as those of Fuchs and Peierls, 'we must, I suppose, lend our assistance, but I think he should be advised that it will lead to a very considerable purge which will presumably have to include a number of very highly placed British scientists'.[23]

After reviewing the case, Guy Liddell concluded that 'as it stands there is really nothing of a positive nature' against either Fuchs or Peierls. On the other hand, 'I do feel that there is a *prima facie* case for investigation, and that where such important issues are at stake we cannot possibly afford to leave matters as they are. I think it would be unwise to make any approach to the Ministry of Supply until we know more about both these people.'[24] A Home Office Warrant on Fuchs was run for two months in early 1947. A fair amount of material was intercepted but there was nothing whatever to cast suspicion on Fuchs of any kind. The intercepts tended to fall into four main classes: family and personal correspondence; technical material connected with Fuchs's employment; curricula vitae of possible fellow-workers; and travel arrangements for a holiday in Switzerland. In the circumstances it was suggested that the HOW be now cancelled. Liddell agreed.[25] C2 also agreed that they did not think that it had sufficient grounds to advise against Fuchs being placed on the permanent staff at Harwell.[26] In order to reach a consensus, Liddell called a meeting on 8 December 1947 with Dick White, Colonel Furnival Jones, Lieutenant Colonel Collard and Roger Hollis. It was agreed that if the Ministry of Supply should approach MI5 about Fuchs, the answer should be that: 'Some slight risk attaches' to the employment of Fuchs because of his alien origin and Communist connections in the past. The group of MI5 officers agreed that while Fuchs had held anti-Nazi views and associated with Germans of similar views, 'we think that the security risk is very slight'.[27]

Wing Commander Arnold, however, was convinced that there was a spy ring operating out of Harwell. When Colonel Collard visited AERE Harwell, on 18 March 1948, Arnold recounted to the MI5 officer an elaborate story, accompanied with diagrams, concerning the activities of one scientist, Seaton-Bull, and Fuchs. Arnold explained that he had warned the head of Bull's department (a Dr Bretscher) about Bull's 'suspect record' (without, incidentally, any reference to MI5). These three, together with Arnold, were amongst the audience at a recent secret colloquium held under Professor Cockroft's auspices at Harwell. Fuchs and Arnold sat at the back of the lecture hall and Bretscher sat facing the audience on the platform not far away from Bull, who sat near the front row. Towards the end of the proceedings Bretscher rose from his seat and strode down to the end of the hall where he addressed Arnold in a loud voice saying, 'I hope BULL is enjoying this.' This, according to Arnold, was undoubtedly heard by Fuchs who, however, moved not a muscle. A few minutes before the colloquium dispersed, Arnold made his way from the hall and from the balcony of a building adjacent to it, proceeded to observe the method of exit of the crowd of scientists. To his surprise, he found Fuchs elbowing his way through the crowd to speak to Bull. Having succeeded in contacting Bull, the two scientists remained in a close huddle for some few minutes under the undetected observation of Arnold 'from his comparatively lofty perch on the balcony'. Arnold concluded from this incident that Fuchs was acquainting Bull with Bretscher's remark at the back of the hall, thus supporting his theory that Fuchs was running an espionage organisation in Harwell. Arnold found further grounds for attributing the Bull-Fuchs conversation to 'sinister motives' in the fact that he had never known Fuchs and Bull exchange verbal intimacies on any previous occasion, despite their long association at Harwell as colleagues. With only evidence such as this presented to him, Collard told Arnold that 'I could not attach very much importance to this story or his suspicions, but that I would be sure to pass them on to the proper section of the office.'[28]

The basis of MI5's VENONA enquiry, in 1949 was that Fuchs was probably active as a spy in the United States in 1944. But it was impossible to estimate, on the information so far available, the probability of him still being active in the United Kingdom 'in the different world conditions of 1949. In 1944 he may have thought himself justified in passing to the Russians,' then allies in war, 'a part of the product of his own brain'. But arguments which in 1944 might have supported such an attitude 'do not now apply. The impulse to treachery (if ever in fact present) may therefore no longer exist' in Fuchs's mind. He may, on the other hand, have long and secretly been a convinced Communist, considering himself 'justified in aiding the Soviet Union by the specialised means within his reach', whether in the conditions of 1944 'or in those of the present year.' The principal object of the present investigation then, was to prove which of these hypotheses was true – to obtain evidential proof as to whether Fuchs 'is or is not still a spy. It will not be easy to prove either, and to prove the negative will perhaps be even more difficult than to prove guilt.'

The first difficulty derived from the delicacy of the original information regarding the 1944 leakage. 'At no stage in the investigation can action be taken which might in any way compromise the security of the source involved. This means that the many investigators who, in their different special fields, have to co-operate in the enquiry, must necessarily act while in possession of only a part of the story, and with the greatest caution, they are thus handicapped from the beginning.' In the second place, the field in which enquiries had to be made was large. If Fuchs was a spy, the number of possible methods by which he might pass his information to the Soviet Intelligence Service was 'almost limitless'.[29]

A meeting was held on 6 September to discuss the investigation of the case. Those present were Furnival Jones and Collard from C2; Martin from B2.c; and Roberston, Reed and Skarden from B2.a. They agreed that a Home Office Warrant should be applied for to cover all correspondence addressed to Fuchs at his home or at Harwell. The HOW should also cover correspondence emanating from Fuchs. As the case was one of unusual delicacy and importance, a check on the bona fides of the GPO staff involved at the local Post Office, including postmen, was to be made. A telephone check on Fuchs's home was to be applied for and:

> A telephone check should also be operated on FUCHS' extension on the Harwell switchboard, provided this is technically possible... Whenever opportunity offers, FUCHS should be kept under observation by B.4.d in London. It was generally agreed that observation in the Harwell area would be risky, and unlikely to produce results of any value... Early steps should be taken to discover where FUCHS banks, and his bank account investigated.

Wing Commander Arnold was to be invited to attend the MI5 office as soon as possible, 'when he will be told that we are anxious, as a routine security measure', to investigate the activities of Fuchs. Arnold would be told nothing of the source involved in the present enquiry, and he would be asked not to pursue any specific lines of investigation 'unless he has been asked to do so by us, or has consulted us'. He was to be strongly warned that Fuchs's suspicions 'must on no account be roused'. Arnold would then be asked to supply MI5 with the following information:

1. All possible information concerning FUCHS' habitual movements, with particular reference to visits to London.
2. All possible information concerning FUCHS' character, habits and acquaintances.
3. Full personal description of FUCHS.
4. Information (to be communicated by telephone direct to B.4.d when appropriate) concerning any intended visit by FUCHS to London.
5. Particulars of the routine at Harwell for circulating Top Secret documents likely to be handled by FUCHS. In this connection Arnold will be invited to make any suggestion regarding the possibility of keeping a check on the time for which documents remain in FUCHS' hands, or of ascertaining whether FUCHS removes them from his office. The possibility of checking finger prints in order to ascertain whether any unauthorised person

has handled a particular document will be considered in this connection.

6. Information regarding the lay-out of FUCHS' home, which Arnold may be able to obtain if invited there, and which may be useful from the point of view of (a)... placing a microphone, and (b) determining whether or not FUCHS has at his home any apparatus for copying or photographing documents.[30]

It was agreed that MI5 policy was not likely to be materially affected by the nature of the official decision as to Fuchs's future at Harwell. 'Whether he goes or stays, his activities will have to be investigated by all the means at MI5's command.' Fuchs, it was felt, 'will be very much on his guard, and the chances of a successful investigation will be lessened if he becomes aware that he is under investigation. Nevertheless, this would not necessarily be disastrous.' Should Fuchs realise that his activities were being investigated, he might act in one of three ways:

1. Immediately cease all contact with the Russians or their representatives, and lie low until he feels that he is safe.

2. Report to [Sir John] Cockroft, or some other senior authority, his suspicions that he is under observation.

3. Continue in contact with the Russians or their representatives but take action to evade observation.

Of these alternatives,

1. Is the least desirable from our point of view, and probably the most likely.

2. Could be countered by informing him that arrangements will be made to keep him under observation in order to see whether or not he is in fact watched, and then denying that this is so.

3. Would be to our advantage, since if FUCHS were observed to take evasive action this would imply guilt.

Up to a point, therefore, and if methods of investigation involving no risk proved unsuccessful, 'we should be prepared to run some degree of risk if this is necessary in order to obtain the evidence we require'. B2.b were preparing an assessment of the situation, and would attempt to indicate in what directions B2.a could most profitably investigate. Meanwhile, it was a reasonable assumption that Fuchs must at some stage (if active as a spy) pass documentary material to the Russians, whether direct or through 'a cut-out, or through a series of cut-outs.

The cut-out (or cut-outs) may be any person whom FUCHS meets for any purpose. The part could be played equally well, for example, by a waiter in a restaurant or by a servant at Harwell itself.'

On the whole it was considered likely that Fuchs would feel himself safer in making his contact outside Harwell than in it. 'Theoretically, however, he might make it anywhere and with anyone. So far, therefore, as is practicable, we shall aim to investigate his activities continuously, whether in Harwell or outside it, throughout the twenty-four hours of each day. With this aim, the following methods of investigation will be used':

1. As agreed, a HOW will be operated on all FUCHS' correspondence. This is already in hand, and the HOW will operate as soon as Col. Allan has effected the necessary security clearance of the GPO personnel involved.

2. As has also been agreed, a telephone check will be operated on FUCHS at his home, and if feasible at his office. As yet, however, there is no telephone in his house... Mr Denman will be instructed at this meeting to ensure that when FUCHS applies for a telephone, the instrument will be prepared...

3. The full resources of B.4.d will be at the disposal of B.2.a if required. Mr Storrier has been warned, and photographs and other particulars of FUCHS will be in his hands tomorrow...

4. As the investigation progresses, all FUCHS' contacts, without exception, will be listed and investigated. Any which cannot be satisfactorily explained will be investigated, having due regard to priorities. This may necessitate the release of some B.2.a staff from their present work on satellite espionage.

5. If the scope of the investigation expands on the lines indicated, it may be more than the staff of B.4.d can manage. It may then be advisable to call in the assistance of the local police in the area in which the investigation, whether of FUCHS or of his contacts, is proceeding. The most likely areas are Birmingham, London and Oxford.

   With this in view, Col. Perfect is being warned that it may be necessary for him to make arrangements with the local Chief Constables.

6. If twenty-four hour coverage is to be maintained, it will be necessary to develop sources in Harwell itself. With this object, we are already consulting W/Cdr. Arnold.... Consideration will then be given to the following suggestions:

(a) The enlistment of FUCHS' secretary (who was selected by Arnold himself) as a source.

(b) The obtaining, from the secretary or from any other suitable source, of a day to day account of the movements of documents into and out of FUCHS' hands, with the particular object of determining whether or not any given document remains in his possession for longer than is strictly necessary. It may be of especial significance if FUCHS is found to have taken with him to some place outside Harwell – for example Birmingham – any document which the overt purpose of his journey might not absolutely require him to have in his possession.

(c) The examination for finger-prints of documents handled by FUCHS and authorised to be handled only by a limited number of persons other than himself. The presence of the finger-prints of any unauthorised person on such a document would establish that it had had more than the permitted distribution.

(d) The use of a microphone in FUCHS' Harwell office.

7. The activities of Professor PEIERLS of Birmingham University, a close friend and associate of FUCHS, will be investigated by means of a telephone check and a HOW on his correspondence. The necessary warrants have been applied for.[31]

On 9 September, Wing Commander Arnold was informed in outline of the case against Fuchs, but not of the Top Secret source involved.[32] On 14 and 15 September, 1949, Jim Skardon visited Harwell with Arnold, on the second day being accompanied by John Hackney of B4.d. Skardon's principal task was to discover whether any profitable enquiries could be made on the spot and particularly what facilities existed for keeping observation on the suspect. Arnold produced a plan of the establishment 'which paints a better picture than any words. In fact Harwell has become so secure that overlooking, i.e. observation, must quickly be detected.' The establishment was isolated. It fronted on to the Newbury-Oxford road and was formerly an RAF Station. The laboratories, workshops and offices were contained by a perimeter fence outside which lay the residential quarters and club house. There were four gates giving access to the establishment. A main gate with a War Department Constabulary (WDC) police lodge to guard it on the road. On the north or Oxford side there were two gates – one pedestrian only and the other to pass vehicular traffic as well. On the south side there was a contractors' gate. Owing to the grouping for security reasons, any MI5 watchers would themselves be quickly observed. Skardon thought it would be idle to suggest that all the staff were known to one another, but to a large extent this was true 'and I am sure that on the spot observation would quickly and certainly be detected by the suspect. We explored all possibilities of controlling an observation from some remote spot. The best suggestion to be made involved internal observation by Arnold and perhaps Sub-Inspector Bushnell of WDC with word to the watchers at the Rowstock Crossroads a mile away through a sergeant of the Berkshire Constabulary.' Unfortunately, Arnold could suggest no fellow scientist to inform on the suspect. And Miss Holloway, the suspect's secretary, 'does not seem to be the sort of person one can safely approach for information on her chief'. Finally, Skardon concluded that it would be difficult locally to house any staff without attracting attention.[33] With this information B4.d decided:

1. That observation in the Harwell area, whether within the perimeter or in its immediate surroundings, is too risky owing to absence of suitable cover and for other local reasons.

2. That following by car in the Harwell area is also unsafe, owing to the scarcity of traffic on the local country roads ...

3. That FUCHS will almost invariably apply for a travel warrant before making any journey away from Harwell. If he does not do this, he involves himself in unnecessary expense. Moreover, he is on the whole unlikely, for any purpose to do with espionage, to travel in a manner which might appear abnormal. As a rule, therefore, but not invariably, advance warning of his intention to travel will be obtained when he applies for vouchers, since this will always be known to Arnold.

4. In addition, there is a reasonable chance of obtaining advance intelligence about any intended journey through (blank) and T[elephone]C[hecks]., which will be installed by the evening of 17.9.49.

In these circumstances, the following plan had been agreed and would come into operation forthwith:

(i) B.4.d will maintain a headquarters staff of selected watchers in permanent readiness in London.

(ii) These watchers will be prepared to act at once on information received from:

(a) W/Cdr. Arnold, who will communicate by telephone through Regent 6050, by day or by night. When using the telephone, Arnold will use the following code names:

RAMSAY = Fuchs.

MATTHEWS = Peierls.

PIPER = Skinner [friend of Fuchs and deputy to Cockcroft].

Other code names will be added as required.

(b) The (blank) and T[elephone]C[heck] operators at Newbury, through B.4.b. Communication between B.4.b and B.4.d for this purpose, whether by day or by night, will be direct.

(c) B.2.a in the event of information being received from any other source.

(iii) On receiving information that FUCHS is preparing to travel by rail, the B.4.d watchers will attempt to reach Didcot Station and take up observation from that point.

If FUCHS travels by car, B.4.d will <u>NOT</u> attempt observation in the Harwell district, but will endeavour to pick up his car on the most likely trunk road, according to his destination.

If information of an intended journey by FUCHS is received by B.4.d too late for either of the courses of action described above, they will aim to intercept him at the railway terminus to which he is proceeding, or at the address which he will be visiting, whether this be in London, or in Birmingham or Oxford, which are his most likely alternative destinations.

(iv) Appropriate instructions will be given to the Night Duty Officer...

The installation of telephone checks (TC) and microphones proceeded in accordance with the plan. Denman reconnoitred the Newbury Post Office premises on 16 September, returning to London at 3 p.m., and reported that he had found suitable accommodation for the GPO equipment. The complete installation would be ready and working by the late afternoon of 17 September. Three volunteers were obtained from the staff of B4.b, and prepared to leave for Newbury this being dependent on A. Division finding suitable accommodation. The intention was to book the necessary rooms in the Chequers Hotel in Newbury. Should it prove necessary for the B4.b personnel to account in any way for their presence in Newbury they were to state that they were GPO relief staff working at the local Post Office. This accorded with the story told by Denman to the Head Postmaster, which was to the effect that they were working on a statistical enquiry affecting calls passing through the Newbury exchange. Communication of information from Newbury was to be done in two ways: '1. A complete paper record of each day's work will be collected daily by a

Headquarters car from London; 2. Information of operational urgency will be communicated by telephone from Newbury to B.4.b.'

With this in view, Denman had made a scrambler telephone available in the room which would be used in the Newbury Post Office. As an additional precaution, a suitable code would be agreed between B4b in London and their personnel in Newbury. There was to be 'NO contact between W/Cdr. Arnold and the GPO personnel in Newbury'. Any information which Arnold needed to have would be communicated to him by telephone from London. Other sources of information would be considered as and when the sources described above began to be productive. They might include:

1. FUCHS' secretary. Mr Skardon decided, in the course of his visit to Harwell on 15.9.49, that it would be unwise to make any approach to FUCHS' present secretary. At a later date, however, it may be possible to arrange for him to have a new secretary, who could be selected by this office. Arnold thinks that the administrative problems involved in this proposal could be overcome without serious difficulty...

2. The owner of the house next door to FUCHS' pre-fab is a Mr DENTON, whom Arnold considers a reliable person... DENTON might be used at a later stage as a source of information about FUCHS' movements out of working hours.

3. The head of the War Department Constabulary at Harwell is regarded by Arnold as reliable, and as capable of being used for our purposes later, if required.[34]

Arnold called on MI5, on 26 September, and had a series of talks with Dick White, B4, Skardon and J.C. Robertson of B2.a, where it was agreed that the drafting of extra War Department Constabulary personnel to Harwell might attract undesirable attention. The use of members of the rank and file of the present WDC staff in Harwell would be too risky, since there would be no certainty of the men keeping the matter strictly to themselves. It was therefore felt by Arnold, Skardon and Robertson that – since additional coverage, especially over the weekends, was badly needed – the best course of action would be to make use of the WDC Chief Inspector (Jennings) and his Sub-Inspector (Bushnell), especially the latter. This was discussed further at 3 p.m. with B4, and also with Captain Wale of the WDC Headquarters in London, and his principal assistant. Wale was well known to B4. and told simply that an intensive security check was being carried out at Harwell which required investigation of the movements of one or two particular individuals, especially at weekends and during off-duty hours. The proposal to use Jennings and Bushnell was submitted to Wale, who could see no objection.

By now Mr K. Blumfield, formerly Arnold's second-in-command, who had left him a month before for an administrative post, had been selected for appointment as Divisional Administrative Officer in the Theoretical Division at Harwell. As such he would personally sign all applications for petrol or for travel warrants from Fuchs, and Arnold arranged to be informed by him at once of any intention on Fuchs's part to travel from Harwell. Blumfield, in his former capacity of Security Officer, had taken part in a course with the Security Service. The use of Fuchs's secretary as a source was further discussed and finally decided upon: the suggestion was considered that a secretary should be found by B4 to replace Fuchs's 'present girl'. But, in Arnold's view was now that the administrative difficulties in the way of this would be insurmountable. In any event, his view was that a secretary would be able to give them little more information than he would himself be in a position to obtain through Blumfield.

It was represented to White by Skardon and Robertson, in the presence of Arnold, that the proposed use of Sub-Inspector Bushnell at Harwell would lose much of its usefulness if it became impossible to arrange for immediate B4.d coverage in the event of Bushnell learning, by direct observation, of Fuchs's departure from Harwell. In the circumstances, Skardon and Robertson's view was that B4.d should reconsider the possibility of establishing a forward headquarters at the Rowstock crossroads, near Harwell, where they should wait with a car for any exit by road on the part of Fuchs. White recognised that this was essential if the aim of twenty-four hour coverage was to be attained. He undertook to consider the proposal. It was pointed out that, to be useful, the proposed increase of B4d coverage should be effective the following weekend (1 and 2 October), experience having shown 'that our present resources are weakest over Saturdays and Sundays'.[35]

During the period of the investigation the only visitor of possible significance to Fuchs had been F.W. Gurney, a British scientist who was considered in 1947 for employment on the Atomic Energy Project in the United States. The only possible security interest appeared to be that his wife, who was of Russian origin, was reported to have had Communist associations in the years 1931–1937, and to have been secretary of the Bristol Branch of the Society for Cultural Relations with Soviet Russia from 1935 to 1937. The Security Service felt that its surveillance had allowed it 'to account satisfactorily' for Fuchs's movements and contacts since the beginning of the investigation. It found that 'he is a reserved man, keeping very much to himself', and having as almost his only intimate friends in the Atomic Energy Research Establishment, Professor and Mrs Skinner. Professor Skinner, who was unofficial deputy to Sir John Cockroft, was expected shortly to take up a physics professorship at Liverpool University, thereafter dividing his time between Liverpool and Harwell. Fuchs's departures from Harwell had been rare, and on those occasions when he had travelled outside the area it had been possible for Security Service Watchers to keep close observation on his movements – as, for example, when he left Harwell for Wembley on 22 September in the company of Professor Skinner and two other Harwell scientists for an official conference in the premises of the General Electric Company.[36]

TC information failed to account for Fuchs from approximately 1 p.m. on 25 September until 4 a.m on 26 September. Arnold thought it possible that Professor Skinner was away from Harwell on the night in question, travelling by sleeper to Liverpool. If so, it seemed that Fuchs may have spent the evening and part of the night, alone, with Mrs Skinner.[37] In short, apart from Fuchs's extra-curricular activities with Mrs Skinner, nothing of any consequence had shown up.

By December 1949 – after three months of investigation and research – the Security Service was satisfied that no person other than Klaus Fuchs fitted the information received from the FBI; equally they were satisfied that they had found no evidence to suggest that Fuchs was currently engaged in espionage. The problem therefore became one primarily of preventive security. Clearly Fuchs could not be allowed to remain at Harwell but, equally clearly, his dismissal would greatly decrease the prospects of obtaining evidence of any current espionage; moreover there was the further danger that to dismiss him summarily might lead to his defection to the Russians. At this point Fuchs himself precipitated the action which was already under consideration, namely interrogation.[38]

On 12 October 1949, Fuchs had come to see Arnold to tell him that his father, then domiciled in Frankfurt, had been offered a chair at Leipzig University which was in the Russian Zone in Germany; Fuchs said he thought Arnold ought to be aware of this fact. Arnold told Fuchs he would like to think this matter over. Arnold discussed the matter further with Fuchs on 20 October, when he asked the scientist whether he thought pressure might not be brought to bear on him through any possible arrest of his father. Fuchs replied that, at the present time, he did not feel he would be induced to co-operate with the Russians but he could not say how he might react under altered circumstances. This interview concluded with Fuchs asking Arnold if he thought he (Fuchs) should resign from Harwell if his father accepted the post at Leipzig University. Arnold told him this was not a matter for a Security Officer to decide but one for the decision of the administrative authorities. Arnold then reported this incident to the proper authorities. Some time during November, Fuchs told Arnold his father had accepted the post. This fact Arnold similarly reported to the proper authorities. Arnold heard nothing more on this matter until he was told by the Security Service that one of their officers would come down to Harwell and interview Fuchs.[39] The opportunity to interrogate Fuchs was 'accepted by the Security Service with the intention that, whatever the outcome, it would be followed by his dismissal.'[40]

On 21 December, 1949, Jim Skardon went to interview Fuchs at the Atomic Energy Research Establishment, Harwell. Before seeing him, Skardon had a discussion with Sir John Cockcroft and told him that he hoped to keep the two parts of his enquiry in watertight compartments, that was to say Skardon hoped to be able to show that whereas the presence of Fuchs's father in Leipzig constituted a security risk which was being actively considered by the Ministry of Supply and upon which MI5 was giving advice, the matters relating to his espionage activities were known solely to Skardon's department. Sir John was satisfied with this division of responsibility, and asked Wing Commander Arnold to collect Fuchs and introduce him to Skardon.[41] Skardon was introduced to Fuchs by Arnold as 'Mr Seddon of the Security Service'.[42] Arnold left them together in his office.

Skardon commenced the interview by telling Fuchs that the presence of his father in the Russian zone of Germany formed a considerable security risk in view of Fuchs's position and standing in the extremely secret work he was doing. Fuchs 'seemed to understand this'. Skardon told him that he wanted to ask him numerous questions, some of which he might think impertinent, 'but that it was necessary that I should do so in order that we might fairly assess the risks involved'. Skardon first questioned Fuchs about his relatives, and discovered that his only close relations were his father, his brother Gerhardt who was in Switzerland and his sister Kristel Heinemann who was living in Cambridge Massachusetts. Fuchs, basically, confirmed every known fact that MI5 possessed about him, volunteering most of the information but being assisted as to dates by Skardon. 'So that a proper appreciation of the atmosphere may be established,' reported Skardon, 'I will merely say that he gave every appearance of being thoroughly frank so far as we knew his history, and volunteered some information not formerly known to us.'

Very early in his discussions with him, Skardon established that Fuchs recognised that his Oath of Allegiance – taken when he was naturalised as a British subject – was a serious matter 'and a thing to be observed'. At the same time Fuchs claimed freedom to act in accordance with his conscience should circumstances arise in Britain comparable to those which existed in Germany in 1932 and 1933, when he would act on a loyalty which he possessed to humanity generally. Skardon established that Fuchs and his father were members of the SPD in Germany (the Social Democratic Party) 'and might fairly be described as Socialists'. In 1932, when Hitler was coming to power, and on the occasion of an election for a Vice-President, Fuchs supported the Communist candidate against the Nazi candidate, in the absence of a Socialist representative. For this Fuchs was expelled from the SPD, and thereafter belonged to a national students organisation which had Communist affiliations. All his political activities until March 1933 were confined to the district of Kiel, where he was living. Fuchs claimed that he knew that the police were interested in him, and he moved to Berlin where he remained until July, 1933, continuing his activities with the students organisation. On the last mentioned date he left Berlin for Paris, having been asked by the organisation to take part in an International congress in Paris under the auspices of Henri Barbusse. This congress was described as the United Front which, Fuchs said, today would be called a Communist Front. It took place late in August 1933, and in September Fuchs came to the UK. Fuchs went to live with a Mr R.H. Gunn at Chunnock Wood, Clapton-in-Gordans, Gloucestershire, and continued to live with him there and at other addresses until 1937. He was introduced to Gunn through the fiancée of a cousin of his, now a Mrs Martini, who had stayed with the Gunns earlier and recommended them to Fuchs. Fuchs described Mr Gunn as a man who had some interest in Soviet cultural organisations but was never a member of the Communist Party. Fuchs studied at Bristol University for his Doctorate of Philosophy, and took no part in politics in Britain where he had found refuge. The only exception to this rule was when he joined a committee for the defence of Spanish democracy, a local Bristol organisation at the time of the Spanish Civil War. During these years he was in the UK, he travelled once to Switzerland for the purpose of seeing his brother, round about 1934 or 1935.

Fuchs then described how he went to Edinburgh University and worked there under Max Born, and how in 1940 he was interned and sent to Camp L, Quebec, Canada. He admitted having taken part in political activities in the camp, but said that these were domestic politics relating to the camp and internees. In these activities he was associated with Hans Kahle and one Abrahamson. Their activities were directed to making representations to the camp authorities against the appointment of a son of the former German Crown Prince as Camp Leader, and also to dealing with anticipatory fears that the Canadians intended to exchange the internees against Canadian prisoners of war held in Germany.

Very early in 1941, Fuchs, having been released from internment, arrived back in Britain and returned to Edinburgh to continue his work there. He stayed there until May 1941, when he moved to Birmingham and a little later commenced work on the Tube Alloys project under Dr Rudolph Ernst Peierls whom he had first met at scientific conferences immediately before the war and with whom he lived for part of the time that he was in Birmingham. When he obtained Government employment Fuchs decided that he must give up his association with Kahle and other people like him who had returned at about the same time from internment. The only contacts he had maintained with these people in the early part of 1941 were occasional visits from them to him in Edinburgh, and one visit he made to Kahle in London when he was taken by him to a Free German Youth organisation which had a restaurant in the Hampstead area. There he met a number of refugees and one, whose name he forgot, attempted to renew acquaintance with him when Fuchs was already employed in Birmingham but he shook him off.

Late in 1943, Fuchs described how he went to the United States where he stayed from 3 December 1943 until August 1944, in New York. While in New York he lived successively at the Taft Hotel, another hotel for a short time, the name of which he forgot, and later still at an apartment. In none of these places did he share accommodation with anyone else, save for a short time in the Taft Hotel on his first arrival. Fuchs said that the work which he was doing occupied all his waking hours and that he had very little time for social activities. He did however manage to visit his sister and her husband in Cambridge, Massachusetts, at Christmas 1943, and again some time during the following April or May.

Having reached this stage of the interrogation, Skardon turned up the heat dramatically: he alleged to Fuchs that he had been in touch with a Soviet official or a Soviet representative and had passed to that person information bearing upon his work. Fuchs's first reaction was to 'open his mouth as though surprised, and then to smile and say, "I don't think so." I then said to him, "I am in possession of precise information which shows that you have been guilty of espionage on behalf of the Soviet Union; for example during the time that you were in New York you passed to them information concerning your work." Fuchs again replied, 'I don't think so.' Skardon told him that this was an ambiguous reply but Fuchs simply said: 'I don't understand; perhaps you will tell me what the evidence is. I have not done any such thing.'

Skardon then told Fuchs that: 'I was not really questioning him about this matter but that I was stating a fact. I should however want to question him about the manner in which he gave the information, how he made the contact and the full extent of his guilt. He repeated that he was quite unable to assist me, and strongly denied that he had ever been responsible for such a leakage. He said that it did not make sense, since he had been doing all that he could to help win the war. He was perfectly satisfied to be in the vanguard of progress of this new scientific development, and could not think it at all likely that sundry pieces of information on some offshoot would be of any real value to Russia or that he would have any reason for passing the information. He knew quite well that a decision had been taken to exclude Russia from sharing the information. Fuchs thought this was quite a good idea from a scientific point of view, since the Americans were well equipped to make all the necessary experiments, and he was not concerned with the political motives underlying the decision.'

Skardon decided then to question him about an entry in Israel Halperin's diary mentioning Fuchs. Halperin was a scientist engaged in Canadian atomic research and was implicated in the Gouzenko defection as a Soviet spy (although he was subsequently cleared). Fuchs at first denied knowledge of the name. Later, when Skardon told him of the juxtaposition of his name with that of his sister in the diary, he remembered 'as though for the first time' that his sister had made representations to Halperin when Fuchs was in internment. Halperin had sent him physical reviews and the like to read in camp. So far as he knew, he had never met Halperin.

At this stage, Fuchs asked Skardon if all his evidence was of the same kind, 'and I told him that I could not break faith with my informants, and that it was only by being trustworthy in this respect that I could hope to carry out my duties. At the same time I pointed out that I would not break faith with him, and if he cared to make a clean breast of the matter he could trust me to ensure that his actions were presented in the most favourable light.' Fuchs did not take up this offer, so Skardon then questioned Fuchs about the composition, duties and security arrangements of the British Mission in New York, of which he was a member. Fuchs replied that he was unable to help Skardon with precise details as to the manner in which the junior staff were recruited, but thought they were supplied by the British Mission, in whose building the diffusion team were working. Fuchs was unable to say whether the secretarial assistance was provided from the Mission or was recruited locally, and seemed to have no recollection of the names of any of the junior staff. Skardon then questioned Fuchs about the security of the papers produced by members of the mission, and the scientist replied that these were duplicated and numbered serially, but he was not aware of the precise steps taken for the security of the duplicated copies. Fuchs thought that in the early days of the Mission the papers were duplicated within the office, but thought that at some stage the stencils were sent out from the Mission to the Kellex organisation for duplication. He believed that he could confirm the date upon which this change in the routine took place, by referring to his own copies of these papers. Shortly before lunch Fuchs took the opportunity, while his secretary was away, to go and collect the papers and show them to Skardon.

From an examination of them Skardon reported that it was noteworthy that the duplication of the papers by Kellex seemed to have commenced in February 1944, which was the notional date of Fuchs's recruitment by the Soviets 'according to our secret information'. In fact it emerged, 'and should be borne in mind', that between January and July 1944, of all the seventeen papers produced by the Mission, ten were the work of Fuchs alone. These papers varied in length, but were all 'obviously wholly abstruse mathematical calculations, and to my unpracticed eye represent extremely solid work throughout the period. I can well believe that he had little time for any social activities. His own story is that during this period he worked from dawn to dusk.' Fuchs went perhaps once or twice a week to see the Kellex people, and occasionally made contact with the Columbia University Laboratory and the SAM Laboratory in Upper Broadway. He made friendships in these organisations but: 'Otherwise his social activities were nil.'

Fuchs had agreed that he habitually carried some papers with him, to study at home or when moving about from place to place, and thought it quite possible that he took papers with him when he visited his sister. He could not, though, believe that they would have afforded his sister any opportunity of passing information from him to some third party. He recognised that his brother-in-law was of Communistic tendencies, although he did not believe him to be a member of any party. During the time that he was in New York, Fuchs said that he paid one visit to Montreal and suggested that his passport would show the precise date at which this took place and whether he went before or after his move to Los Alamos. (In fact MI5 knew of one journey to Montreal in November 1945, from Los Alamos.)

The interrogation was broken from about 1.30 p.m. to just after 2 pm, while they had lunch, and Skardon deemed it prudent to allow Fuchs to lunch alone and think about what had been said. But upon his return Fuchs had nothing fresh to tell Skardon, 'and this remained his attitude in spite of the many opportunities I gave him to confess'. In addition Skardon sought to make it quite clear to Fuchs that the decision as to whether he would remain at Harwell, having regard to his father's domicile in the Soviet zone, was one which the Ministry of Supply was actively considering and one where they would seek the advice of MI5. Skardon told Fuchs that he felt quite sure that whatever the Ministry decided to do, 'we should advise that a big risk would be taken' by the continued employment of Fuchs on this top secret work in such conditions. 'Whether the Ministry would take our advice or not would be a matter for them.' Skardon explained to Fuchs that the knowledge that he had been engaged in espionage was shared with no one outside MI5, and any decisions to his future at Harwell would be taken upon the basis of his father's location. Skardon took the opportunity of course to point out that a favourable report from MI5 might have the effect of keeping him at Harwell, where he had said he would be most happy to stay. Fuchs professed to:

recognise the extremely difficult situation in which we were placed and said that he was so sensible of my inability to produce my evidence to him that he had been able to restrain himself from instinctively pounding the table and demanding that the evidence against him should be produced. In the absence of the production of the evidence against him, he felt that he was utterly unable to help the enquiry. He also made the point that since he was under suspicion he might upon reflection think it quite impossible to continue to work at Harwell, and if he came to that conclusion he would offer his resignation. He thought it would be perfectly simple for him to obtain a University post. He also foresaw that there would be no particular financial disadvantage in his doing so. At the same time he made it quite clear that his great interest is in the work upon which he is at present engaged.

The pair separated after over four hours together, and Fuchs left with a clear understanding that Skardon was the only person he knew who could discuss the espionage angle of his case with him. Skardon gave Fuchs the opportunity of making contact with him at any time, through Arnold, should he change his mind or think of any useful piece of information. In accordance with his instructions Skardon concluded the interview by referring again to the security problem raised by Fuch's father, and asked him why he had thought it proper to bring this fact to the attention of Wing Commander Arnold. Fuchs replied that he thought it quite possible that the Russians would seek to make political use of the fact that his non-Communist father was working peacefully in the Soviet zone. He also thought it possible that his father might get himself into trouble on his own account. Whereas his father seemed to be impressed by what he saw in the Soviet zone at the present time, the day might well come when he would disagree, 'and will say so quite strongly'. Fuchs claimed that he had not considered the likelihood of pressure being brought to bear on him through his father, until this suggestion was made by Arnold. Skardon said that he thought this was an important matter for consideration 'and I did not regard it as a very remote possibility'. Fuchs agreed that the Russians were quite capable of using the opportunity presented to them in such a manner.

In his report on the meeting Skardon admitted that he found it 'extremely difficult to give a conclusive view' about the guilt or innocence of Fuchs. 'His demeanour during our interview could have been indicative of either condition. If he is innocent it is surprising that he should receive allegations of this kind so coolly, but perhaps this squares with his mathematical approach to life. It could also be argued that he is a spy of old standing and was prepared for such an interrogation.' Reviewing all the facts in the light of the interrogation Skardon felt sure that 'we have selected the right man, unless by chance someone in the nature of a twin brother was in New York when he was there'. In fact there was no one in such close daily contact with him as would provide MI5 with another candidate, and it was difficult, 'unless he had a colleague using his name and the background of his life as a cover, or alternatively a secretary completely in his confidence', to find any candidate for the suspect other than Fuchs himself.[43]

On 30 December, 1949, Skardon had a further interview with Fuchs at Harwell. On this occasion Skardon's impending arrival had been announced to Fuchs by Arnold. Fuchs again appeared to be quite calm and self-possessed, and answered Skardon's preliminary questions: (a) had he thought of anything which would be of assistance and (b) had he decided to make a clean breast of his espionage work on behalf of the Russians; in the negative. He said that he had given a lot of thought to Skardon's allegations, but could think of no way of accounting for them. Skardon questioned Fuchs at great length about the movements of his sister, Kristel Heinemanns, and her husband. According to Fuchs, his sister went to America in 1936, travelling via England. He saw her in Britain. In the USA she attended, he believed, a Quaker college, her subject being psychology. They were irregular correspondents, only one or two letters a year passing between them. Fuchs claimed, therefore, to know very little about his sister's movements or mode of life in the USA. He was unable to suggest how his sister made contact with Israel Halperin, or how it was arranged that physics reviews had been sent to him in internment. He confirmed that he paid two visits to the Heinemanns in Cambridge, Massachusetts: one at Christmas 1943, and one which he thought took place shortly before he went to Los Alamos. Fuchs was quite sure that although a trip was projected, his sister did not in fact visit him in New York, and so far as he knew she did not visit New York after his departure for Los Alamos. He thought she may have given him the names of one or two friends of hers in New York, but he did not take up these introductions. The position, therefore, was that he knew of nobody in New York at the relevant time who might be described as a mutual friend of his sister and himself. Since Kristel had three small children, the youngest born in November 1943, she was very much tied to the house, and so far as Fuchs was aware she only left her Cambridge home for a holiday at the coast in mid-1944. When Fuchs travelled to Cambridge he believed that he travelled by night, as this was a journey of six or seven hours from New York.

Skardon questioned Fuchs about his finances while he was in the U.S., but he denied receiving any financial payment, either by way of a fee, gift or in any other manner. He did not give any lectures for which he was paid, nor render any services for which he might have expected a reward. Skardon asked him about his contacts with students, and he answered that he had made none. The only university with which he came into contact was Columbia, and his visits were confined to their laboratories to see Dr Cohen. On this point he confirmed that Dr Cohen was the one person in New York with whom he struck up any sort of friendship, and he was on visiting terms to his house.

His projected departure for Los Alamos was something which Fuchs deemed to be most secret, and accordingly he was careful not to tell anybody about it. Fuchs said that he may have dissembled when questioned directly by Cohen as to where he was going, and the latter therefore may have deduced the truth, but he did not in fact pass on the information to anybody. Fuchs maintained that while in New York he met nobody who might be said to be connected with his earlier life. This was in answer to questions as to whether Hans Kahle pursued him, either in person or through some agent there. Fuchs denied that he had any contact with anybody, either directly or indirectly, touching upon his past life.

After this, Skardon told Fuchs that the Ministry would undoubtedly, although with reluctance, decide to dispense with his services, since his father's presence in Leipzig did form a substantial security risk. Skardon repeated 'that he should keep the other subjects I had discussed with him to himself, and made it plain that should other people learn of them it would only be through his lips. I expressed the view that he would find himself settled fairly soon in some university atmosphere, and indicated that it was quite certain that I should desire to question him again. He understood, and expressed willingness to see me at any time.' In closing the interview Skardon told Fuchs that he could be reached at any time through Arnold, should he desire either to confess or pass on information. Fuchs thanked Skardon. Later Skardon reported that Fuchs 'was not in the least discomposed by the interview or my questions, and the only sign of nervousness which I detected was to be found in his parched lips, which I noticed just before he left the office'.[44] After this conversation, Skardon returned to MI5 HQ to tell Dick White: 'You're barking up the wrong tree... Fuchs is innocent.' White urged him to continue: 'Sincerity ... is a wonderful disguise. Go back and continue the questioning.' White explained his thinking: 'I sought to create understanding rather than obedience. I wanted people like Skardon to understand and agree what was worth doing. It taxed my wits to win at the end of the day.' Arthur Martin supported White, telling Skardon: 'I know he's guilty.'[45]

In the meantime, Sir John Cockcroft, as Director of the Atomic Energy Research Establishment at Harwell, told Fuchs that, on the advice of the Security Service, as the presence of his father in the Soviet Zone of Germany presented a security risk which the Department of Atomic Energy ought not to run, it had been decided that he must leave Harwell and transfer himself elsewhere, e.g. to a university. Although Cockcroft and Fuchs had been at Harwell since 1946, Sir John had only since met him in the course of their work and on various social occasions; their association 'never developed into one of friendship'.

It was not until Cockroft was in America on official business in the autumn of 1949 that he had any reason to suspect the loyalty of Fuchs. During their three years of association, recalled Cockcroft, Fuchs 'had always been meticulously careful in all matters of Security'. In America however Cockcroft had received information which for the first time caused him to distrust Fuchs's loyalty.[46] Yet soon Cockcroft was telling Fuchs that he could help him to find a job, and suggested that Professor Skinner might be ready to take him on at Liverpool. He went on to say that there was a post in theoretical physics vacant at Adelaide University, and that possibly Professor Oliphant might help. Fuchs was delighted. Cockcroft then told Fuchs that the only chance of the Security Service changing its advice was that Fuchs should give every assistance in providing full information about himself, his life and background. The interview closed with Cockcroft offering Fuchs six months leave of absence starting at about Easter, and suggesting that Fuchs should think over this interview and come and see Cockcroft in a few days time.

When Cockcroft informed MI5 – in the person of J.H. Marriott – of this they were not pleased: the position now was that Fuchs had been told that he had to leave Harwell, but that no date had been fixed, nor had any agreement been arrived at as to the form which his departure would take or as to the reasons for his leaving. In addition, a 'grave complication' has been introduced in the shape of the suggestion that he might go to Australia. Marriott told Cockcroft and Michael Perrin, the Deputy Controller Atomic Energy (Technical Policy) Ministry of Supply, that 'I was disturbed' at the idea of Fuchs remaining at Harwell until Easter and that he should have to obtain the DG's advice as to the extent to which MI5 could undertake, during that period, to keep Fuchs under supervision.[47]

On the same day that Marriott received this unwelcome information – 13 January 1950 – Skardon saw Fuchs again, at Harwell. The object of Skardon's visit this time was primarily to discover Fuchs's New York address. He lost no time in telling Fuchs that it was for this purpose that he had come, and the scientist immediately said, 'Oh yes, the Barbazon Plaza.' Skardon then pointed out that although he was interested to know the name of the second of the two hotels at which Fuchs had stayed, it was the address of his apartment which the MI5 man required. Fuchs thought that if he had a map he might be able to locate his apartment on it, and Skardon produced one for him. After studying it carefully he decided that it was on West 77th Street, near Central Park and in the middle of the block between Columbus

Avenue and Amsterdam Avenue. Fuchs believed that when he left New York he probably gave as his forward address, to the janitor of his apartment, the Washington office. There was just a chance, he said, that if he had been given permission to do so, he would have given the Box Number at Santa Fé, which was the usual address for people employed at Los Alamos. His firm belief was, however, that he did not do this. When Skardon revealed to Fuchs that it was known that a representative of the Russians had called at his New York apartment after his departure, 'and that it was for this reason that we wanted to make direct enquiries there. He was not in the least alarmed at this possibility, but on the contrary he thought it extremely unlikely that such a visit had occurred.'

Fuchs denied once again that he had ever passed any information to the Soviets or to their representatives and Skardon told him that if he were speaking the truth 'it was my duty to make such enquiries as would clear him and it would be to his advantage to help in this matter'. Fuchs, noted Skardon:

> was completely composed, and I questioned him about his present position. He said that he had been told that he must go, but that there was nothing very urgent about it and he had not so far made any positive enquiry to find any job. He thought the task would not be too hard, and mentioned that Sir John Cockcroft had offered him the choice of two posts, one at Adelaide and the other with Professor Oliphant, also in Australia. He thought that he would not like to work with Oliphant, although he hardly knew him. In reply to a direct question he said that he thought he might take some leave, but had made no plans at all up to the moment.'[48]

On 19 January, Sir Percy Sillitoe wrote to Sir Archibald Rowlands, at the Ministry of Supply, relating how Cockcroft had told Fuchs he could no longer remain employed at Herwell. This was in line with the long-term policy agreed at a meeting held by Lord Portal on 5 January. Unfortunately, explained Sillitoe, 'there still remains a short-term problem of considerable difficulty from our point of view'. Cockcroft, he understood, gave Fuchs no fixed date of notice and suggested in general terms that he might stay on at Harwell at least until Easter. If Fuchs did remain where he was for that length of time it involved 'a very heavy burden on our resources of investigation which frankly I can well do without'. By this stage Fuchs's activities had been under intensive investigation for more than four months. It had been an investigation of special difficulty owing to the fact that Fuchs spent the greater part of his time inside Harwell 'where you will appreciate that the task of maintaining continuous observation without arousing his suspicion produces a series of awkward problems. We have used in this case every kind of resource available to us for the purposes of investigation and this has tied up a large part of the time of our specialist officers. These resources are badly needed in other directions.'

Since it had been generally agreed that Fuchs's continued employment was a constant threat to security 'and since our own elaborate investigation has produced no dividends', Sillitoe declared that he would be grateful if Rowlands would be kind enough to arrange for Fuchs's departure from Harwell 'as soon as is decently possible'.[49] And then, suddenly, before anything else could be done, the badly needed breakthrough in the case came.

Wing Commander Arnold telephoned J.C. Robertson at 10 a.m. on 23 January 1950 to report that Fuchs had asked to see him, in order to have a 'long quiet talk'. As a result he arranged to lunch with Fuchs later that day. Arnold asked for guidance as to the attitude he should adopt. This situation was reported to B2 and Dick White at once. It was quickly agreed that Arnold be instructed, in his talk with Fuchs, that he should reveal no knowledge of the situation surrounding the resignation of the latter, other than that Fuchs was recently interviewed by a security official, that this interview was connected with the presence of Fuchs's father in the Soviet Zone of Germany, and that Fuchs's resignation was a consequence. Arnold's principal aim should be to hear Fuchs out, and to do what he could to make Fuchs tell him everything which was on his mind. If Fuchs supplied any information additional to that which Arnold was supposed already to know, it would be necessary for Arnold to make clear to him that this information would have to be reported by Arnold to the authorities. Arnold should, however, postpone any statement to this effect until the latest possible stage of the conversation. Similarly, if Fuchs supplied Arnold with new information, and if he gave Arnold any lead for mentioning the interest of Mr Seddon (Skardon) in such information, Arnold had to make it clear that everything related to himself (Arnold) by Fuchs should also be related to Seddon by Fuchs. Again, any such statement should be left as late as possible. MI5 were worried that, before talking to Arnold, Fuchs might attempt to obtain some form of advance guarantee – as for example of immunity 'in the event of frankness'. Arnold 'must on no account commit himself to a guarantee of any kind, or make any promise whatever' to Fuchs. 'If he has to give reasons, these should be firstly, that he has no authority to give guarantees; and secondly, that in any event his knowledge of the whole affair is too limited for him to be justified in committing himself to anything of the kind.' Robertson passed these instructions to Arnold by telephone at 12.15 – fifteen minutes before he was due to lunch with Fuchs. Mrs Grist of B4b was also informed of the situation and asked to report any relevant intelligence that might be obtained through T.Cs.[50]

Arnold lunched with Fuchs at the Old Railway House Hotel, Steventon. He told Arnold, that he would like to have another interview with Skardon as he had something else to tell about the matter under enquiry. Fuchs seemed to Arnold 'to be under mental stress' and appeared anxious to continue his conversations with Skardon. He told Arnold that he did not want this further interview to take place either at Harwell or in London and Arnold accordingly arranged for Skardon to meet Fuchs at his private house on 24 January 1950.[51] Skardon saw Fuchs the next day at his home, at 11 a.m. and he began by saying to Fuchs, 'You asked to see me and here I am', to which he replied, 'Yes, it is rather up to me now.' Thereafter, for nearly two hours, he related the story of his life, but during the course of this made no admission of any espionage activity, though he did tell Skardon about his work for the Communist underground in Germany. It was clear to Skardon that Fuchs 'was evidently under considerable mental stress, and I told him that it seemed to me that whereas he had told me a long story providing a motive for acts, he had told me nothing about the acts themselves. I suggested that he should unburden his mind and clear his conscience by telling me the full story.' Fuchs replied, 'I will never be persuaded by you to talk.' At this stage they went off to lunch. During the meal Fuchs 'seemed to be resolving the matter and to be considerably abstracted', and towards the end he suggested that they should hurry back to his house. On their arrival there Fuchs announced that he had decided that it would be in his best interests to answer Skardon's questions. He had a clear conscience at present but was very worried about the effect of his behaviour upon the friendships which he had contracted at Harwell.

Skardon then put 'certain questions' to Fuchs, and in reply the scientist told the MI5 man 'that he was engaged in espionage from mid-1942 until about a year ago. He said there was a continuous passing of information relating to atomic energy, at irregular but frequent meetings. This illegal association commenced on his own initiative, no approach having been made to him.' Fuchs had spoken to an intermediary who arranged the first rendezvous, and thereafter future interviews were arranged at the current meeting, with an alternative arrangement to meet every eventuality. For a long time Fuchs confined the information 'to the product of his own brain', but as time went on this developed into something more. His contacts were sometimes Russians but were often of other unknown nationality. Fuchs had realised he was carrying his life in his hands but that he had done this from the time of his underground days in Germany. He said that there were pre-arranged rendezvous and recognition signals to be exchanged. Fuchs admitted that the association continued during 1944, in New York; for a period at Los Alamos, and later on in London when he returned to England. There had been no sign that his contacts had endeavoured to renew arrangements with him after he failed to keep the last rendezvous in February 1949.

Generally the meetings were of short duration and consisted of Fuchs passing documentary information and of the other party arranging the next rendezvous. At times some questions were put to him, but he always thought them to have been inspired from some other quarter 'and not to be the work of the brain of his contact'. Fuchs admitted that the worst thing that he had passed to his Russian contacts was the manner of making the atomic bomb. He said that it was impossible for him to do more than explain the principle of the bomb and that it would still have been required to be developed from an industrial point of view by the Russians. Fuchs was somewhat surprised when the Russian atomic bomb was detonated in 1949, for whereas he believed that scientifically they might be sufficiently advanced, he did not believe that they would be 'up to it' from a commercial and industrial standpoint.

For the last two years of his association with the Russians there was a gradual reduction in the flow of information which Fuchs passed, since he was beginning to have doubts as to the propriety of his actions. He still believed in Communism, 'but not as practised in Russia today. He thinks that as practised by the Soviet Union it is something to fight against.' Fuchs had decided fairly recently that he could only settle in England. He had been terribly worried about the impact of his behaviour upon his friendship with various people, in particular Wing Commander Arnold.

Fuchs further claimed that his sister knew nothing of his illegal association with the Russians. She may have seen something in Boston but would have been likely to think it merely a continuance of his underground activity in which she had earlier joined in Germany. While based at Los Alamos, he had meetings with his Soviet contact in Santa Fé. So far as the London rendezvous were concerned, he remembered that a typical one was at Mornington Crescent in the street. No alias was used at any time and Fuchs could not remember any particular recognition message. He admitted to accepting his expenses in the early days of the relationship and to taking the sum of £100 shortly after his return to England in 1946, saying that he regarded this as a symbolic payment signifying his subservience to the cause.

At the end of the conversation Skardon told Fuchs that MI5 'should want some more detailed information upon this association', and it was agreed that they should meet on 26 January, so that Skardon might question Fuchs further. When they met, Fuchs told the Security Service man that he was most anxious that his position should be resolved as quickly as possible. He wondered whether the authorities would clearly understand his position and Skardon asked him whether he would like to make a written statement incorporating any details that he thought ought to be borne in mind. Skardon suggested three possibilities: that he should write out a memorandum himself, that he should dictate a statement to a secretary or that Skardon should write down a statement at his dictation. Fuchs said that he would like to avail himself of Skardon's services, and they therefore made arrangements to meet in London the next day, 27 January, for this purpose.

Skardon then questioned him further about his espionage activities and Fuchs said that he thought it was a little later than October 1941, after he was cleared for Top Secret work with Professor Peierls in Birmingham, that he indicated to a friend that he desired to pass over the important information that he was receiving to the Russians. An introduction was arranged and the first meeting took place at a private house in London on the south side of Hyde Park. He there met a man whom he believed to be Russian, who was alone and seemed to be familiar with his surroundings and may have been in uniform. After this first meeting there were further rendezvous at intervals of two or three months, possibly six meetings in all, covering the period before he went to New York in December 1943. The first meetings were in London and at one stage he visited the Soviet Embassy in Kensington Palace Gardens. Other meetings took place with a foreign woman in a country road near Banbury.

After his arrival in New York Fuchs kept an appointment, and subsequently three or four meetings took place in New York, always with the same individual who was possibly a Russian. He later went to Los Alamos and he believed he made forward arrangements for a rendezvous at Boston at Christmas 1944. It was his belief that this meeting did not take place but that he attended an alternative rendezvous at the same place in February 1945. Following upon this there were possibly two more meetings which took place at Santa Fe before his return to England in 1946. All Fuchs's meetings in the U.S. were with the same man. Fuchs thought that there were possibly two meetings in Boston in February 1945, the first to re-establish contact and the second to hand over information which he had written out about the atomic bomb between the meetings. After his return to England he thought that the first new meeting was at the beginning of 1947; thereafter they took place at two-monthly intervals and on every occasion until his last rendezvous in February or March 1949, his meetings were with the same man, probably a Russian.[52]

By this stage Fuchs had already admitted to Wing Commander Arnold that he was a spy. It was on the morning of 26 January, 1950, shortly before the scientist saw Skardon, that Arnold asked Fuchs whether he had 'disclosed certain very important items to the Russians'. Fuchs replied that he had disclosed information regarding initiators and the broad principles of the new 'Super Bomb'. Arnold 'told him that this was a dreadful blow to me and that it hurt me deeply. He seemed much affected'.[53]

On 27 January, Skardon met Fuchs at Paddington Station and took him by car to Room 055, at the War Office, where he finally cautioned Fuchs and asked him whether he still wanted Skardon to write down his statement. Fuchs said: 'Yes, I quite understand and I would like you to carry on.' At his dictation Skardon wrote down the statement.[54] It began:

> My father was a parson and I had a very happy childhood. I think that the one thing that most stands out is that my father always did what he believed to be the right thing to do and he always told us that we had to go our own way even if he disagreed. He himself had many fights because he did what his conscience decreed even if these were at variance with accepted conventions. For example he was the first parson to join the Social Democratic Party.

Fuchs explained how he did not take much interest in politics during his school days 'except insofar as I was forced into it by the fact that of course all the other pupils knew who my father was and I think the only political act at school which I ever made was at the celebration of the Weimar Constitution when there was a celebration at school and all the flags of the Weimar republic had been put up outside whereas inside very large numbers of the pupils appeared with the Imperial badge. At that point I took out the badge showing the colours of the republic and put it on and of course it was immediately torn down.'

When Fuchs got to the University at Leipzig he joined the SPD. 'I found myself soon in opposition to the official policy of the SPD for example on the question of naval rearmament, when the SPD supported the building programme of the Panzercreuzer. I did have some discussions with Communists but I always found that I despised them because it was apparent that they accepted the official policy of their party even if they did not agree with it.' Later Fuchs went to Kiel University. It occurred to Fuchs, 'though it may not be important', that at Leipzig he was in the Reichsbanner which was a semi-military organisation composed of members of the SPD and the Democratic Party.

> That is a point at which I broke away from my father's philosophy because he is a pacifist. In Kiel I was at first still a member of the SPD, but the break came when the SPD decided to support Hindenburg as Reich President. Their argument was that if they put up their own candidate it would split the vote and Hitler would be elected. In particular this would mean that the position of the SPD in Prussia would be lost when they controlled the whole of the Police organisation. The election was I think in 1932. My argument was that we could not stop Hitler by co-operating with other bourgeois parties but that only a united working class could stop him. At this point I decided to oppose the official policy openly and I offered myself as a speaker in support of the Communist candidate.

Shortly after the election of Hindenburg, Papen was made Reich Chancellor and he dismissed the elected Prussian Government and put in a Reichstadhalter.

> That evening we all collected spontaneously. I went to the headquarters of the Communist Party because I had in the meantime been expelled from the SPD, but I had seen many of my previous friends in the Reichsbanner and I knew that they were gathering together ready to fight for the Prussian Government, but the Prussian Government yielded. All they did was to appeal to the Central Reich

Court. At this point the morale of the rank and file of the SPD and the Reichsbanner broke completely and it was evident that there was no force left in those organisations to resist Hitler. I accepted that the Communist Party had been right in fighting against the leaders of the SPD and that I had been wrong in blaming them for it. I had already joined the Communist Party because I felt I had to be in some organisation.

Some time before this Fuchs had also joined a student organisation which contained members of the SPD as well as members of the Communist Party. This organisation was frowned upon by the SPD, but they did not take steps against Fuchs until he came out openly against the SPD's official policy. Fuchs was made the chairman of this organisation 'and we carried on propaganda aimed at those members of the Nazis whom we believed to be sincere'. The Nazis had decided to start propaganda against the high fees which students had to pay,

> and we decided to take them by their word convinced that we would show them up. I carried on the negotiations with the leaders of the Nazi group at the University, proposing that we should organise a strike of the students. They hedged and after several weeks I decided the time had come to show that they did not intend to do it. We issued a leaflet explained that the negotiations had been going on but that the leaders of the Nazis were not in earnest.

The policy did have a measure of success because some members of Fuchs's organisation succeeded in making personal contacts with some of the 'sincere' Nazis. The Nazi leaders apparently noticed that because some time later they organised a strike against the rector of the university. That was after Hitler had been made Reich Chancellor. During that strike they called in the support of their paramilitary SA from the town who demonstrated in front of the university. In spite of that, Fuchs went there every day to show that he was not afraid of them. On one of these occasions 'they tried to kill me and I escaped'. The fact that Hindenburg made Hitler Reich Chancellor 'of course proved to me again that I had been right in opposing the official policy of the SPD'. After the burning of the Reichstag:

> I had to go underground. I was lucky because on the morning after the burning of the Reichstag I left my home very early to catch a train to Berlin for the conference of our student organisation and

that is the only reason why I escaped arrest. I remember clearly when I opened the newspaper in the train I immediately realised the significance and I knew that the underground struggle had started. I took the badge of the hammer and sickle from my lapel which I had carried until that time.

[Fuchs was now] ready to accept the philosophy that the Party is right and that in the coming struggle you could not permit yourself any doubts after the party had made a decision. At this point I omitted to resolve in my mind a very small difficulty about my conduct of the policy against the Nazis. I received of course a great deal of praise at the conference in Berlin which was held illegally, but there rankled in my mind the fact that I had sprung our leaflet on the leaders of the Nazis without warning, without giving them an ultimatum that I would call to the student body unless they made a decision by a certain date. If it had been necessary to do that I would not have worried about it but there was no need for it. I had violated some standard of decent behaviour but I did not resolve this difficulty and very often this incident did come back to my mind, but I came to accept that in such a struggle things of this kind are prejudices which are weakness and which you must fight against.

All that followed helped to confirm the ideas Fuchs had formed. Not a single party voted against the extraordinary powers which were given to Hitler by the new Reichstag while in the universities there was hardly anybody who stood up for those who were dismissed either on political or racial grounds 'and again you found that people whom you normally would have respected because of their decency had no force in themselves to stand up for their own ideals or moral standards'.

Fuchs was in the underground until he left Germany. He was sent out by the Party because they said that he must finish his studies, because after the expected revolution in Germany people would be required with technical knowledge to take part in the building up of the Communist Germany. Fuchs went first to France and then to England where he studied,

and at the same time I tried to make a serious study of the basic Marxist philosophy. The idea which gripped me most was the belief that in the past man has been unable to understand his own history and the forces which lead to the further development of human society; that now for the first time man understands the historical forces and he is able to control them and that therefore for the first time he will be really free. I carried this idea over into the personal sphere and believed that I could understand myself and that I could make myself into what I believed I should be.

Fuchs also 'accepted for a long time that what you heard about Russia internally could be deliberate lies'. But then he had his doubts for the first time on the foreign policy of Russia: the Russo-German pact was difficult to understand 'but in the end I did accept that Russia had done it to gain time, that during that time she was expanding her own influence in the Balkans against the influence of Germany'. Finally Germany's attack on Russia seemed to confirm that Russia was not shirking and was prepared to carry out a foreign policy with the risk of war with Germany. Russia's attack on Finland was more difficult to understand but the fact that Britain and France prepared for an intervention in Finland at the time when they did not appear to be fighting seriously against Germany made it possible to accept the explanation that Russia had to prepare its defences against all possible Imperialist powers. 'In the end I accepted again that my doubts had been wrong and the party had been right.'

By the time Germany started the 'real attack' on France, Fuchs had been interned and for a long time he was not allowed any newspapers. He did not know what was going on outside 'and I did not see how the British people fought at that time. I felt no bitterness by the internment because I could understand that it was necessary and that at that time England could not spare good people to look after the internees, but it did deprive me of the chance of learning more about the real character of the British people.'

Shortly after his release Fuchs was asked to help Professor Peierls in Birmingham on some war work. He accepted it and started work without knowing at first what the work was: 'I doubt whether it would have made any difference to my subsequent actions if I had known the nature of the work beforehand.' But when he learned about the purpose of the work:

I decided to inform Russia and I established contact through another member of the Communist Party. Since that time I have had continuous contact with persons who were completely unknown to me, except that I knew that they would hand whatever information I gave them to the Russian authorities. At this time I had complete confidence in Russian policy and I believed that the Western allies deliberately allowed Russia and Germany to fight each other to the death. I had therefore no hesitation in giving all the information I had even though occasionally I tried to concentrate mainly on giving information about the results of my own work.

[In the course of this work, Fuchs began] naturally to form bonds of personal friendships and I had to conceal from them my inner thoughts. I used my Marxist philosophy to establish in my mind two separate compartments: one compartment in which I allowed myself to make friendships, to have personal relations, to help people and to be in all personal ways the kind of man I wanted to be and the kind of man which, in a personal way, I had been before with my friends in or near the Communist Party. I could be free and easy and happy with other people without fear of disclosing myself because I knew that the other compartment would step in if I approached the danger point. I could forget the other compartment and still rely on it. It appeared to me at the time that I had become a 'free man' because I had succeeded in the other compartment to establish myself completely independent of the surrounding forces of society. Looking back at it now the best way of expressing it seems to be to call it a controlled schizophrenia.

[In the post war period, Fuchs] began again to have my doubts about Russian policy. It is impossible to give definite incidents because now the control mechanism acted against me also in keeping away from me facts which I could not look in the face but they did penetrate and eventually I came to a point where I knew that I disapproved of many actions of the Russian Government and of the Communist Party but I still believed that they would build a new world and that one day I would take part in it and that on that day I would also have to stand up and say to them that there are things which they are doing wrong.

During this time Fuchs was not sure that he could give all the information that he had to the Soviets. However it became more and more evident to Fuchs that the time when Russia would expand her influence over Europe was far away 'and that therefore I had to decide for myself whether I could go on for many years to continue handing over information without being sure in my own mind whether I was doing right. I decided I could not do so. I did not go to one rendezvous because I was ill at the time. I decided not to go to the following one.' Shortly afterwards his father told Fuchs that he might be going into the Eastern Zone of Germany. At that time:

my own mind was closer to his than it had ever been before because he also believed that they are at least trying to build a new world. He disapproved of many things and he had always done so but he knew that when he went there he would say so and he thought that in doing so he might help to make them realise that you cannot build a new world if you destroy some fundamental decencies in personal behaviour. I could not bring myself to stop my father from going there. However it made me face at least some of the facts about myself. I felt that my father's going to the Eastern Zone, that his letters would touch me somewhere and that I was not sure whether I would not go back. I suppose I did not have the courage to fight it out for myself and therefore I invoked an outside influence by informing security that my father was going to the Eastern Zone. A few months passed and I became more and more convinced that I had to leave Harwell. I was then confronted with the fact that there was evidence that I had given away information in New York. I was given the chance of admitting it and staying at Harwell or of clearing out. I was not sure enough of myself to stay at Harwell and therefore I denied the allegation and decided that I would have to leave Harwell.

However, it then began to become clear to Fuchs that in leaving Harwell in those circumstances he would do two things. He would deal a grave blow to Harwell, to all the work which he had loved,

and furthermore that I would leave suspicions against people whom I loved who were my friends and who believed that I was their friend. I had to face the fact that it had been possible for me in one half of my mind to be friends with people, be close friends and at the same time to deceive them and to endanger them. I had to realise that the control mechanism had warned me of danger to myself but that it had also prevented me from realising what I was doing to people who were close to me.

Fuchs then realised that the combination of the three ideas:

which had made me what I was, was wrong, in fact that every single one of them was wrong; that there are certain standards of moral behaviour which are in you and that you cannot disregard. That in your actions you must be clear in your own mind whether they are right or wrong. That you must be able before accepting somebody else's authority to state your doubts and to try to resolve them; and I found that at least I myself was made by circumstances.

Fuchs knew that he could not go back on that 'and I know that all I can do now is to try and repair the damage I have done'. The first thing was to make sure that Harwell would suffer as little as possible and that he had to save for his friends 'as much as possible of that part that was good in my relations with them. This thought is at present uppermost in my mind and I find it difficult to concentrate on any other points.' He claimed that there was nobody he knew by name who was concerned with collecting information for the Russian authorities. There were people 'whom I know by sight whom I trusted with my life and who trusted me with theirs and I do not know that I shall be able to do anything that might in the end give them away'. They were not inside the project but they were the intermediaries between Fuchs and the Russian Government.

At first Fuchs thought that all he would do would be to inform the Russian authorities that work upon the atomic bomb was going on. They wished to have more details 'and I agreed to supply them'. Fuchs concentrated at first mainly on the products of his own work, 'but in particular at Los Alamos I did what I consider to be the worst I have done, namely to give information about the principle of the design of the plutonium bomb'. Later on at Harwell, Fuchs began to be concerned about the information he was giving, 'and I began to sift it, but it is difficult to say exactly when and how I did it because it was a process which went up and down with my inner struggles'. The last time Fuchs handed over information was in February or March 1949. Fuchs concluded his confession with a remarkable statement that gave an inclination into how his attitudes had changed: 'Before I joined the project most of the English people with whom I had made personal contacts were left wing, and affected to some degree or other by the same kind of philosophy. Since coming to Harwell I have met English people of all kinds, and I have come to see in many of them a deep rooted firmness which enables them to lead a decent way of life. I do not know where this springs from and I don't think they do, but it is there.'[55]

After making his statement Fuchs said that he was most anxious to discover what his future was to be and did not want to waste any time in getting the matter cleared up. Skardon told him that it was under active consideration, and that whereas 'I wanted to take up his offer contained in the statement to provide all technical information relating to his espionage activities' and was prepared to see him on 28th and 29th if he so wished, 'I thought that a rest would do him good.' Fuchs agreed and asked for a rest, suggesting he meet Michael Perrin of the Ministry of Supply on Monday 30 January to impart to him full details of his technical disclosures to the Soviets.

On 30 January, Skardon again met Fuchs at Paddington, at 10.45 a.m., and took him once more to Room 055, at the War Office, where he saw Perrin. Before the arrival of Perrin, Fuchs 'said that he had something to say to me, and he then indicated that he thought that during his contact with the Russians there was some other person passing information to them'.[56] Fuchs then gave Perrin the full details, in chronological order, of how from 1942 to end of 1943, while working at Birmingham University for the 'Directorate of Tube Alloys', he passed to the Russians copies of all the reports which contained the results of his own personal work. This covered two aspects of the atomic energy project: 1. The basic theory of the gaseous diffusion process for separating the isotopes of uranium; 2. The development of mathematical methods for calculating the critical size and efficiency of an Atomic Bomb using pure uranium 235.

Fuchs denied passing, during this period, any detailed information which was the work of anyone other than himself. Nevertheless he did give the Russian agents the general fact that this work was being passed to the U.S. where similar work was being very actively prosecuted. He did not give any detailed practical or technical details of the apparatus involved. During this period all his information related to the possible use of uranium 235 as an atomic bomb. He did not then realise the possible significance of plutonium, nor did he pass any information about this.

From December 1943 until August 1944, while he was in New York as a member of the British Atomic Energy 'Diffusion Mission', Fuchs had access to the knowledge of the design and progress of the American full scale diffusion plant and, to a lesser extent, of the Electromagnetic Isotope Separation Plant which was to be built and used in conjunction with it. This general information was passed to the Russian agent in New York with whom he was then in contact. He then handed over copies of all the detailed reports of a theoretical or mathematical nature which he wrote on the Gaseous Diffusion Process while in New York. At this time he also gave the agent some information of a practical nature on the membranes which constituted the essential element of a Gaseous Diffusion Plant. While in New York Fuchs learnt that serious work was being carried out on the Atomic Pile Process for the production of plutonium, but its significance was still not fully clear and he did not specifically pass it to the Russian agent. He did, however, describe the general scale of the American effort and the approximate time programme to which they were then working.

From August 1944 until the summer of 1946, Fuchs was working in the American Atomic Weapons Establishment at Los Alamos, New Mexico, as a member of the British Atomic Energy Team. When he arrived at Los Alamos, he learnt for the first time all the principles on which the whole American Atomic Energy programme was based. He learnt in particular that plutonium would become available as well as pure uranium 235 and could be used as material in an atomic bomb. Fuchs himself was engaged on the extremely difficult problems involved in using plutonium for this purpose. He made his first contact with the Russian agent since his arrival at Los Alamos in February 1945 in Boston, Massachusetts. He there wrote a report summarising all that he had learnt of the technical problems of using plutonium in an atomic bomb, and then handed it to the Russian agent. In particular in this report he stated *inter alia* the need for using a highly complicated and specialised procedure for detonating a plutonium bomb such as would not be required for a uranium 235 bomb.

His next meeting with the Russian agent was at the end of June 1945. He then handed him a report which he had written at Los Alamos with access to all the relevant American information. In this report he described the first plutonium bomb which was due to be tested in the following month in New Mexico. The report included a sketch of the bomb with all leading dimensions and full technical details as to its various component parts. In the report he also mentioned the date when the test would be made. At subsequent meetings with the Russian agent, he gave further information of a theoretical and mathematical nature about the atomic bomb, and some details of the properties of plutonium. He did not, however, pass any information on the technique of producing or handling this material.

From the summer of 1946 to February 1949, Fuchs was employed as Head of the Theoretical Physics Division of the Atomic Energy Establishment at Harwell. During this period, the information which Fuchs passed to a Russian agent in the UK partly related to further amplification of the information he had acquired at Los Alamos, and partly to the post-war British Atomic Energy programme. As to the American information, this mainly concerned mathematical and theoretical treatment of the problems of the atomic explosion, but it included a reference to the possible use of a mixture of plutonium and uranium 235 in an atomic bomb which would be of special value to the Americans in that they had plant capable of producing both materials.

As to British information, Fuchs told the Russian agent in the middle of 1946 and the beginning of 1947 the general outline of the programme for building atomic piles, their designed output of plutonium, and the arguments which led to the decision to build air-cooled rather than water-cooled piles. He did not answer a specific question as to how uranium metal rods were fabricated, but did, during the second half of 1948, provide extracts from a particular report which he was asked to obtain about a device used in the British air-cooled piles. He also passed information about different types of nuclear reactors which were being studied at Harwell, and also told the agent of the British proposal to build a plant for separating the uranium isotopes. He was asked for information about the solvent extraction process for the chemical separation of plutonium from uranium and gave some information of a limited nature which he was able to extract from the appropriate British report available to him at Harwell. During 1947 he was asked specifically for information about the so called Hydrogen Bomb and about a highly secret component material used in connection therewith. He gave to the Russian agent the essential nuclear physics data and the general picture as far as it was then known to him of how the weapon would work.[57]

The scale of Fuchs's treachery was truly staggering. When Dick White was told of the information that Fuchs had passed to Russians he was incredulous, for it was: 'Nothing less than the full design of the atomic bomb'. Yet, even after learning of the scale of Fuchs's betrayal he could not help having a degree of understanding for the scientist: 'His motives... were relatively speaking pure. A scientist who got cross at the Anglo-American ploy in withholding vital information from an ally fighting a common enemy. They were easily led astray by the spy rings on the other side of the Atlantic. These consisted of men carefully selected to prey on such motives.' 'Marx' remarked White, 'has a peculiar appeal' for scientists like Fuchs.[58]

Remarkably, despite Fuchs's confession, MI5's legal advice was that the evidence supporting a prosecution the Official Secrets Act was not clear cut and consisted entirely of voluntary statements made by Fuchs to Skardon, Perrin and Arnold. There was no other evidence available to prove his espionage activity and it would not be possible for the Security Service to obtain any further evidence. Any prosecution therefore had to rest on Fuchs's voluntary statements but this was complicated in view of the 'possible inducements' to confess made by Skardon at his interview with Fuchs on 21 December, and then by Sir John Cockcroft on 10 January: 'these possible inducements render the voluntary statements inadmissible in evidence'. It could not be denied that these inducements were made, although it was suggested that the evidence tended to show that Fuchs 'did not act on these temporal inducements but rather on the moral urge to repair the damage he had done, and to put himself right morally with his friends at Harwell'.[59] As Fuchs was a naturalised British subject the only way to prevent him leaving the country – and the knowledge in his head – was by the institution of criminal proceedings. Faced with this prospect the Legal Adviser of the Security Service finally came to the conclusion that sufficient evidence did exist to make out a *prima facie* case for prosecution of Fuchs. The fact there might be a successful prosecution did not automatically mean that Fuchs would face charges: the final decision lay with the Prime Minister.[60] Attlee gave permission. Fuchs was arrested by Commander Burt, Special Branch, at 3.30 p.m. on Thursday 2 February 1950, at the Atomic Research Department, Ministry of Supply, on the following charges:

> 1. That he, for a purpose prejudicial to the safety or interests of the State, on a day in 1947, communicated to a person unknown information relating to atomic research, which was calculated to be, or might be, directly or indirectly, useful to an enemy.
> 2. That he, being a British subject, for a purpose prejudicial to the safety or interests of the State, on a date in February, 1945, in the USA., communicated to a person unknown information relating to atomic research, which was calculated to be, or might be, directly or indirectly, useful to an enemy.

These were read over to Fuchs by Commander Burt, and, after being cautioned, the scientist asked to see Michael Perrin, to whom he said: 'Do you realise the effects of this at Harwell?' Fuchs was then taken to Bow Street Police Station where he was formally charged and cautioned. The charges were read over to him and he was again cautioned, but he made no reply. Fuchs appeared before Sir Laurence Dunne, Chief Magistrate, Bow Street Magistrates' Court, at 10.30 a.m. on 3 February. After evidence of arrest had been given by Commander Burt, the prisoner was remanded in custody.[61]

The Fuchs affair was very damaging to MI5's reputation. Damage limitation was necessary. Bernard Hill, MI5's Legal Advisor, prepared a brief for officers of the Security Service who might 'be led into discussing the case with their official contacts'; 'some guidance on facts may, therefore, be helpful', thought Hill:

> Criticism will probably crystallise into three questions to which answers are given below:

1. Why was FUCHS taken on for employment in Atomic Energy?

Application for FUCHS' first employment with an Atomic Energy research team was made in August 1941 – at the end of the second year of the war against Germany.

The British Security authorities had been aware since August 1934 that, in that month, the Gestapo had objected to the issue to FUCHS of a new German passport on the grounds that he had been an active anti-Nazi and a Communist in 1932/33 (an allegation which had been groundlessly made against countless other refugees who later made a notable contribution to the allied war effort). They were also aware that, although his private views had probably always been to the left – he was a member of the Social Democratic Party in Germany until 1932 – he had taken no active part in political activities nor come to the unfavourable notice of the police throughout the whole of his eight years residence in Britain. He had spent these years, between the ages of 22 and 30, first at Bristol and later at Edinburgh Universities and it was in response to the highest possible recommendation from Edinburgh University that he was released after six months from internment under the 1940 General Order covering all enemy aliens.

The work for which he was required in August 1941 was of the greatest importance to the war effort against Germany and it was decided that no other person was available with such suitable qualifications.

In accordance with normal practice the responsible employing department on the facts presented by the Security authorities assessed the security risk by weighing the adverse information then available against the lack of confirmatory evidence obtained during his residence in Britain. It was decided that FUCHS could be employed.

Thereafter, although his case was kept under periodic review – more particularly when the security context changed after the war against Germany – the assessment of his case was increasingly weighted in his favour by the growing confidence felt in him by his colleagues and by the outstanding contribution he himself was making to the Atomic Energy project. Whatever his private thoughts may have been, his conduct and behaviour so far from encouraging those most closely associated with him to call in question the correctness of the assessment of his case, did in fact cause him to be regarded throughout his eight years service as an exceptionally security-minded officer.

2. Why was FUCHS' espionage activity not detected?

Dr FUCHS first made contact with the Russians not on their but on his own initiative and, as is now known, he had already acquired considerable experience in conspiratorial techniques during his 'underground' work in Germany. The habits of self-discipline and the ability to lead a double life were already acquired. There was therefore no prolonged period of recruitment and training when the Security authorities might have had their best opportunity of detecting his activities. Moreover the first three years of his espionage career were during the war when the attention of both the British and American security authorities were directed primarily against German agents.

The system of contact was exceptionally secure and involved the use of no intermediaries and the passage of no incriminating communications. Meetings took place at intervals of two to three months or even longer (at one period they ceased altogether for over a year) and lasted only the few minutes necessary for passing reports and receiving instructions. The reports were not official documents but manuscript summaries written by FUCHS himself, and many of them were original products of his own brain.

It can fairly be said that the technique employed would have made the detection of Dr FUCHS an exceptionally difficult problem in any democratically governed state.

3. Why is it that the Americans appear to have known all about Dr FUCHS' Communist history but not the British?

There is no official evidence to suggest that the Americans possessed any information which would have modified the British assessment of Dr FUCHS' security record. It would have been normal practice for the American security authorities, on finding that Dr FUCHS was a British citizen, to have warned the British authorities of any serious security record, had they possessed it. No such warning was received.

In August 1949 the American authorities supplied the British with certain very valuable general information about Soviet espionage activities in the United States. The British security authorities were able to develop this information to the point when suspicion fell upon Dr FUCHS. Thereafter the two authorities worked in the closest collaboration and each was able to contribute to the compilation of a full record of Dr FUCHS' history.[62]

On 28 February 1950, Klaus Fuchs was sentenced to fourteen years imprisonment.

BODYBLOWS

The fallout from the Fuchs case was enormous. The Prime Minister defended MI5 in the House of Commons, calling the case 'exceptional';[1] but Attlee's main concern was to minimise the damage done to Anglo-American relations. Within MI5, Percy Sillitoe exploded in anger at the shortcomings he perceived in the initial investigation of Fuchs. In one meeting he raged at White, Liddell and Ronnie Reed: 'In future... you'll do as you're told!' Liddell calmed him down by pointing out that it was impossible to act on every suggestion that someone should be checked out. Counter-espionage was not like policing. When Sillitoe and White went to brief the Prime Minister, it had already been decided to conceal the degree of concerns raised about Fuchs: it was argued that much of the material concerning Fuchs's earlier affiliation to Communism was 'unreliable'. MI5 were now claiming that there had been 'a thorough police investigation' that had not raised any concerns.[2]

But more bad news was to follow: Wing Commander Arnold reported that Bruno Pontecorvo, an Italian-born, but naturalised British subject, experimental physicist, who worked at Harwell (and had been based in Canada during the war working on the atom project), had not returned from his holiday in Europe.[3] A few months previously, on 1 March 1950, Arnold had reported to MI5 that, in a recent conversation he had with him, Pontecorvo disclosed that he had a brother, also a scientist with an international background, who was an active Communist. Arnold added that Pontecorvo had recently been offered a job at Liverpool University and that this provided an opportunity for Harwell to be rid of any security risk that might attach to his continued employment. The following day, a report was received from SIS in Sweden to the effect that Pontecorvo and his wife were 'avowed Communists'. MI5 asked for details of the reliability of the source. Arnold, meanwhile, reported on a further talk that he had with Pontecorvo, on 6 April, when the scientist admitted that not only was one of his brothers, Gilberto, a Communist but his brother's wife, also, was a Communist; and one of his sisters was a Communist while another was sympathetic towards Communism. Pontecorvo denied that he or his wife were Communists but said that his politics, if any, were Labour. Arnold informed MI5 that his opinion was that Pontecorvo's views were 'definitely Left, but I found it difficult to assess exactly how Left they were' and that he thought Pontecorvo would 'quite readily change his nationality again should it be to his scientific advantage to do so'. As a result of this, MI5 informed the Ministry of Supply, on 25 April, that: 'As Bruno Pontecorvo has access to Top Secret information, from the security standpoint it is considered that a potential security risk exists.' Three days later the Security Service was informed that the Swedish report, received from SIS, was from an 'absolutely reliable source.' By the beginning of May, the Ministry of Supply were advised by MI5 to hasten the arrangements for Pontecorvo's transfer to some post where he would not have access to secret information, such as that at Liverpool.[4] But before this transfer took place, Pontecorvo and his family disappeared.

On 23 October, Guy Liddell had the dubious honour of informing the Prime Minister about the case. The Deputy Director General informed Mr Attlee that Pontecorvo had left the country in July with his family and had now been traced as far as Helsinki where he arrived on 2 September. There was a press rumour that he had gone on to Soviet Russia but this was, at the moment, unconfirmed. The Prime Minister asked how far Pontecorvo had had access to vital information. Liddell replied that the Department of Atomic Energy had expressed the view that, for several years, Pontecorvo had hardly had any contact with secret work, having been mainly concerned with cosmic ray projects. But, in the earlier period of employment in Canada, he had been employed in atomic pile work. Liddell explained to the Prime Minister that, on the information available, that had been no grounds for bringing Pontecorvo before the 'purge committee' and that, therefore, the Department of Atomic Energy had concentrated on 'eliminating him amicably so as to avoid, if possible, the course he has now apparently taken. This course could not have been prevented unless there had been evidence of an indictable offence; in fact there was none.' It was impossible, the DDG told the Prime Minister, to say whether Pontecorvo had committed acts of espionage in the UK or in Canada 'which might have made him feel that he could only be secure behind the Iron Curtain, or whether he had gone to Russia from purely ideological motives'.[5]

A frantic search of files began to find out who had vetted Pontecorvo – whether it was MI5 or SIS, given that the scientist would have been cleared for atomic research while outside the UK. To the relief of both organisations it was neither: Pontecorvo had been vetted by the now defunct wartime British Security Co-ordination Organisation. The Security Division of the BSC, based in New York and Washington, comprised eighty-three staff under the direction of Sir Connop Guthrie, was responsible for the administration of the Consular and Industrial Security Organisations in the States; for various security services carried out in the States on behalf of the British Government and its Missions there; and for security liaison with US Government Departments and Services and with Dominion Governments. The overseas organisation fell to the Security Executive in London, because foreign countries were outside the ambit of MI5 and security measures, and, as distinct from the gathering of intelligence, outside that of SIS. From April 1942, the BSC's Security Division no longer reported anything to SIS in London but the Security Executive only save that on 4 January 1943 it was agreed that the BSC should enter into direct correspondence with MI5 on 'unique interests' to the latter such as 'suspect seamen and methods of sabotage'. Those connected with clearing Pontecorvo were Colonel K.M. Bourne and E.K. Balls. Bourne was taken on as a local employee by Guthrie in Ottawa and employed for a few months in BSC's Security Division in Washington; Balls was also a local employee. Neither was connected to SIS.[6] On 30 November 1942 the following communication was sent from BSC: 'Referring to your letter of November 4th addressed to Colonel K.M. Bourne, we have now received a rather detailed report on Dr Bruno Pontecorvo. This is entirely clear and would indicate that he is quite satisfactory from the point of view of security for employment by any British agency. It is noted that he is Italian by birth and Hebrew by race but his record makes it quite clear that he is entirely in sympathy with the allied cause.' On 3 March 1943, additional information was sent by BSC: 'Re Dr Pontecorvo. We have now received a final report on the above which indicates that his record is entirely clear for security.'

But the FBI had received, and passed on to the BSC, reports that Pontecorvo was a Communist. These reports reached the BSC after Pontecorvo had been appointed to the Tube Alloy team in Montreal but before the second BSC report on his satisfactory clearance, dated 3 March 1943, had been sent. What action BSC took on these reports was, MI5 found, 'impossible to say' but the information was not passed on to the RCMP. An FBI report of 2 February 1943 was copied, by the Bureau, to their liaison officer in London but was not passed on by him either to MI5 or SIS. The report stated that a search of Pontecorvo's residence in Oklahoma had resulted in a find of numerous books and pamphlets on Communism. MI5 were unable to say why these reports were not, apparently, taken into consideration when BSC made the final clearance of Pontecorvo, but it seemed certain that the reports could not have been seen by the officer who made the clearance, 'and it must therefore be assumed that by some organisational error they were not connected with the other Pontecorvo papers. None of these reports were brought to the notice of the Security Service in London.' Nor was any adverse information passed on to the RCMP.

The Security Service entered the picture in the autumn of 1946 when the foreign scientists employed in Canada, began to return to the UK and MI5 asked the RCMP to supply them with any adverse information which they might have about any of them. Of course, nothing adverse on Pontecorvo was known by the RCMP. On 24 November 1947, MI5 vetted Pontecorvo for the Nationality Division of the Home Office in connection with his naturalisation proceeding and replied 'nothing Recorded Against'. He received his British naturalisation in absentia in Canada on 7 February 1948, on the special application of the Directorate of Atomic Energy. Had Pontecorvo been in the UK he would have been submitted to the full naturalisation enquiries of the police – although it was by no means clear that this would have made any difference to the final decision.

On 26 November 1947, the Ministry of Supply had asked MI5 to vet Pontecorvo following the Deputy Chief of Staff's request to employ the scientist, indefinitely, at Harwell. As MI5 had nothing on Pontecorvo, they asked Wing Commander Arnold to obtain answers to a series of questions relating to his reliability and loyalty. Arnold replied that 'after making discreet enquiries from those who know him well, I would say that he is not politically minded. He certainly expresses no political views. Dr Cockroft has confirmed this opinion.' After completing further enquiries, Arnold wrote, again, on 6 January 1948, summing up his views on Pontecorvo: 'The opinion I have formed of Pontecorvo is that he is a straightforward fellow with no political leanings.' On receiving the results of these enquiries, MI5 wrote to the Ministry of Supply in March stating: 'In the exceptional circumstances of the case we do not wish to advise against Pontecorvo being granted permanent status in Government service.' The 'exceptional circumstances' were that he was said to have done outstandingly good work for the Department in Canada and could not be adequately replaced. On 7 July 1949, MI5 were again asked, by the Ministry of Supply, to vet Pontecorvo before his case was submitted for the waiver of the Department's nationality rule. This was simply to check if any new information had come in since the previous vet. None had, so the Security Service reported thus.[7] From a simple clerical error in the BSC no concerns about Pontecorvo were raised until Arnold raised some in 1950.

Pontecorvo's disappearance soured relations between MI5 and the FBI. Patterson, the Security Service's Liaison Office with the Bureau, had 'restrictions' placed upon his access to FBI intelligence. Sir Percy Sillitoe was despatched to the States to try and repair the damage. On 1 November 1950, Sillitoe had to brief the Prime Minister on how his meeting with J. Edgar Hoover had gone and on developments concerning the case, generally. He told Attlee that FBI/MI5 relations had deteriorated since the Fuchs case: this, he put down to the misrepresentations that had one FBI individual, Clegg, had on put on their conversations putting 'poison' into his reports on that occasion. Nevertheless, Clegg, in the DG's opinion, seemed to be unpopular in the FBI. Sillitoe had found that: 'One remarkable instance of Mr Hoover's suspicion or hostility before his meeting with the Director General had been a week's delay in his answer to the invitation from the Embassy to attend there for his KBE investiture. This invitation was only answered after their meeting.' Sillitoe had spoken 'very frankly' with Hoover who, in turn, had been pleased to say that he liked plain speaking and that what he disliked was a 'liar'. Sillitoe asked Hoover to 'restore proper working relations' between the FBI and MI5. The DG was careful not to use the word 'restrictions' and pointed out that the access that the FBI's counterpart had to all Security Service information in London. Hoover, in his reply, stated that the 'restrictions' – this was the first time the word had been used in the conversation – on Patterson would be removed immediately. The subsequent investiture ceremony at the British Embassy impressed Sillitoe so much so that he told the Prime Minister of the admiration for the way in which Sir Oliver Franks, the Ambassador, had conducted the event and 'bore witness to the great impression it had made on Mr Hoover and his entourage'. Speaking to Hoover, after his investiture as a Knight of the British Empire, Sillitoe told him that the Prime Minister took a personal interest in the relationship between the FBI and MI5 and mentioned that, if Hoover were to visit the UK the following year, he felt sure the Prime Minister would wish to see him.

Later Sillitoe reported back to his senior officers that the Prime Minister had 'showed himself to be rather critical' of MI5's role in the Pontecorvo affair. Attlee first of all asked why he had not been told of the SIS report from Sweden. Sillitoe answered that he had not been informed at the time, but pointed out that action was immediately taken on receiving this report. The Prime Minister then asked why Pontecorvo's activities had not been discovered by investigation, to which Sillitoe replied that 'we had "no magnet to find the body".' The DG asked the Prime Minister to bear in mind that MI5 had not seen the information given by the FBI to the BSC and that 'even if we had' the evidence against Pontecorvo was by no means damning since it referred to Communist literature which 'might have been found in the houses of a large variety of people in 1943'. When Attlee asked why Pontecorvo had been allowed to go abroad, he was told by Sittitoe that he knew of no powers to stop him. The Prime Minister wondered whether it was not suspicious that Pontecorvo had gone abroad with his wife and family, to which the DG pointed out that Mrs Pontecorvo's Swedish background offered a good reason why they had visited Sweden. The Prime Minister then wanted to know what the Pontecorvo incident 'really meant and why it happened'. Sillitoe could only reply that 'at present we could only surmise' but it seemed quite possible that Pontecorvo had no intention of decamping to Russia when he first went abroad on his holiday. There was a possibility that he had been blackmailed in Italy on the basis of information about his past Communist connections: 'Blackmail was a typical technique of the Russian Intelligence Service.' The Prime Minister was 'evidently impressed by this idea and was prepared to accept it as a reasonable explanation'.[8] MI5 never got to the Pontecorvo affair. The missing scientist, though, later turned up in Moscow.

While all this was happening MI5 continued to search for the high grade Soviet mole in the Foreign Office as revealed by VENONA. By early 1951, by a process of elimination, the focus was narrowed down to six suspects in the British Embassy in Washington. Arthur Martin's efforts had been aided by a helpful message from Kim Philby, the SIS Liaison Officer in Washington, whom Martin had known and respected during the war. Philby suggested that MI5 refer to the disclosure by a Russian defector, Walter Krivitsky, in 1940 that Soviet Intelligence had recruited a young Foreign Office official of good family who had been educated at Eton and Oxford. This was, in one way, a key clue that had been ignored for years; on the other hand quite a lot of the diplomatic corps were of good family and who had been educated at Eton and Oxford. Indeed, Martin had not placed much importance on the defector whose description was too wide to be meaningful. But now Martin's list of suspects roughly matched Krivitsky's description. He sought access to the Foreign Office personnel files. Vetting had only recently been introduced and the files were devoid of detailed information. But then Carey Foster, the Security Officer at the Foreign Office, discovered that the FO held two files on each employee: a personnel file and a private file. Back in MI5's HQ, Dick White was 'surprised' and then 'annoyed' when told that Sir William Strang, the Permanent Under Secretary at the Foreign Office, had denied the Security Service access to the private files. By the time Strang's opposition was removed, Philby had visited London and called on Carey Foster. Philby was briefed on all aspects of the investigation. Carey Foster used the opportunity to invite White to discuss progress in the case. In the course of a brief meeting, White suggested: 'You should look for someone who is unstable, living on his nerves. That will be our man.'

Martin, meanwhile, read the private file of Donald Maclean, head of the Foreign Office's American Department. He would have been surprised to find a letter from a Secretary at a British embassy to Robin Hooper, the head of Foreign Office personnel. Maclean, the secretary revealed, had declared to her in a drunken stupor: 'I am the English Alger Hiss.' Hooper had minuted this letter to the Foreign Office's chief clerk: 'It seems that D.M. is up to his old tricks.' Martin showed the letter to Carey Foster. 'I was astonished,' he told White. 'I never saw the file before.' Carey Foster had forgotten that, less than two years earlier, he had approved psychiatric treatment for Maclean. The doctor's report mentioned Maclean's marital problems and his repressed homosexuality. Then Carey Foster had taken no action.[9] Now Maclean became MI5's prime suspect.

Donald Maclean had been born in London in 1913, the third of four sons and five children of Sir Donald Maclean, a Liberal politician and Cabinet minister, and his wife, Gwendolen Margaret. He was educated at Gresham's School, Holt, where the headmaster, J.R. Eccles, enforced the so-called 'honour system' with the aim of maintaining the highest moral standards. In October 1931, Maclean went up to Trinity Hall, Cambridge, with an exhibition in modern languages. He soon joined the university Socialist Society. Maclean, standing 6ft. 4in. tall, was prominent both physically and intellectually among his contemporaries. In June 1934 he graduated with first class honours in part two of the modern languages tripos, having gained a second class in part one in 1932. He entered the diplomatic service in 1935, serving in the League of Nations and Western Department of the Foreign Office. In 1938 Maclean was appointed Third Secretary at the Paris Embassy. There he met an American student, Melinda Marling, eldest daughter of Francis Marling, a Chicago businessman. Maclean and Melinda were married in Paris in 1940 at the time of the evacuation of the city. Back in London he was promoted to Second Secretary and employed in the General Department until April 1944, when he was transferred to the Washington Embassy, and soon after promoted First Secretary. Early in 1947 he became Joint Secretary of the Anglo-American-Canadian Combined Policy Committee, a post that gave him access to the American Atomic Energy Commission. When Maclean left in September 1948, on promotion to Counsellor and Head of Chancery in Cairo, he was the youngest officer in his new grade. In Cairo, however, 'an all-round deterioration set in', culminating in a drunken spree that caused him to be sent back to London and subjected to psychiatric examination. The Foreign Office, believing that he had recovered, appointed him in November 1950 to be head of the American Department.[10]

Soon it became clear that MI5 were closing in on their man. In March 1951, the Armed Forces Security Agency, in the States, deciphered another VENONA message to Moscow transmitted in 1944, reporting that HOMER had visited New York to see his pregnant wife. A quick search by the Security Service revealed that Maclean had undertaken just such a journey. This was the breakthrough. HOMER's identity was transmitted to the FBI in Washington. Since MI5 used SIS communication's channels, Kim Philby read the message on its arrival. In London, Carey Foster rushed to break the news to Strang: 'I told him about our discovery as we were walking through St James's Park. He went white.'

A meeting was convened in Strang's office at which Sir Percy Sillitoe, Guy Liddell, White and Foster attended. 'Similar to Fuchs,' said White. The decrypts proved Maclean's guilt and MI5's task was to secure the evidence which could lead to a conviction without revealing how the suspicion had first arisen. The most desirable outcome, White believed, would be to observe Maclean in contact with a Soviet intelligence officer. Surveillance would be a combined Special Branch and MI5 responsibility. White's liaison with the Branch was James Robertson, 'a dour Scotsman' who had run XX cases from Cairo during the war. White, in the meantime, assigned Commander Felix Johnston, retired from the Royal Navy, to examine Maclean's office and files. Maclean was also slowly withdrawn from the circulation list of Top-Secret papers. Maclean's telephone at home and at the Foreign Office was tapped and his mail intercepted. The five, it was agreed, would meet again within one week. Sillitoe decided to inform the FBI of MI5's plans. The messages would be sent through SIS's communications channel. Automatically, they were seen by Philby. Secondly, there was a report from James Robertson that Special Branch and the MI5 Watchers had vetoed surveillance around Maclean's home in Kent on the basis that the Watchers thought they would 'stick out like a sore thumb'. In the second week of May, surveillance was increased but was still not carried out beyond London. Special Branch officers always followed Maclean to the ticket barrier at Charing Cross Station but insisted that further unobserved surveillance was impossible and beyond their resources. 'I saw Maclean in Pall Mall yesterday,' reported Carey Foster. 'The watchers were ridiculously close. Maclean must have seen them.' 'He knows that we're on to him,' agreed White but did not dispute Special Branch's decision. Sillitoe wanted 'to push him to do something foolish'. Special Branch reports listed the names of those seen with Maclean. Among the names was Guy Burgess. White paid no particular attention to Burgess.[11] He, like the rest of British Intelligence (with one notable exception in Washington), had no idea that Burgess was also a Soviet agent – indeed the one that recruited Maclean in the first place.

Guy Francis de Moncy Burgess was born in 1911, in Devonport. He was the elder son of Commander Malcolm Kingsford de Moncy Burgess RN and his wife, Evelyn Mary. Burgess's father died in 1924 and his mother subsequently married John Retallack Bassett, a retired lieutenant colonel. Following a period at Eton College, Burgess spent two years at the Royal Naval College, Dartmouth, but poor eyesight ended his naval prospects and he returned to Eton. He won an open scholarship to read modern history at Trinity College, Cambridge, in 1930, gained a first in part one of the history tripos (1932) and an aegrotat in part two (1933), and held a two-year postgraduate teaching fellowship. He became a member of the Apostles, home to the intellectual élite of the arts and sciences, and he was already well known for his drinking and homosexuality. He joined the Communist Party while at university. And he was recruited as a Soviet agent.

Soviet Intelligence appeared to value him for his 'ability to meet useful people'. In 1935–1936 he was secretary to Captain Jack Macnamara, a Conservative MP, having joined the Anglo-German Fellowship to hide his Communism. In October 1936, Burgess accepted a prestigious post in the BBC's talks department. In March 1938 he was a courier between Chamberlain and Daladier, and in September he urged Churchill to repeat his warning against Hitler to Stalin; he received a signed copy of Churchill's *Arms and the Covenant* as a reward. In December 1938, Burgess, thanks to the contacts he had cultivated, was appointed to Section D of SIS, dedicated to sabotage and subversion. He helped secure the entry of his friend from Cambridge, Kim Philby, into SIS. Burgess rejoined the BBC in 1941 and spent the next three years in the European propaganda department, liasing with the Special Operations Executive and SIS. On 4 June 1944, Burgess joined the Foreign Office news department. In December 1946 he became Private Secretary to Hector McNeil, then Minister of State at the Foreign Office. He, naturally, informed his Soviet controller about his advance to the centre of British foreign and defence policy-making. He was appointed to the Information Research Department a secret unit created to combat Soviet propaganda. In August 1950, Burgess was appointed Second Secretary to the Washington Embassy.[12] While in Washington he had been staying at Kim Philby's home. And, the SIS officer was, of course, also a Soviet agent.

Harold Adrian Russell (Kim) Philby was born on New Years Day 1912 at Ambala in the Punjab, the only son and eldest of four children of Harry St John Bridger Philby (1885–1960), civil servant in India, explorer, and orientalist, and his wife, Dora, daughter of Adrian Hope Johnston, of the Indian public works department. They nicknamed him Kim. He was educated at Westminster School and Trinity College, Cambridge, where he joined the university Socialist Society and became a Communist. At Cambridge, Philby befriended Guy Burgess. Philby obtained a third class in part one of the history tripos (1931) and a second class (division I) in part two of the economics tripos (1933). In 1933 he went on a trip to Vienna, where he met Alice (Litzi) Friedman, an Austrian Communist, whose father was Israel Kohlman, a minor government official of Hungarian Jewish origin. They witnessed the street fighting which ended with the defeat of the Socialists in February 1934, when they had a hurried marriage and left for England. By this time she had persuaded him to become a Soviet agent. In June 1934, at a secret meeting in Regent's Park, Philby was approached by Arnold Deutsch. Philby agreed to become a Russian spy. Another of his controllers was Teodor Maly. Beginning his career as a journalist, Philby was instructed to sever all links with his Communist past and swing over to the far right. Like Burgess, he was involved with the Anglo-German Fellowship. First as a freelance and later for *The Times* he went to Spain in February 1937 to cover the Spanish Civil War from the point of view of General Franco (whose planned assassination was part of his original brief), who awarded him the Red Cross of Military Merit. He left Spain in August 1939 and, during the Second World War, was recruited into SIS. He joined Section V in 1941. By 1944, Philby had risen to become Head of Section IX, whose remit was 'to collect and interpret information concerning communist espionage and subversion'. When Section IX was merged with Section V in 1945 he alerted Moscow to the intended defection in Istanbul of Konstantin

Volkov, who could have unmasked Philby as a Soviet agent. Philby was even appointed OBE in 1946. And, by 1949, Philby was SIS's representative in Washington, where he kept Moscow informed of Anglo-American intelligence collaboration.[13]

Philby, then, was in an extraordinary position of influence. But his prime concern, in 1951, was to save Maclean. He drew up a scheme to help Maclean escape. It would involve his old friend Burgess – and that is where it almost went wrong. Philby assigned Burgess to warn Maclean in London. The plan was for Burgess to get himself arrested three times in one day for drunken driving in Virginia, forcing Sir Oliver Franks, the British Ambassador, to send him home. That part of the scheme was easy – and perfectly in character for Burgess to be convincing. Confident that Maclean would soon be safe, Philby forestalled any possibility of suspicion on himself by giving the investigation 'a nudge in the right direction... I wrote a memorandum to head office suggesting that we might be wasting our time in exhaustive investigations of the Embassy menials.'

Meanwhile, on Monday 21 May, the group of senior MI5 officers met in Strang's office at the FO. Dick White remained silent as Percy Sillitoe argued that, while surveillance had proved unsuccessful, no action could yet be taken because the formal identification of Maclean as the proven suspect had not yet been passed to the FBI. There was also one small issue arising out of the VENONA decrypts of the Soviet wartime messages which also needed clarification. Once this was clarified Maclean would be handed over to the Security Service the following Monday. That day, Philby wrote to Burgess, now back in the UK after his latest disgrace. The letter concerned the fate of Burgess's second-hand Lincoln, which had been impounded by the Ambassador following the traffic offences: 'Urgent measures must be taken on the Lincoln, otherwise it will be too late and the car will be sent to the dump.' Philby added: 'It is very hot here.' Meanwhile, Yodi Modin, a Soviet intelligence officer was walking along Oxford Street. In a travel agent's window he spotted an advertisement for day trips on the *Falaise* to St Malo. On Saturday morning, Maclean did not appear for work. A colleague reported that, the previous day, Maclean had announced that he would be collecting his sister off a ship at Tilbury docks. He had taken the day off. 'Carey Foster never told us that Maclean had been given leave,' complained Dick White. 'It would have been crucial.'

White was told, however, at 10.15 a.m. on Monday 28 May 1951, by Carey Foster that: 'Maclean's disappeared'. Foster had just had a call from Maclean's wife Melinda. She asked 'if we might know where Donald is'. She said that he walked out of their house on Friday night and had not come back. He left with someone called 'Roger Stiles'. White agreed with Liddell that Maclean, suffering a breakdown, had probably disappeared for a 'drunken spree with the unknown Stiles'. The Home Secretary, Herbert Morrison, was informed by Liddell and Foster. Then a Special Branch report came through that a car had been abandoned by two passengers on the Southampton dockyard quay before boarding the *Falaise* for the Continent. The driver had shouted to a dockside worker: 'We'll be back on Monday!' When it was revealed that the car had been rented by a Mr Guy Burgess, Carey Foster looked at Liddell: 'He was clearly shocked. Amazed'. When Carey Foster gave the news to White, the latter hid his reaction, remaining outwardly calm. But inside White 'couldn't believe it. It really was very challenging to one's sanity to suppose that a man of Burgess's type could be a secret agent of anybody's.' Burgess had posed as 'Roger Styles' rather than 'Roger Stiles' – taking the name from two Agatha Christie novels: *The Mysterious Affair at Styles* (1921) and *The Murder of Roger Ackroyd* (1926).

Yet again the fallout from another spy scandal was enormous. It sparked decades of speculation, both privately and publicly, as to how far Soviet Intelligence had penetrated the British state – even as far as the position of Prime Minister. There were searches for a 'Third Man' who had aided the absconding diplomats, followed by searches for a 'Fourth Man' and then a 'Fifth Man'.

As White and his colleagues slowly put the pieces together the finger of suspicion pointed to a common link to a number of intelligence failures – Kim Philby. Eventually, against SIS's wishes, Philby was subjected to an interrogation by Helenus Milmo, in Leconfield House. Philby, White hoped, would be intimidated by the professional MI5 interrogator. The interrogation went badly. Asked to explain why the Soviet radio traffic between London and Moscow and Istanbul had increased after Volkov's offer to defect, Philby pleaded ignorance and repeated that answer to every question and proposition. 'I just had to make sure' Philby subsequently told Yuri Modin, 'that I didn't contradict what I had said previously and volunteer nothing'. Milmo launched into a tirade to force Philby into a confession. White watched aghast: 'It all became a shouting match with Milmo accusing Philby of everything. I was surprised and disappointed that Milmo did not use more legal subtlety.' It did not work. As Philby departed after just three hours of questioning White sneered at Philby: 'You may think you've had the last laugh, but bear this in mind – we'll haul you back when we're ready, not before. Then the last laugh could be on you.'

When White presented his case to C, the MI5 man 'insisted that Philby could no longer be employed by SIS'. But C disagreed and a 'terrible argument' ensued. White concluded that 'trust and loyalty are so much of English nature' that 'Sinclair refused to let one of his chaps down'. Philby, believed C, was a victim of circumstance and told White: 'You're in breach of Crow's Law. Do not believe what you want to believe until you know what you ought to know!' So Philby escaped justice – eventually defecting in 1967.

A small consolation was the discovery of another member of the Cambridge spy ring: John Cairncross, a wartime Bletchley officer who had moved to the Treasury and then the Ministry of Defence. Among the papers in Burgess's flat, Jane Archer found official documents written by Cairncross. Cairncross was tailed and, at Ealing Common Tube station, he stood smoking, apparently waiting for someone. His KGB controller, Yuri Modin, was in fact hovering nearby identifying three MI5 Watchers before leaving without making contact. Cairncross later walked away. Cairncross was a non-smoker – it was a warning to his Soviet contact. Cairncross was twice interviewed by Jim Skardon and made a limited confession of carelessness with official papers. He then resigned from the civil service. After his resignation he moved to America.[14]

There were some successes, though: Michael Goleniewski, a Pole working for Soviet Intelligence, defected to the West in 1961. His information led to the exposure of George Blake – an SIS officer who had betrayed many Western agents on the other side of the Iron Curtain. In 1950, Captain Vivian Holt, British Minister in Seoul, was authorised to withdraw with his staff. The decision was left to him and he decided to remain with George Blake, his Vice-Consul, and another member of his staff. They were captured by North Korean forces and taken to the North's capital, Pyongyang; it was a year before they were reported safe and well. They were released from a North Korean prison camp in the spring of 1953 and taken to Moscow via Peking on April 20 of that year. Two days later they returned by RAF transport aircraft to Abingdon with other internees taken in Seoul. From the time of his release there was not an official document of importance, to which George Blake had access, that he did not pass to Soviet Intelligence. While interned in Korea, Blake decided, in the autumn of 1951, to join the Communist side in establishing 'a more just society'. After his trial in camera, Blake was sentenced by Lord Parker of Waddington, the Lord Chief Justice, to a total of forty-two years' imprisonment. Parker, before he imposed the longest term of imprisonment that could be recalled at the Central Criminal Court, stated the case was 'akin to treason, one of the worst that can be envisaged other than in time of war', and showed 'conduct that in many other countries would have carried the death penalty'. Sir Reginald Manningham-Buller, QC, the Attorney General, prosecuted.[15]

Other defectors, including Anatoli Golitsin, contributed to the capture of an important Soviet spy in Naval Intelligence: John Vassall. Vassall got a secondary education at Monmouth Grammar Sohool, which he left in 1941 at the age of sixteen. He was extremely sensitive as to his social position, and a number of people thought him a snob. His readiness to give the impression of 'having a good family' was probably one of the influences supporting the widespread, if vague, idea among his colleagues that he enjoyed some private means. The general judgment of his capacity as a clerical officer in the Civil Service (he was not found fit for promotion on either of the two occasions when he came before a promotions board in 1958 and 1961) was that he was 'defective in the power of judgment and of limited intellectual capacity'. But nearly everyone found him pleasant to work with, a 'discreet, reserved, and obliging man, well spoken and in appearance neat and well dressed'. In June, 1952 he was posted to the War Registry (the Admiralty's central communications centre), and while he was serving there saw a circular inviting applications for the post of clerk to the Naval Attache in Moscow. He applied and was selected out of some forty volunteers on a short list of eight.

Vassall arrived in Moscow at the beginning of March, 1954, and was an attached member of the Embassy staff without actually being a member of the Foreign Service. There was not then a special security officer on the Embassy staff. The Foreign Office had, in March 1953, and March 1954, circularised British embassies behind the Iron Curtain with specific warnings about dangers arising from unofficial contacts with Russians. Another memorandum contained two paragraphs on the risks of contrived compromise by hostile agents. Each year the memorandum on security was circulated to all members of the Embassy staff who had access to classified material; a new arrival was required to read and sign it on arrival. The Regional Security Officer stationed in Vienna, who annually visited Moscow to review security arrangements, noted, in 1955, but not in 1954, that the memorandum had not been seen by all newly arrived staff. The inference was that in 1954 he was satisfied everyone had seen it. There was also a regular initial briefing from the Head of Chancery about local conditions, including a warning that contacts with the Russians must be reported to him. Vassall's claim, on the contrary, was that he had never seen the memorandum on security and that no one gave him any specific warning or guidance about Russian contacts until August 1955, when the entire Embassy staff received addresses on the subject. The occasion was a Russian-arranged compromise of a woman employee, which necessitated her immediate return to the United Kingdom. By this time Vassall himself was 'already in their toils.'

No one had noticed any change in Vassall's demeanour. He played a full part in the social life open to the diplomatic colony in Moscow, mixing freely in contacts with other embassies. 'It was impossible not to see that he was thoroughly enjoying himself.' He was discreet about his personal affairs and whatever homosexual partners he may have had in Moscow. 'No one, it seems clear, thought him a practising homosexual.' Yet by November 1954, about eight months after his arrival in Moscow, the Russian Secret Service had perceived this and got the photographs they wanted at their 'compromise party'. This, it was believed, had been through the aid of a member of the Embassy's locally engaged staff, Sigmund Mikhailski. He was supplied to the Embassy as a junior interpreter and administrative officer by the Russian agency through whom local staff had to be engaged. He became the agent to lure Vassall into contacts with other Russians.

Mikhailski was engaged early in 1954, and supplied by the Burobin agency. The circumstances themselves were suspicious, since a week or so before in Gorki Park he had approached one of the Embassy staff who was Russian speaking, and inquired about the chance of employment. He was referred to the Burobin agency. It was known that to refuse anyone offered by Burobin was normally followed by months of delay. 'So he was engaged. He was evidently a man of insinuating and attractive manners.' He was, or said he was, a Pole, and in conversation with people at the Embassy he would indicate a lack of sympathy with the Soviet regime. He made himself very useful to several of them with small but appreciated services. There was no doubt that he quickly made a nurmber of friends and before long was received as a guest at parties given by members of the Embassy staff and accompanied some of them when dining out at Moscow restaurants. The senior staff, most of whom, seemed, unlike the junior staff, to have disliked and distrusted him from the first, were unaware of the extent to which Mikhailski had made himself familiar with many members of the Embassy. The matter came to a head in 1955. One member of the staff became increasingly concerned at the pattern of attempted penetration by the Russian Secret Service, and in particular had kept an eye on Mikhailski. He had pressed Mr Slater, the Head of Chancery, for more effective action, and questioned whether Mikhailski should be retained. Slater was not easy to persuade, but in December, just before leaving for Britain on holiday, had issued a circular to all members of the Embassy staff reminding them of their duty to report Russian contacts. Two days later a second circular mentioned Mikhailski by name.

Vassall's social ambitions were 'gratified' by many contacts in the varied diplomatic circle of Moscow and, under the tutelage of Mikhailski, he soon began to go out to Russian restaurants and to make what he believed to be Russian friends. None of these contacts or the invitations that followed them was reported by him to the Embassy. No one knew of his Russian contacts except the man who shared his flat, and even he had no idea how far they had gone. Vassall spent his two-and-a-quarter years in Moscow in various apartments in a block of flats in Ulitsa Narodnaya, in which were lodged some other members of the British Embassy staff, some of the staff of other embassies and some non-Russian press correspondents. He presented to the general observer the appearance of a young man who was taking a normal part in the life of the embassy. Vassall did not offer his services to the Russians: rather they captured him under a deliberately-contrived plan he was first introduced to and then cultivated by Russian agents and his vanity flattered, then enticed to a party and photographed in 'indecent homosexual positions, and finally surprised in a homosexual assignment with a Russian officer'. He was threatened with prosecution and exposure and by the summer of 1955 had been 'brought into subjection'. Monetary inducement was not held out at the time but, 'in accordance with the usual technique of compromise' money was passed to him later and irregularly thereafter 'as long as he was a servant of the Russians'. He thus drifted ito acting as their agent without visible indication that anything compromising had happened at all.

Vassall had no reputation in the Embassy of being a homosexual. The women members of the Embassy, with whom he was evidently popular and among whom he had a number of friends, neither thought him homosexual nor had heard any rumours that he was. Only one of the six women had spoken of 'some gossip'. A woman member of the Embassy staff with security training said explicitly that she never thought of Vassall as a homosexual or as a security risk; he seemed happily engaged on his social activities and for that reason less vulnerable. The Naval Attaché who succeeded Captain Bennett and under whom Vassall worked for some six months never suspected his homosexuality nor did the Assistant Naval Attaché who was there for most of Vassall's time; and a colleague who shared a flat with Vassall for most of the whole period thought him not to be a homosexual.

The Naval Attaché when Vassall first joined the Embassy staff was Captain Bennett, with whom for a time he shared a room at work. He entertained 'a suspicion that Vassall might be a homosexual'. When Vassall first joined him, Captain Bennett was very dissatisfied with him. He found him indolent and incompetent, and after three months of exasperation gave him a stern warning that he would have to go back to the UK if he did not improve. Socially he regarded him as a misfit in the Embassy. But then Vassall began to give much better service and, by the end of 1954, Captain Bennett reported that his work was in general satisfactory, that he was trying hard to please and that he was socially acceptable 'despite his handicap of an irritating, effeminate personality'. In the autumn of 1954, Bennett brought the matter up at a talk with Sir William Hayter, the Ambassador, who thought the allusion was made half jokingly. In November 1955, Bennett wrote his second report on Vassall, just before he himself left his post. This said: 'After a poor start he has developed into a first rate clerk who, except for occasional lapses into inaccuracy, can be trusted to work hard and well. I should be glad to have him for my secretary almost anywhere... A pleasant young man of first-class appearance and manners. Never ruffled. Always helpful. His moral standards are of the highest. A distinct social asset to the embassy staff.' Bennett, a few weeks later, when handing over to Captain Northey, mentioned the suspicions he had or had had that Vassall was a 'possible latent homosexual'. The latter did not recall this though he thought it was not unlikely. His own opinion of Vassall was that he was a 'rather pansy little man' but not a homosexual.

At first Vassall had given his Soviet interrogators oral information about people employed in the Embassy. But, by about September 1955, he had begun to abstract documents from the Naval Attaché's office. The general system of safeguarding the custody of documents belonging to the Naval Attaché's office was an efficient one. All documents of any security classification were kept in a specially protected room, the registry. The Naval Attaché had a cupboard for his papers in this registry, and Vassall as his clerk had access to the cupboard when the registry was open, but had no access to the registry itself until it was opened for him by one of the registry clerks who alone knew the combination control. These clerks kept the keys to the Naval Attaché's cupboard in the registry and would hand them to Vassall when he asked for them. It was Vassall's duty to get the papers for the day out of the cupboard in the morning and to put them away in the evening and for the luncheon break when the Naval Attaché's office would be empty. Normally the Attaché's incoming mail was brought to him by Vassall in a sealed envelope, without first being opened by the registry clerks. Papers were then logged in by Vassall and filed, except that certain papers of special secrecy were seen only by the Naval Attaché himself and then kept in sealed envelopes with his signature across the flap. Neither Captain Bennett nor his assistant attaché recalled any difficulty or suspicious delay in tracing a document when it was called for. Confidential papers when ready for destruction were torn up in the office and then taken down in a sack to be burnt in an incinerator in the Embassy grounds. It was Vassall's duty to carry out this task with naval papers. He gave no reason to suppose that he had made use of his trips to the incinerator in order to abstract any of the documents he took.

Vassall's controllers would give him an appointment at some rendezvous in Moscow three weeks or a month ahead. He had to bring with him a document or documents of value to them, which they photographed at once and returned to him. The danger of a document being found missing increased the longer it was absent. Vassall, therefore, kept to an overnight plan which minimised his risk. He took the paper out of a tray or off his table on the day he was going to meet them, slipped it into a despatch case, or later in accordance with instructions, into an envelope, and then between the pages of a magazine, carried it out of the office with his belongings at the end of the day and put it back next morning. He was, therefore, limited to a choice of such documents as came into his hands in the ordinary course of his duties.

When Vassall came back to work in the Admiralty, in London, he continued to operate the same methods. The postive vetting system that had been introduced to prevent potential or actual enemy agents penetrating Whitehall failed. But it was not the system of vetting that failed, rather the judgement of those involved in the process. Vassall's post in the Naval Inteligence Division was one in which he would have regular access to Top Secret defence information, including information from international defence organisations and some access to classified atomic energy information. The decision to place him in the Intelligence Division, which was essentially a repository of secret matter, was primarily due to a policy of employing for a time in that Division returning clerks who had served naval attachés abroad in a country in which the Intelligence Division was interested. Russia was 'obviously within this category'.

At that time the posts which were subject to positive vetting were: those which required regular and constant access to top secret defence information and material; and those which gave access to classified atomic energy information. Because the special investigators carrying out the field inquiries involved in the vetting process were heavily overloaded and there was a serious backlog of investigations, departments were necessarily employing many people in the first category of posts who had not been positively vetted. No such dispensation was permitted in the second category. Initially, this affected Vassall's employment in the NID. He was allowed to undertake those duties which involved access to top secret defence information without awaiting positive vetting clearance, but did not undertake those which would give him access to classified atomic energy information until the full positive vetting procedure had been completed. Vassall completed a standard security questionnaire, nominating two referees. Although they might have been well acquainted with Vassall some twelve years previously, they were now out of touch with him and he was asked to nominate two others with more recent knowledge of him in his private life. He gave the names of two ladies who had known him and his family for nine and ten years respectively, and satisfactory replies were received from them.

The investigating officer conducting the field inquiries in Vassall's positive vetting was E.S. Sherwood, a Security Officer, Grade II who worked under the supervision of C.F. James, Security Officer Grade I and the head of the investigating team H.W. White. Sherwood was not an inexperienced officer, having served for eleven months in the investigating team and having previously served in the Nigeria police. His investigations followed closely the standard pattern, and he formed the opinion that Vassall was being straightforward and fully co-operative. He interviewed the two referees, the three supervisory officers under whom Vassall served between 1947 and 1953, and H.V. Pennells, the Civil Assistant to the Director of Naval Intelligence, who was able to give some information about the period 1954–1956, when Vassall was in the Moscow Embassy. 'The total impression of Vassall created by these interviews' was of 'a reserved, sober and reliable young man, of good character and unquestionable loyalty, who lived quietly with his parents and his brother at the family home in St. John's Wood, who has as his main interests classical music, bridge and the theatre, and who possessed a strong dislike of communism and the Soviet way of life. There were no suggestions of any kind against his character.'

Except for a few short periods when he was working for the Civil Lord, in the Admiralty, and the Civil Lord's secretary was away, Vassall did not work in a room by himself or without two or three colleagues at work at other desks. 'But no one seemed to have noticed his acts of smuggling.' The Russians discouraged the use of a brief case, presumably fearing he might be caught out in a snap check at the Admiralty doors. His instructions were to bring newspapers or magazines in with him in the morning, as many other civil servants would be doing, and to carry out the purloined documents concealed in the folds of these papers. The documents themselves were slipped into large envelopes, of which he was supplied with a stock by the Russians. His practice was to note a single paper or docket which seemed to him of value to the Russians and which was not likely to be called for at short notice, usually one which had come to him from higher up after being dealt with and was therefore waiting to be put away or filed, or one which for some reason was for the time being safely in suspense, and to transfer this from his desk or tray to the envelope, either directly or by keeping it in a drawer until a convenient moment arrived. He was always careful not to keep a paper out of the office longer than overnight. This went on intermittently through six years of employment in the Admiralty. No one noticed or suspected Vassall, 'presumably because though rooms were shared by three or four people or more, each individual was concentrated on his own work at his desk, and the man who wishes surreptitiously to slip a paper away in the course of the day has only to watch for his chance and then to act unobtrusively'.

At Christmas 1957 the Russians decided that Vassall should have a camera to be able to photograph the documents in his own home. He was given the money to buy one, and after that was never without one or more cameras. This greatly extended the range of his service to the Russians since, though he continued to keep documents out of the office for one night only, useful documents could be taken and photographed on any day that they came to him without regard to the date of his next Russian appointment. This was an 'important change'.

Vassall did not like the work in the NID and asked if he could change. In June 1957 he was transferred to the private office of the Civil Lord, T.G.D. Galbraith, MP, where it was intended that he should work as clerical officer assisting the Civil Lord's private secretary. Vassall's Russian controllers were not pleased with his assignment to this office. Though he continued his abstractions during the two-and-a-quarter years he was in the office, it was probably not an important period from the point of view of his spying activities. In 1959 he was posted to Military Branch 11, the secretariat which served the naval staff in the Admiralty. A large volume of highly classified material passed through it and he was placed at the centre of one of the Admiralty's most sensitive branches. His clerical duties brought him into touch with material concerned with technical matters such as radar, communications, torpedoes and antisubmarine material, gunnery trials, Allied technical publications, Allied tactical publications, Allied excise publications, Fleet operational and tactical mistructions, and also with general matters concerning naval liaison with Commonwealth countries. After arrests in the Portland spying case – including the *illegal* Soviet agent George Lonsdale – were made in January, 1961, (once again thanks to information from Goleniewski) Vassall was at once told by his Russian controller that though he was not himself compromised he was to stop all espionage work until further notice that it was safe to resume. This notice was not given to him until some time early in 1962, but from that time on until his arrest he was actively at work for the Russians on the same lines as before.

While Vassall's ordinary work when he was moved to Military Branch probably did not give him regular access to much really significant material, there were occasions during 1962, one only shortly before his arrest, when the temporary absence of the clerical officer who normally assisted the head of his section placed Vassall, as her deputy, in a position to handle a volume of documentary matter which carried a very high security classification. The undelivered films which he took of some of these papers and which were recovered from his flat when he was detected 'did not suggest that he was either slow to seize his opportunities when they came or that by that time he was reluctant to obtain for his masters the richest spoil that he could put into their hands'.

By June 1962, Vassall was under suspicion as a possible spy, and by August 'certainty began to turn on him'. The inquiry into Vassall's activities concluded that the success of his 'somewhat complicated existence as an ordinary civil servant of junior rank, quiet, obliging and moderately efficient, and as an agent of the Russian Secret Service' was based on the fact that it was essential that the two sectors of his life should never overlap. But it was noticeable how in other sectors too Vassall succeeded in keeping separate activities from impinging on one another. His long immunity from suspicion could only be understood in the light of the impression of himself that he created among his office colleagues. Their general impression was that he was a man of good family with some private means. It was known that he lived a fairly active social life, going to theatres, restaurants and concerts, away for weekends and for holidays abroad. But he had no close friends of his own in the Admiralty. There was no single person sufficiently far in his confidence to have any comprehensive picture of his social and personal life as a whole. 'And without such knowledge no concrete idea would have emerged as to the level of his general expenditure. Moreover, without independent cause of suspicion, such activities are as much indicative of private means as of some criminal source of profit.' It was not unknown in the office that he lived in Dolphin Square, or more vaguely, in the West End. But he might have been living with his parents, or sharing with a friend, or helped by a family allowance or using some private means of his own. In fact, to the ordinary acquaintance the Dolphin Square address probably contributed to the attribution of private means. He was to many people though by no means all, 'something of a joke, for they thought him a social climber and a hanger-on of rich old ladies, with an eye to the main chance'.[16]

The lesson of the Vassall case was that the vetting process was only as good as the vetters themselves. In the sexually conservative 1950s to be a homosexual was to be considered a sexual deviant. The moral atmosphere then pervading made men like Vassall desperate to conceal their sexuality for fear of prosecution. And it left men like him open to blackmail. But blackmail was a weapon available to the Soviets that could be used against any heterosexual too. Anybody, making an error of judgement, could be entrapped.

MI5 were not culpable in missing Vassall or lapse in failing to discover him without the aid of a defector: as in the war, with ISOS, one makes use of whatever tools give one an advantage. It is almost certain that many other agents – on both sides of the Iron Curtain – went undetected by either side in the Great Game. But MI5 emerged with far less excuses when it was revealed that one of their own – albeit retired – officers was a former Soviet agent: Anthony Blunt.

In late 1963, MI5 were informed by the FBI that an American citizen, Michael Whitney Straight, had told them that Blunt had recruited him for the Soviets while they were both at Cambridge University in the 1930s. Arthur Martin flew over to interview Straight, who confirmed the story, and agreed to testify in a British court if necessary. Blunt was offered immunity after the matter had been cleared with the Attorney-General. When he was confronted by Arthur Martin, in April 1964, Blunt almost immediately admitted his role as Soviet talent spotter and spy. This was a shocking revelation to those who had worked with Blunt during the war. In particular, wartime MI5 colleagues of Blunt, such as Victor Rothschild, were devastated by the news. Rothschild's main concern, as soon as he was told the truth, was how to break the news to his wife, Tess, who had formed an even closer relationship with Blunt than her husband had. When war broke out, Tess Mayer, as she then was, joined MI5, and, during this period, she had rooms in Bentinck Street along with Blunt and Guy Burgess. She would recall how 'Anthony used to come back tight to Bentinck Street, sometimes so tight that I had to help him into bed'. Victor Rothschild realised that the Service would need to interview his wife now that Blunt had confessed, 'but he dreaded telling her the truth'.[17] It was Burgess, it appears, who suggested that Blunt be recruited, at Cambridge, by the Soviets.[18]

Blunt claimed that he became a Communist, or more particularly a Marxist, in 1935 or 1936. He had been on a sabbatical, and on his return to Cambridge found that his friends and 'almost all the bright undergraduates' had become Marxists under the impact of Hitler. The 'most intelligent' was Burgess, who convinced Blunt that the Marxist interpretation of history was correct. When Burgess put it to him, Blunt decided that the best way of opposing fascism was to become a talent spotter – that is, he gave Burgess the names of likely recruits. Blunt claimed that he spotted very few before he left Cambridge in 1937 to work at the Warburg

Institute[19] – although, ironically, one of those was Michael Straight – his ultimate betrayer. Blunt also recruited John Cairncross, before the entire NKVD London residence was recalled to Moscow and caught up in Stalin's purges in the summer of 1937. It was then that Blunt left Cambridge to work at the Warburg Institute in London, where he met a generation of Jewish émigré academics who greatly influenced his art history. He had no further contact with Moscow until the NKVD's London resident re-established contact in December 1940 and was amazed to discover that Blunt had joined MI5.[20]

Although Blunt had been rejected by Military Intelligence when he applied for a posting at the beginning of the war, he was accepted by the Intelligence Corps and served in France until the evacuation of the BEF in 1940. On his return to Britain he joined MI5, 'largely because of the old-boy network'. He received 'only a routine vetting because everybody was too busy'. The Ribbentrop-Molotov Pact, he convinced himself, was a tactical necessity to help the Soviet Union gain time and prepare for war, and while working at MI5 he passed on information to the Soviets. With the Russians as allies he continued his espionage activities with a 'clearer conscience'. Blunt passed the information to English friends and a Soviet agent, whom he met in London. He did not know his name, but assumed he was attached to the Soviet Embassy. Blunt claimed that he ceased to report to the Russians after the war. He could have contacted them through Burgess, but he had nothing to report – certainly nothing from Buckingham Palace, where he was employed as Surveyor of the King's Pictures. Nevertheless, he kept in touch with Burgess but not Maclean, who was frequently posted abroad. Burgess could be 'tiresome and difficult' but was highly intelligent. They discussed everything except politics.[21]

It turned out that, when Burgess had arrived in London, back in 1951, sent there by Philby to engineer Maclean's flight from MI5, he had first called upon Blunt, who by coincidence, was due to meet his Soviet contact, Yuri Modin, the following day. It was the Soviet Intelligence Officer who, surprised to hear that Burgess was in Britain, suggested that Burgess and Maclean meet, 'not in an office or unusual place, but in their club'. Burgess was to report back, via Blunt, about Maclean's reaction to his predicament.[22]

On the morning after Maclean had failed to turn up at work, Blunt had telephoned Guy Liddell. Liddell, who trusted his former MI5 colleague implicitly, confided that Burgess had disappeared.

Blunt pretended to be shocked. Believing that the Soviet plan was for Burgess to return, he reassured Liddell that there were no grounds for suspicion. Liddell then asked Blunt to obtain the keys to Burgess's flat so as to avoid MI5 formally applying for a search warrant. Blunt did obtain but first searched the flat, taking letters which compromised himself.[23] Blunt's treachery was yet another blow to the morale of the Service. Some asked how many more Soviets moles were in the Service; how far up; and where would the trail end?

6

Spycatchers:
The Hunt for the Soviet Mole

In July 1969, Stella Rimington started work in MI5's headquarters in Leconfield House at the Park Lane end of Curzon Street. Looking back, she recalled:

> Leconfield House is now the glitzy London headquarters of banks and property companies. In 1969, like many government offices in those days, it was dreadfully run down. The inside had not been painted for an age, the windows were dirty and everything about it was dark and gloomy. There was a canteen on the top floor. The most you could say about that was that it functioned. The lady in charge was one of those office 'characters', with whom everyone seems to be on good terms but whom they secretly despise. She would slop the food onto the plates with a huge spoon and a great splat, making it, if possible, even more unappetising than it looked in the container. Out of the grimy windows you could watch the rich and famous going in and out of the White Elephant Club and the other gambling dives on the other side of the road or driving up to the Bunny Club on the corner of Curzon Street. The contrast was acute. I thought the whole set-up was grim, and after one lunch there, I never went again.

A partitioning of Leconfield House had left some of the rooms without windows and the size and shape of cupboards, 'but I was put to work in a long narrow room with about ten or so other people, mostly women'. This was the section where all new joiners, whether they were men (officers) or women (assistant officers) were put for a few months to be trained and it was presided over by a couple of training officers, two well-bred ladies 'of a certain age', from the 'twin-set-and-pearls brigade'. On Rimington's first day 'I was intrigued when at noon, these two opened their desk drawers and produced exquisite cut glasses and bottles of some superior sherry, and partook of a rather elegant pre-lunch drink. I realised then that I had arrived in the land of eccentrics and that this promised to be a lot more entertaining than spending my days in Woking.'[1]

As a newcomer, having arrived fresh from living and working in India, 'I felt like a real outsider. I could not quite see how or where

I was going to fit into this very curious set-up. It was indeed, as the recruitment process had made clear, unashamedly male-dominated.' The men were the 'officers' and the women were the 'other ranks' in military parlance, and there were 'still quite strong military overtones'. The men, Rimington found, were largely from a similar background:

> To me it seemed that they all lived in Guildford and spent their spare time gardening. Many had fought in the armed services during the war; some had performed heroically and some, perhaps not surprisingly, seemed drained by their experiences. I remember one, who had been a Dambuster and had flown the most dramatic and dangerous sorties when he had been very young. He regularly withdrew into his office and locked the door after lunch. I used to jump up and down in the corridor to look over the smoked glass in the partition, to see what he was doing, and he was invariably sound asleep. No one thought it appropriate to comment.

Rimington discovered that many of the men had come in to MI5 from a first career in the Colonial Service. They had come in little groups as each of the colonies had become independent, and there were circles of friends known as the Malayan Mafia or the Sudan Souls. They had come in as 'officers', broadly equivalent to Principal in the old Administrative Class of the Home Civil Service, but they were given no promise of progression through a career. Most had a pension and a lump sum which had enabled them to buy a house, so they were not on the breadline. Though some did well and rose to senior positions, others did not and, not surprisingly in the circumstances, 'many of them lacked any motivation or drive and did not exactly exert themselves'. In fact:

> Some of them, far from exerting themselves, seemed to do very little at all and there was a lot of heavy drinking. I remember one gentleman, who was supposed to be running agents against the Russian intelligence residency in London. He favoured rather loud tweed suits and a monocle. He would arrive in the office at about 10 and at about 11 would go out for what was termed 'breakfast'. He would return at 12 noon, smelling strongly of whisky to get ready to go out to 'meet an agent' for lunch. If he returned at all it would be at about 4 p.m., for a quiet snooze before getting ready to go home. Eventually, he collapsed in the lift returning from one of these sorties and was not seen again.

'Maybe it was not as bad as I remember,' wrote Rimington, years later; 'I was very lowly in the hierarchy and from low down you often get a very partial view of what is going on. But I know the various drinking clubs around Soho were much frequented by the older MI5 officers in those days, because occasionally I went with them.' These were the kind of places where drinks were available at all hours; 'you signed your name in a book as "Mr Smith and two guests" and you could drink all day.' Rimington found the women 'a curiously mixed bunch'. There were 'still some of the debs around, the generals' and admirals' daughters who had peopled MI5 as clerks and secretaries during and just after the war – recruited more for their obvious reliability, for whom they knew and who could vouch for them, than for their brains or education – though some of them were very bright women being seriously underemployed.' Although there were some women, like Rimington with a good degree, starting to be admitted to the Service, she found that 'not much regard was paid to your qualifications or ability if you were a woman'. The nearest the women got to the 'sharp end of things in those days' was as support officers to the men who were running the agents. They would be asked to go and service the safe house where the agent was met – 'making sure there was milk and coffee there and the place was clean and tidy', and 'very occasionally' they might be allowed to go with their officer to meet a very reliable, long-standing agent on his birthday or some other special occasion: 'This attitude to women seems incredible now, looked at from the standpoint of the 21st century. So much has changed in women's employment expectations since those days. But I don't think it ever occurred to my male colleagues that they were discriminating against us and in those days it was not really questioned inside the Service. And to be fair to them, even I, coming in from the outside, did not question it at first.'[2] Stella Rimington would, one day, go on to become the first woman Director General of MI5.

It was in the early 1970s that Rimington was invited to work in the Counter-espionage branch. The Director of Counter-Espionage was Michael Hanley, 'a large, gruff, red-faced man, who had a reputation for being abrupt and having a fierce temper'. This, reflected Rimington, was 'perhaps not surprising considering that he had himself fallen prey to the paranoia of the 1960s and '70s and had been investigated as a possible KGB mole because he appeared to fit the description produced by a defector from the Eastern bloc'. Rimington was surprised to be called into his office to be welcomed into the counter-espionage branch: 'His kindly interest was unusual in those days when personal contact between directors and junior staff was rare.' Hanley moved on shortly afterwards to become Deputy Director General and then in 1972, Director General. Rimington's section consisted, 'as usual', of a number of male officers supported by a collection of female assistant officers:

> I worked in an office with two men who had been friends in the Colonial Service. They fell firmly into the cynical camp and while they were together, not a great deal of useful work was done. They spent a lot of time in the office telling jokes about their colonial experiences, and took extremely long lunch hours. It was routine for them to return from lunch at about four in the afternoon (they had some 'arrangement' with a pub up the road), and then we all settled down to afternoon tea laced with whisky accompanied by peppermints in case the boss called them to a meeting. He rarely did and the days passed quite peacefully, with them occasionally going out to interview someone and me sitting at my desk writing summaries of files and sorting out papers. I used to go home to my baby daughter some evenings rather the worse for wear if the whisky tea had been too well laced. I suppose there was some plan in what we were doing and some strategic direction somewhere, but I certainly did not know what it was – perhaps I was too lowly to be told.

And, in and out of all this 'strode the extraordinary figure of Peter Wright. I believe he had at one time been regarded as an effective counter-espionage operator, but by the time I knew him well he was quite clearly a man with an obsession and was regarded by many of the newer arrivals in the Service and even by some of the older hands as quite mad and certainly dangerous.' He had briefly been made the Assistant Director of the section Rimington was working in, 'but according to rumour, he had been so bad at giving any direction or leadership that he had been "promoted"' to be a special adviser to the Director. Rimington pointed out counter-espionage work 'is not a glamorous business, however it has been presented by the spy-story writers. It is hard work.' It was all about 'painstaking and rigorous analysis, the detailed following up of snippets of information and perseverance in the face of disappointment. A bit of luck helps of course.' In particular,

> it is not the quick jumping to conclusions and the twisting of the facts to meet the theory which Peter Wright went in for in those days.

He was in fact by then everything which a counter-espionage officer should not be. He was self-important, he had an over-developed imagination and an obsessive personality which had turned to paranoia. And above all he was lazy... It is hard to explain why he was allowed to stay for so long. As Special Adviser he had the right to pick up anything he liked and drop it when he tired of it. He used to wander around, finding out what everyone was doing, taking cases off people, going off and doing interviews which he never wrote up, and then moving on to something else, while refusing to release files for others to work on. He always implied that he knew more about everything than anyone else, but that what he knew was so secret that he could not possibly tell you what it was. That gave him the right to disagree with everything anyone else thought without challenge.[3]

Peter Maurice Wright was born in Chesterfield, Derbyshire, on 9 August 1916: it was said that he arrived prematurely because of shock to his mother, Lois Dorothy, caused by a nearby Zeppelin raid. His father, George Maurice Wright (who became chief scientist at Marconi), had served in SIS during the First World War, enabling Wright to claim that 'the thread of secret intelligence work had run through the family through four and a half decades'. A sickly child, he had a terrible stammer, suffered from rickets, and wore leg irons almost into his teens. Brought up in Chelmsford, Essex, he attended Bishop's Stortford School until 1931, and then worked for a while as a farm labourer in Scotland before joining the School of Rural Economy at Oxford in 1938. That year he married Lois Elizabeth Foster-Melliar with whom he had two daughters and a son. Although without formal qualifications, Wright worked for the Admiralty research laboratory during the Second World War. At its end he sat entry exams for the scientific civil service, passing out joint first. For four years he was a principal scientific officer at the services research laboratory and in 1950 he began working as an adviser for the Security Service, joining MI5 full-time in 1955. On his appointment Dick White, then head of MI5, told him, 'I'm not sure we need an animal like you in the Security Service,' but they shared a bond, both having been educated at Bishop's Stortford School. Told from the start that his late entry would deny him any of the agency's directorships, he quickly came to regard most of his colleagues as snobbish: they in turn regarded him with undisguised contempt as a technician, and not as a gentleman. At MI5 he was highly proficient in developing microphones and bugging devices.[4]

Most importantly, Wright became the central figure among a small group of officers convinced that MI5 had been penetrated to the highest level by the Russians. He began a personal crusade – or witch hunt – to discover a Soviet mole. Evelyn McBarnet, an MI5 research officer, 'with a large birthmark running down one side of her face', had always believed there was a penetration of the Service. She had spent years working in counter-espionage research and was a 'walking compendium of office life and a shrewd, if somewhat morbid, judge of character'. One day, with Wright present, she opened her safe and pulled out a small exercise book with a black cover. She gave the book to Wright and told him to read it. It listed details of cases from the 1940s and 1950s, some of which Wright knew about vaguely, and others he did not, which the author had collated from the MI5 Registry. Each one contained an explicit allegation about a penetration of MI5 or SIS. The book had been compiled by Anne Last, a friend of McBarnet who had worked in MI5 until she had left to have a family.

The name of Maxwell Knight (long since retired) figured frequently in the first few pages. During the war he was convinced there was a spy inside MI5, and had minuted to that effect, although no action was taken. There were dozens and dozens of allegations. Many of them were 'fanciful, offhand comments drawn from agent reports; but others were more concrete', thought Wright, like the testimony of Igor Gouzenko, the young Russian cipher clerk who defected to the Canadians in 1945. According to Anne Last, Gouzenko claimed in his debriefing that there was a spy code-named 'Elli' inside MI5. He had learned about Elli while serving in Moscow in 1942, from a friend of his, Luibimov, who handled radio messages dealing with Elli. Elli had something Russian in his background, had access to certain files and his information was often taken straight to Stalin. Gouzenko's allegation 'had been filed along with all the rest of his material, but then, inexplicably, left to gather dust'. That evening Wright 'joined the commuters thronging down Curzon Street toward Park Lane, my head humming with what I had learned from Evelyn. Here was a consistent unbroken pattern of allegations, each suggesting there was a spy in the office, stretching from 1942 to the present day. For too long they had gone uninvestigated, unchallenged. This time the chase would be long and hard and unrelenting. I paused to look back at Leconfield House. This time, I thought, this time there will be no tip-offs, no defections. This one will not slip away.'[5]

The first serial Wright investigated was that of would be Soviet defector Konstantin Volkov gave a list of departments in which Soviet spies operated. He then disappeared before he could supply the names – most likely thanks to Kim Philby's treachery. Wright decided to have the entire document retranslated by Geoffrey Sudbury, the GCHQ officer who ran the VENONA program. Sudbury was a fluent Russian speaker, but most important of all, from the VENONA programme he was familiar with the kind of Russian Intelligence Service jargon in use at the time Volkov attempted to defect, whereas the British Embassy official in Turkey who made the original translation was not. One entry in Volkov's list puzzled Wright in particular. In the original translation it referred to his knowledge of files and documents concerning very important Soviet agents in important establishments in London. According to Wright, when the case against Philby was first compiled in 1951, MI5 assumed that the last spy referred to by Volkov was Philby, who in 1945 was fulfilling the duties of head of a department of SIS Counter Intelligence, responsible for Soviet counter intelligence. A few days after he gave Sudbury the Volkov list, he rang Wright up to explain that the translation should read: 'I know, for instance, that one of these agents is fulfilling the duties of head of a section of the British Counterintelligence Directorate.' Sudbury pointed out that 'the British Counterintelligence Directorate' was MI5 – and not MI6/SIS as everyone had assumed. For Wright: 'The meaning was crystal clear. If Sudbury was right, this was not Philby, and it could not be Blunt either, since he was never acting head of anything. Only one man had been acting head of a section of the British Counterintelligence Directorate in 1944–1945. His name was Roger Hollis.'

A new investigation – FLUENCY – re-examined the case of Elli in great detail. The essence of Gouzenko's story was simple. He said he knew there was a spy in 'five of MI.' He had learned this from a friend, Luibimov, who had worked alongside him in the main GRU cipher room in Moscow in 1942. The problem, for Wright, with Gouzenko's story was that over the years, since he had first told it in 1945, he varied the details. 'Five of MI' became MI5. Theoretically, 'five of MI' could be taken as referring to Section V of MI. In 1942, Philby was working in Section V of SIS – or MI6. The other problem with Gouzenko was that by the mid-1960s 'he was an irretrievable alcoholic' and memory was at best unreliable for events which occurred more than twenty years before. When Gouzenko defected, an SIS officer, Peter Dwyer, travelled up to Canada from Washington to attend his debriefing. Dwyer sent back daily telegrams to SIS headquarters in London outlining Gouzenko's information. Dwyer's cables were handled by the head of Soviet counter intelligence in SIS – Philby. Philby, in the following week, 'was to have to face the pressing problem of Volkov's almost simultaneous approach to the British in Turkey. By good luck he asked that his opposite number in MI5, Roger Hollis, should go to Canada to see Gouzenko instead of him.' Was this coincidence, Wright wondered, 'or an arrangement made in the knowledge that Hollis was a fellow spy and could be trusted to muddy the waters in the Gouzenko case?' But then Wright knew, from VENONA, that the KGB was unaware of the existence of a GRU spy in MI5 when Hollis travelled to Canada and interviewed Gouzenko.[6] What made all this even more explosive than it normally would be was that, by now, Sir Roger Hollis had succeeded Dick White as Director General of MI5. The idea that the spy could be the head of the Security Service was dynamite.

Hollis was born at Wells, Somerset, in December 1905, the third of the four sons of the Reverend George Arthur Hollis, Vice-Principal of Wells Theological College and later Bishop-Suffragan of Taunton, and his wife, Mary Margaret, the daughter of Charles Marcus Church, Canon of Wells, a great-niece of R.W. Church, Dean of St Paul's. His elder brother, (Maurice) Christopher Hollis (1902–1977) became a Conservative MP. Roger Hollis was educated at Leeds Grammar School, Clifton College, and Worcester College, Oxford. At school he was a promising scholar who went to Oxford with a classical exhibition. But at Oxford he read English and in the view of his contemporaries seemed to prefer a happy social life to an academic one. Because of this he went down four terms before he was due to take his finals. After only a year's work in the Dominions, Commonwealth, and Overseas branch of Barclays Bank, Hollis left Britain to become a journalist on a Hong Kong newspaper. He did not stay long in this job either and in April 1928 he transferred to the British American Tobacco Company (BAT), in whose service he remained for the following eight years of his time in China. His work there allowed Hollis to travel widely in a country torn by the almost continuous conflict between Chinese warlords and Japanese invaders. An attack of tuberculosis led to his being invalided out of BAT. He returned to England in 1936 for a further brief spell with the Ardath Tobacco Company, an associate of BAT. On 10 July of the following year he was married in Wells Cathedral to Evelyn Esmé, daughter of George Champeny Swayne, of Burnham-on-Sea, Somerset, a solicitor in Glastonbury. Their one child, Adrian Swayne Hollis, became a fellow and tutor in classics at Keble College, Oxford, and a chess player of international reputation. Hollis joined MI5 in 1938. Dick White later commented: 'By qualities of mind and character he was in several ways well adapted to it. He was a hard and conscientious worker, level-headed, fair-minded, and always calm.' He 'managed' during the war, 'with small resources to ensure that the dangers of Russian directed communism were not neglected'. Consequently, when the war was over and the Security Service turned to face the problems of the Cold War, Hollis 'had already become one of its key figures'.[7] Hollis was always dressed in a black jacket and pinstripe trousers[8] and this image of the unflappable English gentleman was confirmed when White recalled how it was always said of Hollis 'by one of his closest collaborators that the hotter the climate of national security, the cooler he became'.[9] Peter Wright, however, was convinced that Hollis was a Soviet agent.

Another FLUENCY allegation centred on the Skripkin case. Yuri Rastvorov, a Second Secretary at the Russian Embassy in Tokyo, was in fact a Lieutenant Colonel in the KGB with whom British Naval Intelligence made contact with in the autumn of 1953 and began negotiations for his defection. His reluctance to defect to Britain was because he knew that British Intelligence was penetrated, although he did not elaborate further. Later, the CIA reported that Rastvorov had given further details of his reasons for believing British Intelligence was penetrated. He said that a friend of his, a Lieutenant Skripkin, had approached the British in the Far East in 1946, and offered to defect. Skripkin made arrangements to return to Moscow, fetch his wife, and then defect on his next visit out of the country. However, back in Moscow, Skripkin was somehow detected by the KGB. He was approached by two KGB officers who pretended to be SIS officers. He gave himself away, was tried and shot. When Wright looked Skripkin up in the Registry he found that he did indeed have a file. The file was dealt with by Roger Hollis, then Assistant Director of F Branch, and a junior officer. Hollis instructed the junior officer to make a file and place it in the Registry, where it lay until Rastvorov told his story in 1954. When the file was retrieved it was 'automatically attributed to Philby by MI5'. This, and other evidence, meant that, for Wright: 'the finger pointed toward Roger Hollis, the F Branch Assistant Director who handled the Skripkin file'. Once the shape of the FLUENCY allegations became clear, Wright 'began the most dangerous task I ever undertook. Without authorisation I began to make my own "freelance" inquiries into Hollis' background. I had to be cautious, since I knew that the slightest leak back would inevitably lead to the sack.'

Wright travelled down to Oxford, and visited the Bodleian Library. There he discovered in the university records that Hollis, although he went up to Oxford in the 1920s, never took a degree. He left inexplicably after five terms. To Wright it seemed 'an odd thing for so conventional a man to do'. He visited Hollis's old college, Worcester, and searched the records there to find out who had lived on the same staircase. In his fourth term Hollis moved to digs in Wellington Square, and Wright checked through the Oxford Calendars, which listed the addresses of every student resident at Oxford, to find those students with whom he shared a house. Wright even tried the records of the University Golfing Society 'in the hope that somewhere there would be a clue to the enigma of Hollis' personality'.

Working without Hollis's record of service, 'I was forced to work blind. I knew from talking to Hollis that he had visited China, so I ran a trace through the Passport Office for the dates of his arrivals and departures from Britain. I made discreet inquiries at the Standard Chartered Bank, where Hollis worked before leaving for China, but apart from an old forwarding address at a bank in Peking, they had no records. I wanted to find some evidence of a secret life, a careless friend, a sign of overt political activity. Every man is defined by his friends, and I began to draw up a picture of those to whom Hollis was close in those vital years in the late 1920s and 1930s.' Two men in particular were of interest at Oxford – Claud Cockburn and Maurice Richardson. Both were left-wing: in Cockburn's case, when Wright ran a check on his file 'I noticed that Hollis had retained the file throughout the war, and never declared his friendship on the file as the Service customs demand. Did he, I wondered, have a reason to hide his relationship with Cockburn, a man with extensive Comintern contacts?'

Out in China 'there was a similar pattern'. China was a 'hotbed of political activity in the 1930s, and was an active recruiting ground for the Comintern'. Wright interviewed Tony Stables 'a brusque, old-fashioned military officer', who shared a flat with Hollis out in China. He remembered Hollis well; he said he never knew his political opinions, 'but always assumed they were left-wing' because he mixed with people like Agnes Smedley, a left-wing journalist and Comintern talent spotter, as well as another man called Arthur Ewert, whom Stables described as an international socialist. Wright broached the subject of Hollis with Jane Sissmore, who was responsible for bringing Hollis into MI5 before the war, and was now Jane Archer (having transferred to SIS and married an MI6 officer). She thought Hollis 'untrustworthy' and did not rule out the possibility he might be a spy.

Then, in November 1965, Hollis 'buzzed down' to Wright and asked him to come up to his office. It was unlike the Director General to be so informal. Wright had never before visited his office without being summoned by his secretary: 'He greeted me warmly by the door,' recalled Wright and said 'Come over and sit down,' smiling broadly and brushing 'imaginary dust off the sofa, and sat opposite me in the easy chair. That, too, was odd. Hollis usually sat in a straight-backed chair. Hollis was anxious to put the meeting on an informal footing. He made rather clumsy small talk about his imminent retirement.' As the chat drew to a close, Hollis turned to face Wright, hunching forward, with his hands on his knees. He was smiling again, 'like a Cheshire cat'. He said: 'Peter, there was just one thing I wanted to ask you before I go. I wanted to know why you think I'm a spy.' Wright was caught unawares and 'had to think very fast. If I told him a lie and he knew I had, I was out that day. So I told him the truth.'

'It's all based on the old allegations, sir,' Wright told him, 'and the way things have been going wrong. You know my views on postwar failure. It's just a process of elimination… and now it's you.' For an hour Wright went through the Volkov list, the retranslation, Gouzenko's Elli, the Skripkin report. 'Well, Peter,' Hollis said, laughing gently, 'you have got the manacles on me, haven't you?' Wright began to interrupt. He held his hands face up to quiet me' before the Director General said: 'All I can say is that I am not a spy.' The meeting finished with, according to Wright's recollection, Hollis saying, 'Well, thank you for your frankness, Peter,' as he rose from his seat. 'I must be getting on. Good to have this chat, though.' Wright 'never saw Roger Hollis again'.[10] Furnival Jones became the new Director General after Hollis retired.

The new Director General who had to deal with the fallout from Wright's investigation was Edward Martin Furnival Jones – known as 'FJ'. Born in 1912, at Barnet, Hertfordshire, he was the third and youngest son of Edward Furnival Jones, a chartered accountant, later to be president of the Association of Chartered Accountants, and his wife, Kathleen Lizzie, née Sedgfield. He was educated at Highgate School and at Gonville and Caius College, Cambridge, where he was an exhibitioner, reading modern and medieval languages and then law. On graduating he was admitted as a solicitor in 1937, working for the firm Slaughter and May until the outbreak of the Second World War. In 1940 he was commissioned in the Intelligence Corps – like Blunt – and in 1941 he was attached to MI5, serving in the War Office and then in the counter-intelligence division of Supreme Headquarters Allied Expeditionary Force where he worked on the deception operation for the D-Day landings. For his work with SHAEF he was mentioned in despatches and awarded the Bronze Star by the Americans. By the end of the war he had been promoted to the rank of Lieutenant Colonel.

In 1946 Furnival Jones became a permanent member of the Security Service, initially working in C Branch (protective security), becoming Director of it in 1953. At that time C Branch 'was seen as a backwater' within the Service. Outside the shadowy world of intelligence, he married, in 1955, (Elizabeth) Margaret Snowball, secretary and daughter of Bartholomew Snowball, an electrical engineer. Then, following Dick White's move from DG to become C, in 1958, Furnival Jones had an opportunity to move. When Hollis became Director General, Graham Mitchell, formerly Director of D Branch (now counter-espionage), became his deputy. Furnival Jones replaced Mitchell as head of D branch. When Hollis retired in 1965, Furnival Jones became Director General. 'FJ', later made an appearance before the Franks Committee reviewing Section 2 of the 1911 Official Secrets Act in November 1971. He, famously, stated that Russian spies had been readily recognisable 'because they wore long coats and curiously shaped hats', and that his definition of an official secret was that 'It is an official secret if it is in an official file.' After he retired from the Service, in 1972, FJ would work, briefly, as a security consultant to ICI and *Playboy*.[11] For now, FJ had to sanction an investigation into his former boss.

'It is always distressing to pursue an investigation into a colleague' recalled Wright, although this did not apply with Hollis who was a 'distant' figure, close to retirement by the time the suspicions against him 'hardened'. But first of all, Wright led the investigation into Michael Hanley: 'Hanley and I knew each other well. We were contemporaries, and although by no stretch of the imagination friends, we had served together amicably on committees for over ten years. His career lay in front of him, and his future was in my hands.' The investigation into the Mole was codenamed HARRIET and the 'most difficult aspect of all' in the case was that the investigation soon revealed that Hanley had had 'a most distressing childhood following the breakup of his parents' marriage. He was left with deep-seated feelings of inferiority, which, according to his record of service, required psychiatric treatment in the 1950s, when he was a young MI5 officer, a fact which Hanley made known to the office at the time.' That Hanley had visited a psychiatrist 'was not in itself unusual' as many senior officers in MI5 had counselling of one form or another during their careers 'to assist them in carrying the burdens of secrecy. But inevitably our investigation had to probe Hanley's old wounds, in case they revealed a motive for espionage.'

Furnival Jones, Patrick Stewart (of D1 (Investigations)), and Wright discussed the problem, and the Director General wrote a personal letter to Hanley's psychiatrist asking him to lift the oath of confidentiality. Wright visited the psychiatrist in Harley Street. He knew Hanley's occupation, and showed no hesitation in pronouncing Hanley a determined, robust character who had learned to live with his early disabilities. Wright asked him if he could ever conceive of him as a spy. 'Absolutely not!' he replied with total conviction. There was no evidence of espionage in Hanley's early life. Everyone who knew him at this time, though, remarked on his 'nagging sense of inferiority, and the consequent lack of ambition'. But what 'aroused our interest was his decision, in 1945, to enrol for a crash course in the Russian language at the Joint Services Language School at Cambridge' which was known as a recruiting ground for the KGB. The Russian language course was the first time Hanley came into contact with Russians, and from then on his career seemed a fit for allegations by the defector Michael Goleniewski. After service in Budapest, where he served on the Joint Allied Intelligence Committee with a KGB officer named by Goleniewski as having made the recruitment of the middling-grade agent, Hanley returned to London. He became the War Office liaison officer with the Soviet military attaché, and dealt mainly with returnee problems. During this time he began to have dealings with MI5, and when he was demobilised in the late 1940s, he applied for a full-time post, and joined as a research officer on Russian affairs.[12]

Hanley was brought in for interrogation. It was conducted by the Director General himself. Throughout the first day Furnival Jones took Hanley through his life. Hanley was 'scrupulously honest, sometimes painfully so. He ducked no questions, hid no details of his life or his inner feelings.' On the second day he was given the details of Goleniewski's allegation. 'He was not shaken in any way. He agreed that he was a perfect fit, but calmly stated that he was not a spy, had never been, and had never at any stage been approached by a Russian or anyone else.' By the end of the process, all were agreed that Hanley had been cleared.[13]

Now it was Hollis's turn. Wright was excluded from involvement in this interrogation on the grounds that he was 'too emotional on the subject'. Which he was, for Wright wondered, as he imagined the interrogation, if Hollis 'would be wearing his Cheshire cat smile. Would he feel humiliated? I wondered. Or frightened? I somehow doubted it. Emotion was never something I associated with him.' In the event, Hollis explained his position in a simple, concise manner. He said he left home because he realised he was not religious but Oxford, he claimed, was no escape. It, too, reminded him of his religious upbringing. The only ambition he had was to play golf, but he realised early on at Oxford that he could never make a career out of it. So Hollis decided to travel. China fascinated him. And, he met the 'odd left-wing person out there, but then that was normal'. He said his health was a constant problem. TB afflicted him throughout this period, and in the end it forced his return to Europe. He travelled back via Moscow. Hollis 'wanted to see what it was like. Awful place. Dirty, depressing. Nobody smiled. Intellectuals were making a tremendous fuss about the place. But I hated it.' He was vague about what he did in his first year back in Britain before MI5. For Wright this vagueness was suspicious. But the Director General would have none of it. FJ claimed Hollis 'was in a mess' when he came back from China – his health was 'shot, he had no career, no prospects'. Wright, on the other hand, thought: 'It did not seem to occur to him that this would have made Hollis much more vulnerable to recruitment.'

Hollis admitted his friendship with Cockburn at Oxford, and was asked why he had never declared the fact on Cockburn's file, as any MI5 officer was supposed to do if he handled the file of an acquaintance. Hollis 'brushed the question aside. He said there was no general requirement at that time to record personal friendships on files' which, Wright noted, 'was a lie, only a small one, true, but a lie nonetheless'. Hollis later acknowledged his mistake. He knew that Cockburn was of interest to the Service as a prominent left-winger and Comintern agent, and since he was a recent arrival, and wanted very much to pursue a career inside MI5, he chose to ignore the regulation in case his friendship with Cockburn were seen as a black mark against him. Hollis was sure he was not the first or last officer to 'break that particular rule'. Later, he denied being friendly with Philby – 'too much of a drinker' – although they had good professional relations. Hollis got on with Blunt, though, and thought he was 'very gifted'. But he saw him less after he left the Service. As for his trip to Canada, there was nothing sinister in Philby's sending the file on to him: Hollis was the 'acknowledged Soviet expert at the time'. It would be 'natural for Philby to refer it to me, particularly because it was a Commonwealth matter'. Hollis's performance effectively closed the case. Hollis's codename in the search for the Mole was DRAT.[14] It might have summed up Wright's frustration.

Wright, however, was not finished yet. More revelations followed. By the end of the 1960s information was coming to MI5's attention which suggested that there almost certainly was Soviet penetration of the Labour Party. As far as Wright was concerned, the 'story started with the premature death of Hugh Gaitskell in 1963'. Gaitskell was Wilson's predecessor as leader of the Labour Party. Wright 'knew him personally and admired him greatly. I had met him and his family at the Blackwater Sailing Club, and I recall about a month before he died he told me that he was going to Russia.' After he died his doctor got in touch with MI5 and asked to see somebody from the Service. Arthur Martin, as the head of Russian Counter-Espionage, went to see him. The doctor explained that he was disturbed by the manner of Gaitskell's death. He said that Gaitskell had died of a disease called lupus disseminata, which attacks the body's organs. He said that it was rare in temperate climates and that there was no evidence that Gaitskell had been anywhere recently where he could have contracted the disease. Arthur Martin suggested that Wright should go to Porton Down, the chemical and microbiological laboratory for the Ministry of Defence. He went to see the chief doctor in the chemical warfare laboratory, Dr Ladell, and asked his advice. Ladell said that nobody knew how one contracted lupus. There was some suspicion that it might be a form of fungus and he 'did not have the foggiest idea' how one would infect somebody with the disease. Wright came back and made his report in these terms.

The next development was that Golitsin told MI5 how during the last few years of his service he had had some contacts with Department 13, which was known as the Department of Wet Affairs in the KGB. This department was responsible for organising assassinations. He said that just before he left he knew that the KGB were planning a high level political assassination in Europe 'in order to get their man into the top place'. He did not know which country it was planned in but he pointed out that the chief of Department 13 was a General Rodin, who had been in Britain for many years and had just returned on promotion to take up the job, 'so he would have had good knowledge of the political scene in Britain'.

'We did not know where to go next,' recalled Wright, 'because Ladell had said that it wasn't known how the disease was contracted. I consulted James Angleton, of the CIA, about the problem. He said that he would get a search made of Russian scientific papers to see whether there was any hint of what the Russians knew about this disease.' A month or two later he sent Wright a paper about lupus which he had had translated from a Russian scientific journal. The paper was several years old and Angleton reported that there were no other papers in the Russian literature that they could find. This paper described the use of a special chemical which the Russians had found would induce lupus in experimental rats. However, 'it was unlikely that this particular chemical could have been used to murder Gaitskell because the quantities required to produce lupus were considerable and had to be given repeatedly'. Wright took the paper to Ladell and, while surprised by this area of Soviet expertise, he confirmed that it was unlikely that Gaitskell could have been poisoned by the coffee and biscuits. But he pointed out that the paper was seven years old and if the Russians had continued to work on it they might have found a much better form of the chemical which would required much smaller doses and perhaps work as a one-shot drug. He told Wright there was no way of proving it without doing a lot of scientific work and Porton was unable to do the necessary work as it was already overloaded.

Back in MI5 the problem was discussed at length and it was agreed that nothing could be done unless there was further evidence of the Russians using such a drug to assassinate people. Over the next few years Wright 'watched out for any evidence and asked Ladell also to watch out for it. Needless to say we had no further example of anybody who was in a vulnerable position dying of lupus.' The absence of proof of any kind could be explained by Wright in the following way: 'If there was a high-level leak in MI5 to the Russians' – which Wright thought there was – 'they would have been informed of our suspicions and I am sure they would have ensured that no other case came our way.'

By now, Harold Wilson had become Prime Minister. Before he became Prime Minister, Wilson had paid many visits to Russia. MI5, recalled Wright, were 'well aware that the KGB will stop at nothing to entrap or frame visitors, were concerned that he should be well aware of the risk of being compromised by the Russians'. Wilson surrounded himself with East European émigré businessmen, some of whom had been the subject of MI5's inquiries. Then, in 1964, James Angleton made a special trip to Britain to see Furnival Jones who was then Director of Counter-Espionage. Angleton came to offer MI5 'some very secret information from a source he would not name'. This source alleged, according to Angleton, that Wilson – the Prime Minister – was a Soviet agent. As Angleton was head of the CIA's Counter-Intelligence

Division, 'we had no choice but to take it seriously'. The decision was taken to refuse to accept Angleton's restrictions on the use to which MI5 could put the information, 'and as a result we were not told anything more'. However, Angleton's approach was recorded in the files under the code name OATSHEAF. After Hollis retired and Furnival Jones became Director General, Wright went to FJ and was given permission to look at the evidence, even visiting Angleton in the States. But no concrete evidence was forthcoming.

But then, with the Czechoslovakian defectors, Frolik and August, arriving in the West they named a series of Labour MPs and trade unionists as successful Soviet recruits. Now 'we received the most damaging information of all from Oleg Lyalin'. While Lyalin was still in place, he told MI5 about a friend of his called Vaygaukas. Vaygaukas was a KGB officer working under cover in the Soviet Trade Delegation in London. Lyalin told MI5 that Vaygaukas had claimed to him to be in contact with a man called Joseph Kagan, a Lithuanian émigré who was a close friend of Wilson's. Kagan had helped finance Wilson's private office, and had even lent him an aircraft during elections, and Wilson had been much photographed wearing Kagan's raincoats, which he manufactured in a factory near Leeds. Wilson, by now back in Opposition, took the investigations personally as an attack on him and the Labour Party. An angry Wilson demanded an interview and told MI5 that he had never discussed confidential matters with Kagan at any time. Kagan himself later admitted meeting Vaygaukas for chess games, 'but strenuously denied that any espionage was involved'.

One afternoon Wright was in his office 'when two colleagues came in. They were with three or four other officers. I closed the file I was working on and asked them how I could help.' The senior officer said that they understood Wright had reopened the Wilson case. Wright refused to talk about it. 'Wilson's a bloody menace,' said one of the younger officers, 'and it's about time the public knew the truth.' It was 'not the first time I had heard that particular sentiment. Feelings had run high inside MI5 during 1968. There had been an effort to try to stir up trouble for Wilson then, largely because the Daily Mirror tycoon, Cecil King, who was a longtime agent of ours, made it clear that he would publish anything MI5 might care to leak in his direction. It was all part of Cecil King's "coup", which he was convinced would bring down the Labour Government and replace it with a coalition led by Lord Mountbatten.' The approach in 1974 'was altogether more serious. The plan was simple. In the run-up to the election which, given the level of instability in Parliament, must be due within a matter of months, MI5 would arrange for selective details of the intelligence about leading Labour Party figures, but especially Wilson, to be leaked to sympathetic pressmen. Using our contacts in the press and among union officials, word of the material contained in MI5 files and the fact that Wilson was considered a security risk would be passed around.' According to Wright, soundings in the office had already been taken, and up to thirty officers had given their approval to the scheme. Facsimile copies of some files were to be made and distributed to overseas newspapers, and the matter was to be raised in Parliament for maximum effect. At first Wright 'was tempted. The devil makes work for idle hands, and I was playing out my time before retirement. A mad scheme like this was bound to tempt me. I felt an irresistible urge to lash out. The country seemed on the brink of catastrophe. Why not give it a little push?' It was Rothschild who talked him out of it.[15] This was Wright's claim anyway.

Despite its internal troubles, the Security Service was still able to catch spies. Douglas Ronald Britten, a Chief Technician in the RAF collaborated with the Russians, and for six years, from 1962 until his arrest, provided them with highly sensitive information about his work in the RAF. In 1968, Britten, then aged thirty-seven, of RAF Digby, Lincolnshire, pleaded guilty to five charges under the Official Secrets Act, and was sentenced by Lord Parker of Waddington to twenty-one years' imprisonment. Searches of his person, his home, his car and other places to which he had access at Digby led to the discovery of espionage apparatus, including a camera disguised as a cigarette case for photographing documents, a timetable of Soviet radio broadcasts, including call signs, frequencies, dates and times. There were also Soviet instructions for enciphering and deciphering coded messages, and directions given to him by his Russian controller for meetings with that controller.

Britten was born in Northampton, had studied engineering at Wellingborough Junior Technical College, and had then taken a job as a centre lathe turner. After another job with a radio firm, he joined the RAF. He had married a member of the WRAF while he was in Cyprus. He returned to England and was posted to RAF Digby, where gradually he got into debt and he began to argue with his wife. He was approached during a visit to the Science Museum in Kensington in 1962 by a person who said he was a Russian shortwave listener. They talked about amateur radio for about ten minutes, and the Russian asked him if he could get a copy of a manual of the 1154 transmitter. Britten said he was shortly going to Cyprus and the Russian said he had a friend who could meet him there. After receiving instructions on how to meet this man in Cyprus, Britten was handed money. The man he met in Famagusta in Cyprus took him for a drive in a car. The man said he would like to obtain some harmless information about whether any of the officers had mistresses or indulged in wife-swapping, or whether any of the wives prostituted themselves to English or local males: 'I think sometime towards the end of 1963 my contact was accompanied by a woman and I was told it was his wife. I think at this meeting I passed to him three names of people who I thought might be of use to them.' At this meeting Britten was given a sum of money.

When another meeting was arranged, Britten 'made a resolve not to attend any more meetings'. But he began to miss the various amounts of money he had received and when he received another calling card, he attended the meeting. 'He (the Russian) showed great displeasure that I had not kept my part of the bargain, and he told me the time had come for me to start producing results. He said the centre in Moscow was getting fed up paying money for no return. I had to co-operate more.' His alleged wife produced a photograph of Britten receiving a 'spy kit'. It included the miniature camera made in the form of a cigarette case, a battery charger and film cassette, a code book and black leather wallet, money, 'and I was told in no uncertain terms that the photographs would be sent to the British intelligence service, and that I could expect some rough treatment at their hands'. Britten 'realised there was no easy way of dropping out of this business, and at the same time my marriage was gradually falling to pieces. I resolved to carry on working with them, but to try and get as much money for as little information as possible, and try to improve my marriage with my wife and family in the mistaken idea that money brings happiness.' He was given four containers in which to hide information: two beer cans with false bottoms, a piece of piping, and a magnetic container, which was to be stuck to the underside of a seat. Later, he was given a Minox camera, and asked to obtain photographs of the interior of his section. At one meeting in Cyprus, Britten claimed he was punched several times and pushed against a wall: 'They said they expected me to work much harder in England, and if there was not a 100 per cent improvement they would arrange for me to disappear, and things would not go well for my family. I was thoroughly frightened and realised what a ridiculous position I had got myself in.'

In October, 1966, Britten returned to England, after agreeing to a rendezvous in Arnos Grove, London: 'I attended the meeting in January 1967, as arranged. I was contacted by a man who called himself Yuri, and we walked around the streets in the area and had a conversation of a general nature. He suggested I should not cease to co-operate, and once more threats were made against me.' Britten's contact did not turn up for a rendezvous in February 1968; so Britten went to Bayswater Road and telephoned to the Soviet consulate asking for his contact. 'I think I was told there was no one to help me and to try another time.' He had then written a letter asking for more money and pushed it through the door of the consulate. Britten was given a piece of paper on which were written a call sign and frequencies. His contact told him that his masters wished to give him instructions from Moscow, and this would be done by radio transmissions. 'Yuri' was identified as Alexsandr Ivanovitch Borisenko, a Russian, who arrived in Britain on 17 May 1966, with an appointment as First Secretary in the cultutal department of the Soviet Embassy. He left the United Kingdom on 20 September 1968 – six days after Britten made his first appearance in connection with this matter at Bow Street Magistrates' Court.[16]

The disappearance of Borisenko gave Sir Martin Furnival Jones, in 1971, the opportunity to push the Conservative Government of Edward Heath to move against Soviet agents resident in Britain. As a result, the British Government cut about a fifth in the number of Soviet officials in Britain. Soviet representation in Britain had risen steadily from 138 in 1950 to 249 in 1960 and over 550 in 1971 (including working wives). Since 1960 the Government had requested the immediate recall of 27 Soviet officials detected in active espionage, and more than 40 visa applications by identified Intelligence Officers had been refused. There were some 280 people connected with the Soviet Embassy and other official agencies who had diplomatic status, and their families, who did not have all the privileges but enjoyed certain immunity. The Soviet Embassy in London was asked by the Foreign Office to arrange for about 90 of the 550 accredited Soviet officials in Britain to leave the country within two weeks. About 15 other Soviet officials who were out of Britain but held valid re-entry visas would not be permitted to return. Ivan Ippolitov, the Soviet Chargé d'Affaires, was summoned to the Foreign Office and handed an aide memoire, by Sir Denis Greenhill, the Permanent Under-Secretary, which contained the Government's request for the withdrawal of the officials. Henceforth, the numbers of officials in (i) the Soviet Embassy (ii) the Soviet trade delegation, and (iii) all other Soviet organisations in the UK would not be permitted to rise above the levels at which they would stand after the withdrawal of the persons named in the attached list. If a Soviet official was required to leave the country as a result of his having been detected in intelligence activities, the permitted level in that category would be reduced by one. The total number of Soviet officials filling posts in Britain, standing at 550, was higher than for any other Western country, including the United States.[17]

It was while Rimington was working on counter-espionage that:

> things were beginning to change inside the Service. The supply of ex-Colonial Service officers was drying up and new sources of recruits had to be found. In those days, recruitment to MI5 was still broadly by a tap on the shoulder from a friend or contact, the method by which I had been recruited. There were a number of contacts in various places with their ears to the ground, actively looking for the 'right sort' of men to come in as officers. Men with previous work experience in some walk of life were much preferred; they were thought to be more mature and therefore likely to make better intelligence officers.

In the mid-1970s, it was decided to seek out men in industry and commerce who, after working there for a few years, might be looking for a change and, as an experiment, also to try bringing in some young men straight from university as officers. Rimington had 'already started to feel disgruntled about my second-class status. By then, I knew enough about the Service and the people in it to know that I was just as capable as many of the men, if not more, and I resented being given less responsible work to do and above all being paid less than they were. I couldn't stand working for people who were less competent than I was.' The 'last straw for me' came one day when a 'nice young man arrived in my section to share my office. He had just come down from university, with a BA in something or another and he was about twenty-three. He had been recruited as an officer. There was I, having been in the Service already for three or four years, having previously had a career in another profession, aged thirty-seven or thirty-eight and still only an assistant officer.' Rimington thought carefully about what she should do. She knew that open protest was not likely to be successful: 'If one got a reputation as a revolutionary, one would be regarded as suspect and written off. So I waited until it was the time for my annual interview with my personnel officer and I took the opportunity to ask what was the reason that prevented me from being an officer.'

The 'poor man was completely taken aback. I felt rather like Oliver Twist when he asked for more.' The personnel officer was an ex-army officer 'with a moustache and a pipe clamped firmly between his lips, given to wearing very hairy tweed suits and khaki braces. I do not think it had ever occurred to him that a woman might want to become an officer in MI5.' Rimington felt that the poor man must have had no idea that she was nurturing a grievance. 'After all, no doubt the women he knew stayed at home and did the flowers, so why was this woman, who had already broken all known conventions by returning to work with a baby, now demanding to be treated as if she were a man? He muttered about all the things one could not do as a woman, which made one less than wholly useful.'[18] But Rimington, through her talent and persistence, did get promoted.

Yet while MI5 was undergoing an organic change internally, to the external world the 1980s revealed a Service in apparent turmoil. The Prime Minister, Margaret Thatcher, found out that (now Sir) Anthony Blunt, keeper of the Queen's pictures, had confessed fifteen years earlier to being a Soviet spy. Thatcher was shocked at the decision to cover up Blunt's treachery and the shock that had been felt by many within MI5 was shared by a great many more outside the Service when she revealed the truth to the House of Commons. Blunt's knighthood was annulled, as was the honorary fellowship he had held at Trinity College since 1967. He resigned from the Society of Antiquaries at their behest, but a row erupted within the British Academy over his continued membership, many members threatening their own resignation if he was not expelled and many if he was. Its council voted narrowly in favour of his expulsion but the members avoided a vote at the Academy's annual general meeting, after which Blunt resigned. The press, radio, and television began a campaign of vilification. His long-term partner, William John Gaskin, attempted suicide. When asked after his exposure how he had managed to survive the strains, Blunt answered, pointing to a glass of whisky: 'With this, and more work and more work'.[19]

The Director General who had to deal with the aftermath of the scandal was Sir John Jones. Jones had come from relatively humble origins: he was born in February 1923 at Easington, County Durham, the son of Isaac Jones, a coalminer, and his wife, Isabel Raine. He was educated at Nelson Grammar School in Cumberland and in 1940 went to Christ's College, Cambridge on a scholarship. During the Second World War he served in the Royal Artillery. After the war he returned to Cambridge to complete his studies, taking a first in part two of the historical tripos and a certificate in education. In 1947 he joined the Sudan government service as a teacher, transferring in

1951 to the ministry of education where he became the establishment officer. In 1948 he married Daphne Redman whose father also served in Sudan. In 1955 Jones returned to Britain and accepted an offer to join MI5, serving first in Hong Kong and then Singapore (1959–1961). After returning to London, he carried out the first feasibility study to computerise MI5's records. He then moved to the overseas branch, which was responsible for supervising the work of MI5 agents in British overseas territories. In 1968, Jones was seconded to the Ministry of Defence as director of the moribund British services security organisation in Germany. He revitalised it, and was appointed CMG in 1972. When he returned to Britain, Jones was for a short time Director of the Overseas Branch before becoming Head of F Branch, which dealt with Counter-Subversion, and later the operations branch. He was appointed Deputy Director General in 1976, and in 1981 the Prime Minister, Margaret Thatcher, made him Director General. He had 'not come up in the traditional way through the more prestigious' K branch (countering Soviet espionage), and Peter Wright described him 'as an F branch man through and through, and his appointment perfectly illustrated the decisive shift in MI5's centre of gravity'. It was shortly after John Jones became Director General, that Thatcher learned about Blunt.[20]

This was just the start. In a 1981 'World In Action' television programme, the now retired Peter Wright stated that he was '99 per cent certain that Sir Roger Hollis was a spy'. This flushed out his former colleague, Arthur Martin, who commented: 'I think that was an exaggeration. My recollection is that, while Hollis fitted the circumstantial evidence more closely than any other candidate, the case against him was not conclusive. It was the evidence of continued penetration of the service after Blunt retired in 1945 until at least the early 1960s which carried complete conviction among those working on the case.' When in 1969 the interrogation of Hollis failed to produce a conclusive answer, it would have been normal practice to continue the search but to widen its scope; 'if it was not Hollis, who was it?' Instead, the investigating team was disbanded and the case allowed to lapse. It was that decision, Martin believed, which led to a decade of unease which still festered. For it was 'inconceivable' that the Security Service would have allowed an investigation to lapse if similar evidence of penetration had been discovered in any other department of government. It had been suggested from time to time that yet another official enquiry into the case should be made. In Martin's view this would be pointless. No amount of re-examination can resolve the case; 'only new evidence will do that. New evidence, if it comes, will be by chance or renewed security service effort... I remember Peter Wright as a dedicated officer, deeply concerned by the threats to his country.'[21] Others, however, found Wright's evidence 'entirely unconvincing'. Sir William Hayter, former chair of the Joint Intelligence Committee and a former ambassador to Moscow, was someone 'who had in the past a slight professional acquaintance' with Hollis; he tore into the hollowness of Wright's evidence:

> If this is the best the critics of Sir Roger can do, they had better shut up. Probably any unprejudiced person asked to choose between judgments by Lord Trend (the former Cabinet Secretary) and by Mr Peter Wright would choose the former. Mr Wright dismisses Lord Trend's acquittal of Sir Roger by saying that Lord Trend 'is not a professional intelligence officer'. If Mr Wright's performance is typical of the reasoning of professional intelligence officers, it only shows on what slender and ill-thought-out evidence they arrive at damaging and indeed dangerous decisions; I am reminded of Somerset Maugham's story, 'The Hairless Mexican', in which an agent of British Intelligence kills an innocent man on the basis of incorrect deductions from unreliable evidence. In Sir Roger's case Mr Wright starts from strong but not watertight evidence that there was a Soviet agent in MI5 (Mr Wright's assertion that the evidence excludes the counter-intelligence section of MI6 was far from proven). He then excludes some figures in MI5 (obviously not all; secretaries and stenographers, for instance, as a recent case has shown, often know as much as their superiors), and focuses on Sir Roger because he could have known what the supposed spy is presumed, on slight evidence, to have known. The gaps in this chain of reasoning are obvious enough. Mr Wright totally fails to deal with the crucial question of motive. There are probably only three motives for spying against one's own country: ideological conviction, blackmail, bribery. Mr Wright produces no evidence for any of these in Sir Roger's case, which, given his general line, he would certainly have done if it existed.[22]

But Wright was not finished yet.

Stella Rimington, meanwhile, was in her new post was as Assistant Director of one of the sections in the Counter-Subversion branch. It involved moving away from Gower Street to Curzon Street House, 'the bunker-like building next door to the Lansdowne Club'. The building had 'two claims to fame – the first, possibly apocryphal, that it had been specially reinforced for use by the Royal family in time of war, the second, true, that it had been the Ministry of Education when Mrs Thatcher as Minister of Education achieved notoriety as "Thatcher the milk snatcher".' Her new section 'turned out to be a bit of a backwater and during my first few weeks at my new desk, the telephone never rang, and no one came into my office to see me. It was a huge change from the agent section, which had been bustling with lots of comings and goings and constant operations and excitements.' However, the period of calm did not last long; 'after I had prowled around a bit to see what was happening, I soon realised that there was a lot to do. As it turned out, this period presented some of the most intellectually challenging problems of my career and also proved to be one of the busiest and most interesting.'

By the 1980s there was considerable political upheaval – the miners' strike, the Greenham Common protests, the height of CND, the growth of Militant Tendency and its activities in Liverpool and a Socialist Workers' Party very active in universities. In Rimington's view, most of the subversive activity, 'as distinct from the political protest', which was going on at that time came from Communists, acting, at least at the centre, on advice and support from the Soviet Embassy, and from Trotskyist organisations. It was, 'by design, focused on particularly sensitive areas of society, local authorities, education, the unions, peace movements and, in the case of Militant Tendency, the Labour Party. These were the areas where the democratic system was judged, by those who wanted to destroy it, to be most vulnerable and where also any interference or monitoring by the secret state was likely to be regarded as most unacceptable. My colleagues and I had the difficult task of deciding what, if any, of this activity should be of proper concern to the Security Service, in fulfilling its function of defending democracy.'

MI5's work against subversion in the 1980s was, stated Rimington, based on the definition of subversion which had been given in Parliament in the 1970s:

> It is the same definition which was later incorporated into the Security Service Act of 1989, the Act of Parliament under which MI5 now operates. Subversion is defined as actions which are 'intended to overthrow or undermine parliamentary democracy by political, industrial or violent means'. The concept of subversion is thus focused on hostility to the democratic process itself; it has

never included political dissent. We worked to the principle that the activities of organisations or individuals with subversive intent was of concern to us; the right to set up and join pressure groups and to protest was not.[23]

Rimington argued that it was 'an established fact' that the anti-nuclear movement, 'in its own right an entirely legitimate protest movement, was of great interest to the Soviet Union'. As part of its 'subversive activities in the West', the Soviet Union 'sought covertly to encourage anti-nuclear, ban the bomb and other such protest in many Western countries, as a way of weakening the defences of their enemies. Of course that does not mean that everyone who joined CND was part of a subversive plot. But Soviet officials encouraged Western communist parties, like the Communist Party of Great Britain, to try to infiltrate CND at key strategic levels by getting their members elected as officers. The idea was that they could then direct the activities of the organisation to suit their own long-term objectives.' MI5's job, 'and what we were doing', was to monitor those activities, not to investigate CND, 'which on its own was of no interest to us. The allegation that we investigated CND has been denied on countless occasions, including by ministers in Parliament but I have come to accept that no one who firmly believes the allegation will ever cease to believe it whatever is said.'

This policy was followed during the 1984 miners' strike as well. It was supported by a very large number of members of the National Union of Mineworkers,

> but it was directed by a triumvirate who had declared that they were using the strike to try to bring down the elected government of Mrs Thatcher and it was actively supported by the Communist Party. What was it legitimate for us to do about that? We quickly decided that the activities of picket lines and miners' wives' support groups were not our concern, even though they were of great concern to the police who had to deal with the law-and-order aspects of the strike; accusations that we were running agents or telephone interceptions to get advance warning of picket movements are wrong. We in MI5 limited our investigations to the activities of those who were using the strike for subversive purposes.[24]

It was against the controversial confrontations of the Far Left with the Thatcher Government and fears of an East-West war that Peter Wright resurfaced with his allegations about Soviet infiltration – this time in a book. He made public allegations that disaffected MI5 officers had 'plotted' against the Prime Minister, Harold Wilson, in the 1970s. Many people were prepared to grant credence to the allegations – not least because Sir Harold Wilson himself was convinced that British Intelligence had conspired against him.

This was a staggering accusation because, as Stella Rimington stated, this 'allegation, if it had been true, would have meant that the service whose role it is to defend our democratic system had sought to act against the democratically elected government, it was taken immensely seriously not least within MI5. Sir Antony Duff, the Director General of the day when Wright's *Spycatcher* was published with the allegations, 'was not an MI5 insider and had no personal knowledge of the Service's activities in the period concerned, was determined that the story should be thoroughly investigated'. Extensive interviews were conducted with those who had known Peter Wright and were still working; 'white-haired gentlemen were dug out of their retirement all over the country and asked to cast their minds back but though much reminiscing went on, no one could recall anything that sounded like what Peter Wright was claiming had happened'. Files were trawled through with the same result. Finally, a detailed report was written for Whitehall and Ministers felt sufficiently confident to state publicly that no such plot had ever existed.

When, much later, Rimington was Director General, 'I decided I would try once and for all to knock on the head the Wilson plot allegation.' She asked some of the old grandees of the Labour Party, most of whom had at one stage been Home Secretary, to come in to Thames House – MI5's new HQ – to talk about it. 'It was clear to me then that the conviction in that generation' of the Labour Party was that the allegations were true.[25] Wilson's successor, James Callaghan, had ordered an internal inquiry that found no evidence of a plot. A subsequent inquiry, ordered by Margret Thatcher, came to the same conclusion. In fact, it was Wright, himself, who gave the game away in an interview on the BBC's Panorama programme of 13 October 1988. He admitted that his figure of thirty officers was greatly exaggerated: 'The maximum number was eight or nine. Very often it was only three.' When pressed further and asked, 'How many people, when all the talking died down, were still serious in joining you in trying to get rid of Wilson?', Wright replied, 'One, I should say.' The interviewer asked, 'Is that part of the book perhaps an exaggeration of what you recall now?' to which Wright responded, 'I would say it is unreliable.'[26]

The damage Wright and his accusations did to the morale and the reputation of the Security Service were still felt for years afterwards. In any situation the allegation that the Director General of MI5 was a Soviet agent would have a devastating effect on the confidence of the Service. The KGB may or may not have had a mole inside the Security Service – as they had in the case of Blunt – but they probably did not need one if one of their aims was to destabilise their British counter-espionage enemy. Wright did the job for them.

Following the seemingly never-ending Wright allegations, MI5 had to deal with the highly embarrassing case of Michael Bettaney, a middle-ranking MI5 officer who tried to offer his services to the KGB, which feared a set-up and did not respond to Bettaney's overtures, and treated his original approaches with great suspicion. Bettaney tried again, but the KGB double agent Oleg Gordievsky eventually exposed his treachery. The subsequent Security Commission report was critical of MI5 for failing to spot the potential troublemaker in its ranks, particularly when it became known that Bettaney was a heavy drinker. Sir John Jones was not personally criticised, but the case led to a demand for reforms in both vetting procedures and management. Jones, who had been created KCB in 1983, resigned in 1985.[27] The Security Commission, 'the body of the great and the good' which existed to report on the circumstances surrounding any prosecution under the Official Secrets Act, and to make recommendations, commented adversely on MI5's management practices and style. It noted and criticised the 'closed culture, the remote management', the things with which those, working in the organisation, had felt discontented.[28] A new Director General was appointed to restore morale – Sir Antony Duff.

Born in 1920, he was the son of Admiral Sir Arthur Duff, and grew up at Vartree, a large country house near Dorchester. He was sent to the Royal Naval College, Dartmouth, in 1933 and passed out top of his term. He served as a midshipman in the battleship *Malaya* and the destroyer HMS *Beagle* before volunteering for submarines in 1940. He was mentioned in despatches in 1941 for Mediterranean war patrols serving in the 'Fighting Tenth' Flotilla, based in Malta, before gaining his first operational command, the submarine HMS *Stubborn*, in 1942. In 1943, *Stubborn* took part in Operation SOURCE, the X-craft midget submarine attack on German capital ships in northern Norway. *Stubborn* sailed from Loch Cairnbawn with X-7 in tow on

11 September, and after some excitements over parted tow lines and the sighting of a U-boat, reached Norway on the 20th. X-7 laid two charges beneath the *Tirpitz*, which severely damaged her. X-7 later sank and its commander, Lieutenant Godfrey Place, was taken prisoner. He was awarded the Victoria Cross. Duff was awarded the DSC.

In February 1944, *Stubborn* sank two ships in a convoy off Trondheim. Two days later, Duff attacked another escorted convoy. There was a heavy and accurate depth-charge counter-attack which jammed *Stubborn's* after hydroplanes in the steepest diving position. With *Stubborn* plunging to a depth of 400 feet, her sailors raced from forward to aft and back again to try to balance the boat. *Stubborn* surfaced violently, and then plunged down again. Here, as Duff said, 'our guardian angel stepped in and provided an entirely unexpected bottom', which *Stubborn* hit hard at a depth approaching 600 feet – well below her designated safe depth. The submarine was stuck on the bottom for several hours while depth-charging continued. Finally, by blowing the main ballast tanks with the last remaining compressed air and running the one remaining motor full ahead and then astern, *Stubborn* broke free and shot to the surface at a bows-up angle of 70 degrees. *Stubborn* was badly damaged, but managed to reach harbour eight days later. For his resolution and cool thinking under pressure, and for bringing his ship's company home without a single casualty, Duff was awarded the DSO. 1944 was certainly an eventful year for Duff: he also married Polly Sword, a young widow who came of a naval family.

After failing an eyesight test in 1946, Duff had to leave the navy joining the Foreign Service. His first post was Athens during the Greek Civil War. After service in Cairo, Paris and Bonn, in 1964 Duff was appointed Ambassador to Nepal, where he enjoyed taking enormously long walks in the hills around Kathmandu. His next posting abroad was as Deputy High Commissioner in Kuala Lumpur, and then in 1972 he became High Commissioner in Nairobi. He returned to Britain in 1975 to supervise all the FCO departments dealing with Africa and the Middle East. Much of his time was taken up with Southern Rhodesia. In 1979 Duff led Lord Carrington's team at the Lancaster House conference that granted independence to Rhodesia, and then went out to Southern Rhodesia as deputy governor to Christopher Soames. Following independence he became a Privy Counsellor, the first at the Foreign Office since Sir Alec Cadogan in 1940.

When Duff had initially attempted to retire from the Foreign Office in 1980, he found himself offered the position of Intelligence

Co-Ordinator at the Cabinet Office; the Prime Minister, Margaret Thatcher had been impressed by his performance during the Rhodesian negotiations. Duff's task was to monitor the priorities and budget of MI5, MI6 and GCHQ. In 1983 he was promoted to the chairmanship of the Joint Intelligence Committee, whose role had been redefined in the wake of the Franks Report on the conduct of the Falklands War. Duff now became overlord of all the intelligence and security services, charged with analysing the agencies' daily reports and with formulating long-term foreign policy. At the JIC, Duff's 'prime achievement was to come out against the prevailing view in Whitehall that the Soviet Union would remain a serious threat to the safety of the West. It was Duff's advice that also led Mrs Thatcher to accept at an early stage that Mikhail Gorbachev was the coming man, and one she "could do business with".'

Thatcher turned to Duff, in 1985, when the Bridge Inquiry reported that 'ineptitude' and low morale were threatening to take a grip on MI5. He was appointed Director General. Duff was 'almost excessively modest', but he also 'possessed a rare talent for leadership, inspiring instinctive trust in his subordinates'. Within a short time of his arrival at MI5 he had made a point of speaking to every member of staff, and proved open to new ideas. In turn, he recalled, 'I found that, except for a handful of old sweats in middle management, they were very anxious to be made honest men through legislation and independent oversight.' He recruited more young people and women. Duff also shifted the emphasis of the Service's work away from countering foreign spies to combatting terrorism. He developed, too, a better working relationship with Whitehall and for the first time since 1939 housed the principal branches of the service under one roof in Curzon Street.[29]

As Rimington recalled: 'It is hardly surprising that management had become an issue. None of those who had the responsibility in those days had any training or relevant experience. What's more, because of the closed and secretive culture of the time, they were isolated from contact with thinking that was going on elsewhere.' Duff, in Rimington's words, went about his task 'with gusto'. He had to 'regenerate the morale of a depressed and demotivated organisation'. Duff was already sixty-five when he arrived, 'a patrician figure, with an ambassadorial style and public school manners. But importantly he was open-minded and prepared to listen.' One of the first things he did was to tour around all parts of the Service, asking the staff at all levels what they thought was wrong and what ideas they had for change. 'This went down extremely well and the fact that he was well plugged in to Whitehall and had the ear of the Cabinet Secretary and the Prime Minister were just what we wanted.' For Rimington though Duff had 'one big downside, for which I never really forgave him. He addressed me as "dear". I found this deeply patronising and thought it meant that he did not take me seriously.' But she was wrong to think this: in 1985, following the retirement of the Director of Counter-Subversion, Rimington was made acting Director responsible for all the counter-subversion sections. This included an agent section similar to the counter-espionage agent section in which she had worked earlier. This 'elevation' was a 'trial run' and lasted only a few months. There was someone else thought to have more of a claim to a Director's post, and when he was available, Rimington was demoted again and put in charge of recruiting and staff security. But she was 'not too upset by this because I was told that I would be a substantive Director before too long. In truth, such elevation was more than I had ever expected.'[30] Things were changing, not just in MI5, but in the outside world too. For, unexpectedly, the Cold War ended. And, despite all the setbacks of that conflict, MI5 had the consolation of finishing on the winning side. And, in the end, was not that the most important thing?

Dirty War:
MI5 & the Troubles

My wife always knew me as an IRA man. Nothing else. Twenty-one years on, I finally told her the truth. She thought I was joking. Nobody – not my closest family, not the highest figures within the IRA – had the slightest inkling of my true identity. Twenty-one years of living a lie. During all that time, I was really working for the British Intelligence services. I was a double agent within the world's most feared terrorist organisation.

I'm not a grass. I'm not someone who crossed over to the other side to save my own skin. I was a British soldier, actively recruited by British military intelligence for the specific task of infiltrating the IRA and working my way up within the organisation. Which is exactly what I did. Such was my efficiency as an IRA man, I was eventually promoted to the 'nutting squad' – the terrorist organisation's feared internal security unit charged with rooting out and killing informants.

Some say that my promotion was testament to my steely nerve and to the skill of my handlers who delighted in the rich irony of this role; others insist that I was actively encouraged to go too far to maintain my cover as a top IRA operative. They say that, in the interests of keeping me on side with IRA chiefs, I was allowed to carry out morally reprehensible acts against my own people. It is true that, as an agent for the British Crown, I helped shoot and kill British soldiers, police informants and members of the Royal Ulster Constabulary. People on my own side. I played a key role in the slaying of army comrades and decent law-abiding members of the police force. It gnaws at my nerves and haunts my every thought. After all, these were people striving for everything I believed in. A night will never pass without stabbings of guilt, without my brain being pulled under by great waves of confusion and doubt.

So why did I carry on? Because, all the while, I was being assured that my work was saving more lives than it was costing. That people's lives hinged on my soldiering on. That the British Prime Minister, no less, was being kept abreast of my great work. All along, I was being assured of something else, too. Over and over again, I was assured that if it all went wrong – if the IRA discovered my true role as a British agent – I'd be pulled out and given a new identity, a new home abroad and a lump sum. Then my usefulness ran out, and I was dumped. Sacrificed.

After dedicating my life to British intelligence, they tried to get me whacked. When that didn't happen, I was abandoned. No new identity, no new home abroad, no lump sum. I was left to fend for myself. I now live life on the run, under a death threat from the IRA. Needless to say, I can't go back to Northern Ireland where my wife and family still live. To this day, British intelligence agencies refuse to acknowledge the full extent of my role in the Dirty War. In truth, they'd like me dead. I'm a nuisance. Along the way, I've also earned the wrath of the RUC and leading dissident IRA terrorists. In short, I don't expect to live long. So why am I telling my story? They all counted on me disappearing, on running for my life. But I don't have a life. I've got nothing left to lose.

'Kevin Fulton' Force Research Unit and MI5 agent.[1]

From 1969 until 2007 the British Army fought the longest campaign in its history: Operation BANNER. It demonstrated an extraordinary commitment, on the part of the British Government, to contain – and defeat – a terrorist campaign while political conditions led to a compromise settlement. Originally deployed to prevent civil war the institutions of the British state – including the Security Service – became embroiled in a counter-insurgency campaign that saw no jury courts; internment without trial; accusations of ill-treatment by the Security Forces; the use of Special Forces including the SAS; controversy with regard to the exercise of lethal force by the police and army; as well as numerous killings by paramilitaries and two attacks that nearly killed successive Prime Ministers. Extraordinarily, this all occurred, not in some far away colony or occupied territory, but within the United Kingdom of Great Britain and Northern Ireland.

Northern Ireland consists of six largely rural counties and two built up areas of significant size: Belfast and Londonderry. It measures roughly 80 miles north to south and 120 miles east to west. In 1969 it had a population of about 1.8 million people. Over 3,600 people died in the 'Troubles'. A majority of Northern Ireland's population – the Protestants – wanted Northern Ireland to remain part of the United Kingdom – as it has been since 1801. The island of Ireland had been partitioned by Britain, in 1920, and most of the Catholic minority within Northern Ireland desired union with the rest of Ireland outside the UK. Westminster had partitioned Ireland, dominated by the Unionists (Protestants) who ruled over the Nationalist (Catholic) minority and set up a devolved Parliament in the North to keep Irish politics out of British politics. But Irish politics landed right back in the centre of British politics when the army had to be deployed in 1969 to prevent civil war between Protestants and Catholics.[2]

There were only three battalions of infantry in Northern Ireland in late 1969, but at the peak of the campaign in the summer of 1972, 28,000 soldiers were deployed. Well over 250,000 members of the regular army served there during the campaign, as well as many tens of thousands in the locally recruited – and overwhelming Protestant – Ulster Defence Regiment and its successor, the Royal Irish Regiment Home Service Force. In the early 1970s rioting in Londonderry or Belfast often went on for days at a time. It was fairly common for over 10,000 soldiers to be deployed on the streets. Thousands of houses were destroyed. Over 10,000 terrorist suspects were arrested. Over 14,000 illegal weapons were used at one time or another. Over 600 soldiers died or were killed due to terrorist action. In the worst year of 1972, 102 British soldiers died or were killed – the largest number in one year since the Korean War.

Violence was largely concentrated in areas such as West Belfast, the Bogside and the Creggan in Londonderry, East Tyrone, Fermanagh and South Armagh. The British Army observed the first period, from August 1969 until perhaps the summer of 1971, as largely characterised by widespread public disorder. The next phase, from the summer of 1971 until the mid-1970s, 'is best described as a classic insurgency'. Both the Official and Provisional wings of the Irish Republican Army (OIRA and PIRA) fought the Security Forces in more or less formed bodies. Both had a structure of companies, battalions and brigades, with a recognisable structure and headquarters staff. Protracted firefights were common. The army responded with operations at up to brigade and even divisional level. The largest of these was Operation MOTORMAN, which was conducted from 31 July to 1 December 1972. It marked the beginning of the end of the insurgency phase. The OIRA declared a ceasefire in 1972 which it never broke. The PIRA 'began a process of transforming itself into a terrorist organisation based on a cell structure. The end of the insurgency merged into the phase characterised by the use of terrorist tactics. PIRA developed into what will probably be seen as one of the most effective terrorist organisations in history. Professional, dedicated, highly skilled and resilient, it conducted a sustained and lethal campaign in Northern Ireland, mainland United Kingdom and on the continent of Europe.'

From 1980 onwards its political wing, Sinn Fein, involved itself in mainstream politics in Northern Ireland and the Republic of Ireland. However, from 1992 or 1993 the level of violence in all areas diminished gradually.

The army defined the differences between insurgency and terrorism as those of mass, means and methods. 'Insurgency' generally included large numbers of insurgents using moderately conventional weapons, organisations and tactics. By comparison 'terrorism' was more selective and often more sophisticated in its means and methods of attack, while employing generally smaller numbers. These features broadly applied to Northern Ireland. 'A different approach would be to define terrorism as a tactic and therefore a terrorist organisation as one which acts largely covertly and deploys terrorism as its main means of violence. Conversely, insurgency presupposes an insurgent body (as OIRA and PIRA could both be described in the early 1970s) which employs fairly direct action to achieve its aims although operating under the cover of the local population. These definitions also generally apply to Northern Ireland.'[3]

Low Intensity Conflict

The key to defeating any insurgency or terrorist campaign is intelligence. And it was the secret war fought by the British Intelligence services that ultimately helped defeat the Provisional IRA. The tragedy was that it took three decades before a unified intelligence approach was finally adopted with a central agency directing operations – this was, in essence, MI5 from around the early 1990s. This mistake was exactly what happened in the first Troubles of 1919–1921 when intelligence arrangements were split between a number of bodies; for, when the new Troubles erupted, there was still a demarcation of intelligence responsibilities. Traditionally, intelligence gathering in Northern Ireland had been the preserve of the Royal Ulster Constabulary Special Branch. This was so even during the Second World War. Covert intelligence operations in independent Ireland fell within the remit of SIS – a decision taken in the 1920s. This did not mean that MI5 did not operate in Northern Ireland. But primacy initially rested with the RUC (SB). With the deployment of the army, its Military Intelligence section operated in Northern Ireland alongside MI5, SIS and RUC (SB). In early 1971, to strengthen the army's intelligence organisation the number of Military Intelligence Officers had been doubled. By April more were earmarked but there was a natural limit to the number that could usefully be employed; moreover the RUC were to a great extent the arbiters of how many could be deployed within their chain of command. At the General Officer Commanding Northern Ireland's Headquarters, in Lisburn, there was now a much larger, and more balanced intelligence staff. This included a GSO1, an MOD Principal to assist in assessment work, and a specialist SIGINT officer. A thorough overhaul of the army intelligence machine was undertaken with the advice of Sir Dick White, now the Prime Minister's Intelligence Co-ordinator.

By April 1971 the army's Director of Intelligence at Headquarters Northern Ireland had established a close relationship with the Head of Special Branch (HSB). This had resulted in the records and reports of Special Branch being made completely available to the army's Senior Military Intelligence Officer operating within Special Branch who had furthermore, gained the complete confidence of the RUC. The Director and the HSB, with the MIO, now worked as a triumvirate and, apart from daily informal contacts, met regularly to produce joint assessments. The quality of these assessments, therefore, steadily rose. But the Director did not have the 'constitutional right' to direct and control Special Branch, which was what would be needed in an ideal organisation, although he was, in practice, achieving a large measure of control by these informal means. The Ministry of Defence considered it extremely important that nothing should be done, either in Whitehall or in Ulster, to upset this hard-won relationship of the Director with the RUC. It was considered that any attempt either to introduce an 'expert Englishman' into the Special Branch hierarchy at the top level, or to give the Director formal command over the HSB would be not only doomed to failure but also a 'very unwise step that would undo all the good work' done.[4] Despite these changes the Joint Intelligence Committee, in Whitehall, made a crucial observation: the army's contribution was probably only about 10 per cent of the total intelligence take – the balance being principally from RUC Special Branch. Thus, 'however much we improve our own arrangements, there cannot be a consequential radical improvement in the intelligence situation as a whole. For this we must look to the RUC (SB)'.[5] If the army acted on intelligence it would only be as good as the RUC Special Branch's sources, the limitations of which would be exposed in August 1971 with the introduction of internment without trial – for, since 1969, the unacceptability of the RUC to Catholics, combined with the IRA's insurgency, meant that Special Branch had been unable to operate in Catholic areas and update its files on Republicans. As a result they were hopelessly out of date.

The chickens came home to roost when internment without trial – Operation DEMETRIUS – was introduced in 1971. Internment had been used several times before. Between 1957 and 1962 – the most recent IRA campaign – it had been applied on both sides of the Border and had been generally effective. But, in 1971 it was not introduced in the Republic of Ireland. The army and RUC were poorly prepared: suspect lists were badly out of date and detention facilities were inadequate. The former led to many of the wrong people being arrested and the latter meant that those arrested could not be properly segregated during screening. In addition the army subjected a small number to deep interrogation techniques which had been developed in other theatres during the 1950s and 1960s. Deep interrogation meant selecting a small number of internees were to be exposed to five techniques of in-depth interrogation. This was known as Operation CALABA.

Wall standing required detainees to stand with their arms against a wall but not in a position of stress. It was supposed to provide security for detainees and guards against physical violence during the reception and search period and whenever detainees were together outside their own rooms in a holding room awaiting interrogation. It was also to assist the interrogation process by imposing discipline. A hood (a black pillow-slip which the detainee was not required to wear while he was being interrogated or while he was alone in his room) was supposed to reduce to the minimum the possibility that while he was in transit or with other detainees he would be identified or would be able to identify other persons or the locations to which he was moved. It thus provided security both for the detainee and for his guards. It could also, in the case of some detainees, increase their sense of isolation and so be helpful to the interrogator thereafter. The continuous hum – 'white noise' – to which detainees were subjected prevented their overhearing or being overheard by each other and was thus a further security measure. By masking extraneous sound and making communication more difficult it might also enhance the detainee's sense of isolation. The diet of bread and water at six-hourly intervals formed part of the atmosphere of discipline imposed upon detainees while under control for the purpose of interrogation. The justification for these methods was that they were used in support of the interrogation of persons who were believed to possess information of a kind 'which it was operationally necessary to obtain as rapidly as possible in the interest of saving lives, while at the same time providing the detainees with the necessary security for their own persons and identities'. It also meant that the internees were completely disorientated and, therefore, more likely to reveal tactical intelligence.

Deep interrogation was carried out by RUC (SB). Wisely, when a request for assistance in the setting up of an RUC Interrogation Centre was discussed on 24 March 1971 at a meeting in the Ministry of Defence with representatives of MI5, the Security Service passed up on the opportunity to help and it was agreed that assistance should be provided by the Joint Services Intelligence Wing which was recognised as the only official school for interrogation training. The fallout from CALABA saw the British Government judged to have been guilty of inhuman and degrading treatment by the European Court of Human Rights in 1976.

The army, in retrospect, considered that Operation DEMETRIUS, the introduction of internment, was in practice 'an operational level reverse'. A considerable number of terrorist suspects were interned: the net total of active IRA terrorists still at large decreased by about 400 between July and December 1971. A very large amount of intelligence had been gained: the number of terrorists arrested doubled in six months. However, the 'information operations opportunity' – propaganda – handed to the Republican Movement was 'enormous'. Both the reintroduction of internment and the use of deep interrogation techniques had a major impact on popular opinion across Ireland, in Europe and the United States. 'Put simply, on balance and with the benefit of hindsight, it was a major mistake.' MI5 had been wise to stand aloof on this occasion. But it also helped cultivate an impression that it was best to restrict involving the Security Service's commitment in the Troubles to a minimum. But this did not mean a total abstinence.

Bloody Sunday

In January 1972 an anti-internment march planned in Londonderry was banned by the Northern Ireland Government. The organisers decided to defy the ban and march anyway. The army had put a number of manned barriers in place to stop the march entering the centre of the city. It was also planned to mount an arrest operation as the march began to disperse, so as to arrest the ringleaders and to deter further illegal marches. Derry had virtually seceded from the authority of the United Kingdom in that constant rioting, often used as a cover for IRA sniper attacks, had made it almost impossible for the Security Forces to operate there. Something had to be done to restore some level of order there.

In the run up to the march the army were concerned that troops might come under fire from the Rossville Flats that overlooked the arrest area. MI5, by now, was running its own agents in Northern Ireland. One of those provided intelligence in the run up to the march. This agent had been an informant since 1970 when he was introduced to an Army Intelligence Officer, referred to as IO1. After becoming acquainted with IO1, the agent began to assist him with what information he could provide. Within a few days of meeting IO1 he introduced him to another Army Intelligence Officer referred to as IO2. He also began to assist IO2 with information. For the first few weeks he passed on information to IO1 and IO2 that he thought might be useful. Then IO1 introduced him to a man called JAMES. The agent recalled how JAMES said, 'I am taking you over, you will not have any more to do with the Army, pass all your information on to me.' JAMES wanted to tell the agent his full name and details, 'but I told him that I did not want to know. He also wanted to put me on the payroll and again I refused. I did, however, later receive payments from IO2 to cover my travelling expenses.' A little later on he was introduced to another man known as JULIAN. Both men were from MI5. Although he spoke to JAMES and JULIAN from time to time his main contacts as far as he was concerned remained IO1 and IO2. On 25 January 1972, the Tuesday before the march, the MI5 agent was in Londonderry and was in the area of the Rossville Flats where he claimed that he saw a group of about forty men between the ages of eighteen and thirty dressed in civilian clothing. One of the men, aged about twenty-eight, with a pale complexion and dark hair, began to issue orders to others. The men then lined up in three rows in front of this man and he shouted to them 'attention!' and then 'at ease!' These words were shouted in Irish. At the time the MI5 agent assumed that he was witnessing the drilling of IRA auxiliaries. He had witnessed auxiliaries before who were affiliated to the IRA but were not full members. The auxiliaries tended to be made up of men who wanted to contribute to IRA operations but were not considered to be suitable material for the IRA's Active Service Units that carried out attacks.

After a short while, the MI5 agent observed the men march across Rossville Street and then enter the Rossville Flats through the main entrance located between Blocks 1 and 2. A few minutes later he saw 'X'. 'I said to him "What is going on?" He replied, "You have noticed them." I said, "I have noticed them, I have seen them practising. What do you think they are up to?" X replied, "They are practising for Sunday. They were here yesterday at the same time." I said, "The best thing for you to do is to keep your head down and get on with what you are doing." X replied that that was exactly what he would do.'

The Security Service agent saw that the men had split up and that they were now spread out along the three landings of Block 2 of the flats. He watched as the men appeared to be practising something. At first they stood on the inside edge of the balconies close to and with their backs to the doors of the flats. On command they moved forward to the outside edge of the balconies, keeping just to the left of each of the columns that were located on the outside edge at intervals. The MI5 agent thought that they stood near the columns in the way that they did so that they would be obscured from the sight of anyone looking towards the flats from the observation post on the city walls. A little later he saw X again. 'I said to him, "What on earth do you think they were practising for?". X and I then discussed the possibility that the Fianna [youth wing of the IRA] were planning to attack the Army to draw them into the area and then fall back, leaving the soldiers vulnerable to sniper fire. I had seen this tactic employed before on a couple of occasions but concluded that given the amount of people likely to be present on the march, they would not do such a thing. X said words to the effect that he would not rule anything out... I telephoned IO1 that evening, describing what I had seen and informing him that I thought there was going to be serious trouble at the march on Sunday... I think that the expression that I used was, "I think you have got a problem on Sunday." IO1 replied, "We are going to have to think on this one, ring me again in the morning." The next morning I telephoned him again. I repeated what I had seen and he asked me, "Do you think that they will do it every day?" I took this to mean practice every day. I said that I did not know.' On Thursday 27 January he saw the men drilling in a similar fashion to that which he had seen on Tuesday. He also bumped into X. 'I said to him, "They are still at it," and he replied, "Every day this week." I telephoned IO1 telling him what I had just witnessed. He said he was looking into it. He seemed very excited by this information.'

The citizens of the Bogside denied that such activities took place. But this was the sort of raw intelligence from such 'No-Go' areas that convinced the army that they were likely to come under fire from the IRA during the arrest operation. And, on the Sunday of the march, following severe rioting, the arrest operation began, involving the 1st Battalion of The Parachute Regiment. Three platoons of 1 PARA debussed in three different areas in the immediate vicinity of the rioters. Almost immediately 1 PARA claimed that shots were fired at them and they returned fire. Within minutes thirteen Catholic unarmed civilians were dead. A fourteenth died later. The day became known as Bloody

Sunday and was the biggest recruiting agent for the IRA before and since.

Naturally, controversy has surrounded the events of Bloody Sunday ever since, with accusations hurled on both sides. The IRA have always denied having fired upon the soldiers during the arrest operation. For many Catholics the actions of 1 PARA on that day were nothing less than cold-blooded murder. But one MI5 agent, INFLICTION, a former friend of Martin McGuinness – PIRA's second in command on Bloody Sunday – claimed that the latter had admitted firing the first shot. Officer A, who rose to become the head of MI5's anti-terrorist section, had been INFLICTIONS's 'minder' for seven months. 'With hindsight,' remarked Officer A, INFLICTION 'was a reliable agent... I say with hindsight, because it is not always possible to judge immediately the accuracy of the information supplied, and it is often years before corroboration of it comes to light.' Over the years INFLICTION had provided MI5 'with many reports about Mr McGuinness, many of which could be verified, some of which we could not. I do not recall any reports that he provided about Mr McGuinness proving to be wrong.' McGuinness denied the allegation calling it a 'sham'. He added: 'Unlike me... the reality is that this person who is making allegations against me will never appear' in public.

Indeed, both wings of the IRA subsequently denied any precipitate action on Bloody Sunday, Reg Tester, the Official IRA Quartermaster, claimed there were no IRA volunteers or auxiliaries drilling in the area of the Rossville Flats. McGuinness described auxiliaries in Derry as people who were of assistance to the IRA: they were not active service volunteers for the purposes of fighting the British Army. Both the Officials and the Provisional claimed they did not plan any offensive action for the day of the march. On Thursday 27 January, McGuinness was told that an approach had been made to his OC by people representing the Civil Rights Movement proposing that the IRA accept that Derry should be peaceful in order to facilitate what was expected to be a huge, peaceful demonstration against internment. The following day, Friday, McGuinness was asked by the OC for his opinion on this request. By this stage McGuinness was aware of the ongoing reports of a substantial military build-up in the city. Taking everything into account he expressed a view in favour of the suggestion. In McGuinness's opinion a march consisting of approximately 20-30,000 people protesting against the Unionist administration and its military forces, as well as internment, would be a very powerful expression of the people's rejection of the Unionist regime and of the repressive methods the British Government were employing.

On Saturday morning, McGuinness met his OC. At this meeting he was instructed to issue orders to all Volunteers that the IRA would not engage militarily with British forces to ensure that the Civil Rights march passed off peacefully. Following the meeting McGuinness spoke with the Command Staff and all active service Volunteers. He replayed the decision taken by the OC: 'Without exception everyone I spoke to accepted that our approach to the march was sensible.' Some concern, however, was expressed that against the backdrop of such a large demonstration which would see a large number of people from the Creegan and Brandywell areas marching to the city centre, the British Army might attempt incursions into these two areas. Instructions were issued that a small number of Volunteers, in the form of two units totalling about eight people, should remain armed and vigilant as a contingency in these two areas. The two Active Service units (ASUs) would be the only armed PIRA units in the Free Derry area on 30 January. No IRA weapons were stored at or near Rossville Flats and there was no movement of weapons in the Bogside area for any purpose prior to or during the course of the march taking place. All PIRA weapons, except those in the possession of the two ASUs, were placed in a closed dump for the duration of the march. McGuinness spent the early hours of 30 January with an ASU patrolling the general Free Derry area. Their task was to oppose any attempt by the British Army to launch raids into the area under cover of darkness. As dawn broke and the likelihood of an army incursion receded, McGuinness and his comrades went to safe houses for a few hours sleep. McGuinness went to a house in the Creegan where he stayed until about 9 a.m. He then had breakfast and went to Mass. After joining the march he remained with it until the end. According to Reg Tester, the Official IRA also had orders not to engage the British Army.

However, this cannot be all true. It was while retrieving a hidden .303 rifle, on Bloody Sunday, that members of the Officials – known as OIRA1 and OIRA2 – were confronted with a situation in which they witnessed an army sniper firing upon a civilian. The army sniper claimed the civilian was a nail bomber. Witnesses denied this. OIRA2 opened fire on the soldier in anger. This admission that the Officials had opened fire on the army took decades to emerge. Reg Tester admitted that the OIRA 'has been economical with the truth' in relation to the firing of a shot by one of its Volunteers. This was because the Army Council decided at the time that there were to be no admissions that any shots had been fired. But there were a number of further shots that were not fired by the army that day: a shot, which hit a wall in Kells Walk, close to Cyril Cave, a BBC cameraman; a revolver shot from 'just below the entrance to the block of flats' i.e. Columbcille Court, fired, as a BBC reporter thought, from the crowd there towards soldiers on a roof; or, as Ciraran Donnelly, of *The Irish Times*, thought, from the crowd throwing stones at a derelict house in William Street near Tanner's Row; and another High Velocity round coming from the direction of Little Diamond heard at the City Cabs' office in William Street by Simon Winchester of *The Guardian* and Nigel Wade of *The Daily Telegraph* and timed by Winchester as being fired at about 4.05 p.m. – again before 1 PARA went in. This may, or may not, have been the same shot as that described by Mr Porter – who was monitoring Security Force radio traffic at the time – who, after seeing a camera crew outside Columbcille Court filming a handkerchief covered in blood, heard the twang of a bullet strike 'to my right and high up in Columbcille Court and then I heard the sharp cutting sound of a high velocity bullet travel from a direction between Stevenson's Bakery and Little James Street.' Finally there was a shot referred to by the Intelligence Officer of 1 PARA as a shot coming from the direction of Rossville Street at about 4.08 p.m. and fired towards Barrier 12. Even discounting the final account of 1 PARA's IO the civilian evidence is revealing: six individuals recall firing before 1 PARA began their arrest operation. Its importance is this: it reveals active gunmen in Derry before 1 PARA go in. If all the IRA weapons – of both organisations – were accounted for then who was shooting at the army? Something in the IRA accounts does not add up.

Shoot to Kill

From early on it was clear that a quick victory over the Provisional IRA was unlikely: the reorganisation of the organisation into cells with each compartment having only a limited awareness of other parts of the structure made it more difficult for the Security Forces to defeat it. But the Security Forces could contain the IRA – although it would have the advantage of staging a number of 'spectaculars' over the years. A multitude of agencies were involved in combatting the IRA. Gradually, the dominant security of the army was replaced by 'police primary': the military acted in support of the Royal Ulster Constabulary except in the most hardcore Republican areas. Intelligence gathering was conducted by a number of agencies: RUC Special Branch ran informers – or 'touts' – within the IRA; MI5 would be called in to plant, for example, bugs; 14 Intelligence – known as the 'Detachment' or 'Det' – was a new arm of Military Intelligence that sent undercover soldiers into Republican and Loyalist areas often at great personal risk to themselves. The Special Air Service conducted surveillance on IRA members – particularly in rural areas such as South Armagh – as well as being used in operations that required the use of lethal force. Other military elements, such as the Force Research Unit (FRU), developed later. If a British agent was identified by the IRA they could expect no mercy: many were found dumped on the Border with a bullet in the back of their head often after a 'confession' had been tortured out of them. Undercover soldiers could also expect no mercy if they were detected by the IRA. When Sir Maurice Oldfield became head of SIS he felt it was more desirable and constitutionally appropriate that MI5 should do the job as Northern Ireland was a part of the United Kingdom. By the end of 1973 the intelligence services in Northern Ireland had been reshuffled and improved much more to C's liking. The SIS officer stationed in the Northern Ireland Office at Stormont Castle was relieved by a senior MI5 officer who became Director and Co-ordinator of Intelligence (DCI), and the SIS Intelligence Controller at army headquarters at Lisburn was replaced by another MI5 man.

But intelligence co-operation still left a lot to be desired. Things came to a head in August 1979: in one day the Provisional IRA delivered a spectacular blow. On the same day, Lord Mountabtten of Burma – and a member of the Royal Family – was killed, along with several others, while holidaying in the Irish Republic; while, in Northern Ireland, eighteen paratroopers were killed in another bomb attack at Warrenpoint, County Down. The Prime Minister, Margaret Thatcher, called Sir Maurice Oldfield out of retirement and asked him to go to Ulster as the Province's new Co-ordinator of Security and Intelligence. It proved a turning point in the war against the IRA although the benefits would take years to manifest themselves because it was still an incomplete overhaul of the intelligence machinery. The police and army were at loggerheads over many aspects of intelligence work. The previous MI5 presence had been unable to resolve this. Oldfield, though, created structures wherein police and military representatives could present their views to one another with him acting as a neutral chair. When temperatures rose, it was the respect in which the quietly spoken Oldfield was held that defused tensions; Sir Philip Goodhart, an NIO minister in 1979–1980 recalled: 'All Maurice had to do when the temperature rose was to say "The flowers that bloom in the summer will wither in the autumn", and everyone would nod wisely and the temperature would be reduced. It was his actual presence that mattered.' Oldfield curbed the enthusiasm of some army officers to act on Special Branch intelligence, gleaned from an informer, thereby liquidating the source. He emphasised the benefits of deep cover informer penetration of the IRA.

By the early 1980s, then, a more effective intelligence network had been developed. In line with the policy of police primacy, an anti-terrorist flying squad, the Headquarters Mobile Support Unit, was set up within the RUC under the control and direction of Special Branch. It was composed of of specially selected officers trained by the SAS and other army units to operate at close quarters. In 1982, the average age of the officers in the HMSU was twenty-eight and the average length of police service nine years. A handful of them were former British soldiers. There were two HMSUs, each with around two dozen officers. A Special Branch inspector was in charge of each unit. The unit was broken down into smaller groups of three or four Special Branch officers, each with a sergeant in charge. They operated in unmarked vehicles, known as 'o' cars. Overall command of the HMSUs rested with a Special Branch superintendent who was answerable to the Assistant Chief Constable at police headquarters, at Knock, and who was also Head of the Special Branch. The key to its operations was intelligence provided by one of the RUC's Special Branch departments, E4.A, often supplemented by information from Military Intelligence and MI5. Unfortunately, the HMSU became involved in a series of operations in which unarmed Republican terrorists were killed. This led to allegations of a 'shoot to kill' policy being employed by the RUC. Some of the information, leading to the interception of the terrorists, had been provided by informers: it was the cover stories that were invented by RUC Special Branch officers to protect these informants that led to an enquiry into the shootings.

Special Branch informers were paid a monthly retainer by MI5 from funds specially allocated by Parliament to the Security Service. Although they were paid by MI5, the agents were 'run' by Special Branch. These agents could only be identified by coded numbers and they were paid thousands of pounds for their information. The 'handler' of these agents and the Special Branch units most closely involved – E3 (intelligence) and E4 (operations) – knew that the first duty was to protect their sources. In addition to a regular income from being on MI5's funds, they received what were known as 'incentive' payments – payment by results. The agent would tip off his 'handler' about the movement of IRA weapons and explosives. His IRA colleagues would then, as if by coincidence, run into a vehicle checkpoint manned by one of the Headquarters Mobile Support Units. This was to create the illusion of a lucky arrest by ordinary police officers. The agent would then be paid. Into this murky world John Stalker, the Assistant Chief Constable of Manchester, was parachuted to investigate the allegations of a shoot to kill policy.

A Special Branch superintendent was the operational head for the whole of the RUC's South Region, which included County Armagh. Information from a variety of souces were fed into the Tactical Co-ordinating Group that decided on what action was required: this came from E4.A, Special Branch, army undercover surveillance teams and informers. The role of the TCG was to ensure that all three intelligence agencies involved – Special Branch, Military Intelligence and MI5 – knew what the other was doing although the details of these covert operations were only available on a 'need to know' basis. Subsequent cover stories, that were designed to prevent the sources being revealed in open court, were invented by 'Chinese Parliaments' – meetings of senior officers designed to conceal the true nature of operations. A 'Chinese Parliament' appeared to be a gathering where a decision was made in such a way that the authors could never be identified. Unfortunately for the Security Forces and MI5 five of the six dead men shot dead in operations by the HMSU had been unarmed. One case in particular was to have profound consequences.

At the end of September 1982, an IRA informant told his handlers about a consignment of fertilizer explosives coming from across the Border and the location in which they were to be stored – a hayshed in Ballynerry Road North. Once the explosives were in place, surveillance bcame a problem. Mounting a Static Observation Post was considered too dangerous as the hayshed was near houses. This was where MI5 were called in – to plant an electronic listening device in the hayshed. A Security Service technical officer planed two listening devices: one in a rafter in the roof; the other under the explosives which would be triggered by any movement. However, the devices did not work as they should have done and, at some point, the explosives were removed from the shed – with disastrous results. On 27 October 1982 the RUC received a call about a robbery in the vicinity of the Kinnego embankment a few miles away from the hayshed. Three police officers investigated. Sergeant Sean Quinn and Constables Alan McCloy and Paul Hamilton were blown up and killed by a landmine along the Kinnego embankment. The explosives from the Hayshed had been used in the bomb.

Two young men – Michael Tighe and Martin McCauley – later approached the hayshed. Also in the shed were some old rifles. Unknown to the young men, the HMSU had been waiting to intercept anyone in the hayshed – which they did. Tighe was shot dead and McCauley wounded. The HMSU claimed that they had issued a warning before opening fire. John Stalker and his team later found out, as they investigated the incident, that the hayshed was bugged by MI5. The bug was still in the shed when Tighe and McCauley were shot. Stalker wanted access to any MI5 tapes and transcripts.

At the end of January 1985, he met with Bernard Sheldon, the head of Legal Services at MI5, in London. Stalker said it was vital that he had access to any tapes or transcripts of the shooting if he was to establish how Michael Tighe died. Sheldon, it seems, agreed and gave a commitment that MI5 would not stand in his way. Stalker then approached the Head of Special Branch in Northern Ireland, Trevor Forbes, and asked for the logs and the names of all the officers involved in monitoring the listening device. The request went up to the Chief Constable of the RUC, Sir John Hermon, who declined. Despite several meetings between the two men, nothing was resolved; Hermon's position was that he had to protect the RUC's sources. He could not allow access to the MI5 tape. Then Hermon moved: Hermon, having given thought to the matter of the tape, said he was now prepared to authorise the release of all material the RUC had in relation to the hayshed. However, he indicated that MI5 had a very considerable interest in it and would require reassurance about the way Stalker proposed to handle the material – although he then surprised Stalker by suggesting that the tape might not exist. An MI5 officer later informed Stalker that, subject to unspecified provisos, he would be advising that the Security Service should give its full co-operation.

In the middle of June 1985, Stalker had another meeting with MI5 in London. Present were Hermon, Bernard Sheldon and MI5's senior officer in Northern Ireland. Sheldon made it clear that MI5 was prepared to release any information which Stalker thought might be used as evidence, given the seriousness of the matters he was investigating at the hayshed. This had apparently been one of the stumbling blocks. The tapes were to be used for intelligence purposes, not evidence. Stalker then asked Sir John Hermon when he could have the tape and the transcripts. Hermon replied that the tape had been destroyed but there was a transcript. Stalker asked when it had happened. Sir John could not answer. He then, one assumes, surprised and dismayed Stalker even further by telling him that he could not hand over the material unless he was directed to do so by a higher authority, namely the DPP or the Attorney General. He told Stalker he wanted him to complete his report and deliver it to him – as constitutionally he had been the authority that had invited Stalker to conduct the inquiry – without the evidence from the tape. Eventually, an angry Stalker agreed to submit an incomplete report because of the huge disquiet over the shootings. But, before he could do so, Stalker was removed from the case over allegations concerning his relationship with a Manchester businessman. To the Catholic community in Northern Ireland this merely confirmed that the state had something nasty to hide and that Stalker had come too close to exposing the Dirty War on the British side. Stalker was, subsequently, cleared of any suggestion of wrong doing.

BOXing Clever

When Stella Rimington became the first woman to become Director General of the Security Service, in the early 1990s, she was determined that MI5 should become the prime intelligence agency throughout the entire United Kingdom for combating Irish terrorism. By the 1980s, MI5 was responsible for the collation, assessment and distribution of all intelligence on international terrorism affecting the UK, on Irish Loyalist terrorism outside Northern Ireland and on Irish Republican terrorism outside the British Isles. While the RUC had the lead responsibility in Northern Ireland, the Metropolitan Police Special Branch was responsible for intelligence against Republican terrorism in the mainland of Great Britain. Rimington began to address the basic problem that had plagued counter-terrorism efforts against the IRA in Great Britain: that efforts involved considerable 'networks of liaison' between departments and agencies. Exercises were held regularly in different parts of the country and abroad 'so that everyone could rehearse their role'. If a terrorist incident, a hijacking or a hostage situation took place anywhere in the United Kingdom, it was the Chief Constable – the civil power – who was in charge, unless and until control was handed to the military.

Rimington considered the Metropolitan Police Special Branch's lead role for intelligence, as well as police work against the Provisional IRA's operations on the British mainland 'a historical anomaly', which had survived the taking on by MI5 of lead responsibility for intelligence gathering, co-ordination and assessment work against all other forms of terrorism outside Northern Ireland. Through the work MI5 had done against the Provisional IRA's European campaign and with the RUC in Northern Ireland, it had learned a lot about how to counter their operations, and felt it had much to contribute to doing the same thing in Great Britain. 'Frankly,' in Rimington's opinion, 'neither the intelligence-gathering techniques nor the assessment skills of the police were, in those days, up to scratch.' It was during John Major's premiership that MI5 assumed the lead role in combating terrorism in Great Britain. Stella Rimington believed that it was the IRA mortar bombing of No.10 Downing Street, which came close to killing Major's Cabinet, that provided the catalyst for change. Kenneth Clarke, the Home Secretary, made the final decision. However, 'patience was not one of Kenneth Clarke's virtues, and, having agreed to the change, he wanted instantaneous results' recalled Rimmngton. In the summer of 1992, just after the decision had been taken, but before it had been implemented and while MI5 were still engaged in 'difficult and detailed' discussions with the police, Rimington, by then newly appointed as Director General, was 'summoned down' to the Home Office. Clarke questioned her 'grumpily on why we had not yet made any noticeable difference to the level of IRA activity. I had to tell him that such things took time. We would make a difference in due course. He just had to wait and give us support and encouragement.' The new Director General did not think 'he found the advice very palatable'. The relationship between Director Generals and their political masters was shaped by their different perceptions of what the consequences of decisions would be. On one occasion, when Rimington went to explain to Clarke that 'we wanted to use a building in a residential part of London as a garage for cars, involving much increased traffic movement, he painted for me a nightmare picture of the large-scale protests on the street that would result, from mothers with placards pushing babies in buggies, fearful that their children would be run over. As it turned out there were no protests and everything went ahead as planned.'

In Northern Ireland, MI5's assumption of the lead role in combatting the IRA in Great Britain rang alarms bells in the RUC. Ian Phoenix, who had become the head of a new RUC specialist surveillance unit feared that this would mean MI5 would seek to expand its empire into Northern Ireland. There had been a dispute between the RUC and MI5 during the running of the mainland operations against an IRA ASU which was planning bombing attacks in London during the early summer of 1993. MI5, or BOX as the RUC referred to the Security Service after its famous nondescript address (PO Box 500), was concerned as to who was 'running the show', according to Phoenix. Shortly after this, on 4 June, Phoenix was told that MI5 wished to have more direct access to his unit's information. This would mean that MI5 not the RUC could effectively take control of intelligence in Northern Ireland. Phoenix observed: 'They were somewhat surprised at our insistence that it would not be welcomed.' MI5 later appeared to have tried to pass it off as a misunderstanding about the issuing of warrants. Phoenix did not believe them, and expressed his alarm to his superior, the Head of Special Branch, at the prospect of the police losing control over such a vital source of information. According to Phoenix: 'The boss was adamant that no direct access would be allowed.' However, MI5 pushed ahead with its demands. A few days later, Phoenix again brought up the subject with another senior Special Branch officer. Phoenix said: 'I expressed my doubts and concerns re plans for direct access from the mainland. He asked a BOX agent to show me the telexes on the subject. During the course of our conversation I told him of my concern of a hidden agenda, in that the phones of MPs, senior civil servants, police officers could be tapped as a means of the future political talks. I realised that it was a *fait accompli* only if we allow it.' He appended two question marks after this remark. Thanks to the BOX office's operational experience in Northern Ireland, he was one of the few members of MI5 for whom Phoenix had great respect and affection. The 'hidden agenda' that concerned Phoenix related to the Government's overall plans for Northern Ireland. The Government had secret contacts with the Provisional IRA throughout 1993 and Phoenix suspected that the British were concerned that any settlement with PIRA would meet resistance within the police force and among the North's Unionist establishment. Without the support of the RUC, no settlement could be guaranteed to work. Hence MI5's desire to remove control of some aspects of intelligence from the police and place it in their own hands – so that they would have first access to sensitive information, deciding what and what not to disseminate. That is, they could withhold from the police whatever they chose, and intercept whomever they chose.

The matter became one of the subjects for discussion at a conference that was held that year at Machrihanish air force base near the Mull of Kintyre between 24 and 26 June. The intelligence chiefs took a Chinook helicopter from Aldergrove Airport, Belfast, to spend two days going over pressing problems in the war against the paramilitaries. MI5 claimed that it was not happy with the Special Branch's 'passage of intelligence' and 'would willingly put some of their people into support us. Kind of them,' Phoenix noted. 'They treat us like thick Paddies,' he observed once to his wife. MI5's offer was 'resisted by RUC', he wrote. This resistance reflected his determination to maintain police independence. Phoenix continued to fight BOX interference in or control of police operations, and insisted that restrictions be placed on the dissemination of intelligence his unit gathered. MI5 expressed concern that Phoenix's unit 'will be independent of them'. Phoenix's objections were not only based on an anxiety about the overall intentions of the British Government and its internal security agency: he was always concerned about allowing individuals who were 'no more than civil servants' to interfere in intelligence-gathering operations. He distrusted their judgement. He once wrote in a paper on terrorism: 'There is a continual source of annoyance for those operational agencies who are forced to liaise with civil servants with little or no operations experience or cognizance.' He regarded some of those working for MI5 in this light – 'as pen-pushers who would be more concerned with forwarding political agendas, or their own careers, than with the fight against terrorism, which he saw as the primary role of intelligence-gathering'. If such people had access to vital information without police input or control, he feared that they would not necessarily use it for the good of Northern Ireland. His fears were intensified by a chance discovery in the spring of 1994. During a meeting with MI5, one of their officers let it slip that there were several more operations in place about which the police knew nothing – neither the identity of the targets nor the type of intelligence being gathered. 'For all we know,' Phoenix once commented to his wife, 'they could be tapping the phone of the Secretary of State or the chief constable.'

Phoenix and several others, including a senior MI5 officer, were killed when their Chinook helicopter crashed on the Mull of Kintyre. In 1994 it was decided that all intelligence information would be rerouted through MI5 headquarters in London and no longer under the control of the RUC. Under Dame Stella Rimington, for the first time since the Troubles began in 1968/69, there was one body directing the intelligence war against the IRA. It was the decisive moment in the intellgience war against the IRA – and they only had themselves to thank for it when they tried to kill John Major.

Endgame

The British Government always had a back channel to the Provisional IRA from 1973 onwards. Frank Steele, a former colonial officer and travelling companion to the explorer Wilfred Thesiger, was an SIS officer transferred to Northern Ireland. Steele 'made it his job' to get out into Catholic ghettos like the Falls Road in Belfast and the Bogside in Derry and to make contacts at all levels. Steele was the first British official to meet the IRA. When he left Northern Ireland in May 1973, his contacts were inherited by his successor, another SIS officer, Michael Oatley, who within a few months of his arrival managed to develop connections with and around the IRA leadership to see whether it might be encouraged in the direction of political activity. Cautious probing had produced three different potential lines of contact to the IRA. The most promising, and the one he pursued, involved a Derry businessman called Brendan Duddy. Duddy was an Irish Republican, but he was a pacifist and a firm believer in dialogue. Referred to as the CONTACT, Duddy worked at great risk to himself over many years. In 1991 it was on his initiative that a meeting between Martin McGuinness and Michael Oatley took place which reactivated the LINK and helped lead eventually to the peace process.

Oatley's initial contacts with the IRA through Duddy were conducted in the utmost secrecy. It was claimed that Merlyn Rees, the Secretary of State for Northern Ireland, was unaware of them. Oatley informed Frank Cooper, the senior British official in Northern Ireland, of the existence of the CONTACT and he in turn consulted Sir John Hunt, the Cabinet Secretary, and the Prime Minister, Harold Wilson. From a British government point of view there were no negotiations. Throughout the series of meetings which occurred at a safe house in Derry, Oatley maintained that the purpose of the dialogue was not to negotiate, but to advise the IRA of what action the British Government and Security Forces might take if there were a cessation of violence.

The talks continued for weeks, with the hawks on the IRA's Army Council sending ever tougher demands. One was that their leaders be allowed to carry handguns when they returned to their areas after being 'on the run' in the Irish Republic. The elaborate British response was to point out that, with the ending of violence, the army would withdraw from Republican areas, senior IRA men might helpfully be designated as official points of contact for crisis resolution, and these contacts might then be given special passes which would make it very unlikely they would be searched if they stayed in their own areas. They reached consensus on an indefinite ceasefire, but needed a cover story for why violence was stopping. It was provided by the parallel talks going on in Feakle in County Clare with a group of clergymen in December 1974, and for nearly twenty years both sides kept secret what had actually taken place in Derry. The ceasefire itself stuttered on for some months and then collapsed in response to renewed Loyalist violence. Oatley had, by then, left Northern Ireland but he continued his relationship with Duddy. Oatley felt that the reliable and secret channel of communication was too valuable to waste, and without any authority to do so he agreed with Duddy that the new IRA leadership, with Martin McGuinness as a central figure, should be told that, while there was nothing now to talk about, the channel remained available against the day when there might be. Oatley was known to the IRA as MOUNTAINCLIMBER. This arrangement gave Duddy continuing access. He worked diligently to maintain the relationship, meeting members of the leadership and providing political discussion and strategy papers in his bid to promote peace.

In early 1991, MOUNTAINCLIMBER was about to retire. Just before he retired Oatley received a call from Duddy who suggested he come to Derry to 'meet someone'. Duddy's neighbour, Bernadette, who had played a vital role in smuggling IRA leaders across the border during the 1975 ceasefire, cooked dinner for the three of them and Duddy's wife, Margo. When dinner was over there was a knock at the back door and in came Martin McGuinness. Duddy had known McGuinness since the late 1960s when he used to deliver beefburgers to Duddy's fish and chip shop. He remembered that McGuinness 'used to chat up the girls behind the counter and had absolutely no interest in politics'. When McGuinness arrived, Bernadette said there was nothing left to eat. 'He's not here for dinner,' Duddy told her. Oatley and McGuinness talked by the fire in Bernadette's back parlour for two hours. Oatley recalled it was 'rather like talking to a ranking British army officer of one of the tougher regiments, like the Paras or the SAS'. He found McGuinness 'a good interlocutor'.[6]

Oatley told McGuinness that while the British Army might never stop the IRA altogether, it would always be able to contain it. Unless a political track were found, the cycle of senseless violence would repeat itself all over again. If the leadership were prepared to move in the direction of politics the British Government might be willing to reopen the link. McGuinness indicated they were ready for such a dialogue and asked what the channel would be. Oatley explained he was retiring but said he would talk to the Government about who might replace him. On returning to London, Oatley went to see Sir John Chilcott, the new Permanent Secretary of the Northern Ireland Office, and told him he had opened a channel to McGuinness who was ready to discuss a political way forward. MI5, however, insisted that the operation had to be mounted by one of their staff and found a retired senior SIS officer who had recently been re-employed by the Security Service. He took over running the link.[7]

Weeks later Duddy got a series of phone calls from someone claiming to be a businessman wanting to create jobs in Derry. The caller was persistent. In the end he agreed to see him. As his visitor talked, Duddy's 'eyes glazed over' until he produced a letter, from the Secretary of State for Northern Ireland, Peter Brooke, introducing the 'businessman' as Michael Oatley's successor. Duddy's reaction was instinctive. 'At that moment, I knew it – the conflict was all over.' His visitor's name was Robert. But Duddy gave the MI5 man the codename 'Fred'. 'Fred' set about building up trust with Duddy and his contacts in the Provisional IRA, supplying advance copies of speeches to be made by British ministers that indicated political flexibility once the IRA renounced violence.[8]

So, in a speech delivered at Coleraine, which Sinn Fein had seen advanced copies of, the new Secretary of State, Sir Patrick Mayhew, challenged the Republican Movement. Noted for his conciliatory tone, Mayhew suggested that an end to paramilitary violence would have profound consequences for the maintenance of law and order, and for the administration of justice in Northern Ireland. Mayhew claimed that it was the Republican Movement that had so far excluded itself from discussions, by its devotion to the methods it followed. If its cause did have a serious political purpose then 'let it renounce unequivocally the use and threat of violence, and demonstrate over a sufficient period that its renunciation is real.'[9]

In 1992, Sinn Fein published *Towards a Lasting Peace in Ireland*, which was their analysis of how the logjam in the North might be broken. *Towards a Lasting Peace* placed the onus on the British and Irish Governments, but particularly the British Government, to work to secure change. It called on the British Government to 'join the persuaders' for a united Ireland and to use its influence to convince Unionists that their future did not lie within the Union with Great Britain but in a united Ireland. It also called on the Dublin Government to persuade the British that partition had failed, to persuade Unionists of the benefits of reunification, and to persuade the international community that it should support a 'peace process' in Ireland.[10] In June, in a significant speech, a senior Sinn Fein figure, Jim Gibney, admitted that Republicans now realised the need for a 'sustained period of peace' before a British withdrawal. Implicit in this was the suggestion that Irish unity would not necessarily be a rapid occurrence.[11]

'Fred' then had a face to face meeting with senior members of the IRA including McGuinness. According to the Republican account of a meeting with the British representative in February 1993, the former emphasised that 'Events [violent activity] on the ground will bring an enormous influence to bear. The IRA needs to provide the space to turn the possibility of meetings into a reality. A suspension [of violence] is all that is being required of them. The British believed that two or three weeks was a sufficient period to convince republicans [that the IRA campaign was unnecessary]. There would be an intensive round of talks.'[12] On 22 February the Prime Minister, John Major, received an extraordinary message that MI5 assured him came from Martin McGuinness:

> The conflict is over but we need your advice on how to bring it to a close. We wish to have an unannounced ceasefire in order to hold dialogue leading to peace. We cannot announce such a move as it will lead to confusion for the volunteers because the press will misinterpret it as surrender. We cannot meet [the] Secretary of State's public renunciation of violence, but it would be given privately as long as we were sure that we were not being tricked.[13]

In their 'reply' to the Republicans, the British Government acknowledged that it understood and appreciated the seriousness of what had been said. They emphasised 'We wish to take it seriously and at face value.' The British attitude to the Provisionals would be influenced by events on the ground; in view of the importance of the message it was not possible to give a substantive response immediately.[14] The Republicans welcomed the possibility of a meeting and offered two representatives, McGuinness and convicted bomber Gerry Kelly, for an exploratory meeting.[15] In their reply, delivered by 'Fred' the British stated that they wished to take seriously what had developed, and were preparing a considered and substantive response. However, in the light of continuing violence, since the first response, the British were not yet able to send a substantive response. The British insisted: 'There must be some evidence of consistency between word and deed.'[16]

On 19 March, the British Government sent a key document, via MI5, to the Provisionals. The British accepted that all of those involved shared a responsibility to work to end the conflict and, employing Republican rhetoric, that 'No one has a monopoly of suffering. There is a need for a healing process.' The British believed that there should be no deception on either side, and also, that no deception should, through any misunderstanding, be seen where it was not intended. It was also essential that both sides had a clear and realistic understanding of what it was possible to achieve, so that neither side could in future claim that it had been tricked. The document emphasised that the position of the British Government on dealing with those who espoused violence should be clearly understood. The British position was that 'any dialogue could only follow a halt to violent activity. It is understood that in the first instance this would have to be unannounced. If violence had genuinely been brought to an end, whether or not that fact had been announced, then progressive entry into dialogue could take place.' It had to be understood, though, that once a halt to activity became public, the British Government would have to defend its entry into dialogue. Crucially, it would do so by pointing out that its agreement to exploratory dialogue about the possibility of an inclusive process had been given because – and only because – it had received a private assurance that organised violence had been brought to an end.

The British Government set out its policy. It made it clear that no political objective which was advocated by constitutional means alone could properly be excluded from discussion in any talks process; that their commitment to returning as much responsibility as possible to local politicians should be seen within a wider framework of stable relationships to be worked out with all concerned; that new political arrangements would be designed to ensure that no legitimate group was excluded from eligibility to share in the exercise of this responsibility; and that in the event of a genuine and established ending of violence, the whole range of responses to it would inevitably looked at afresh. However, the British explicitly stated its rejection that it should seek to 'persuade' Unionists that their best interests lay in a united Ireland:

> The British Government has no desire to inhibit or impede legitimate constitutional expression of any political opinion and wants to see included in this process all main parties which have sufficiently shown they genuinely do not espouse violence. It has no blueprint. It wants an agreed accommodation, not an imposed settlement, arrived at through an inclusive process in which the parties are free agents.[but] The Government does not have, and will not adopt, any prior objective of 'ending partition'. The British Government cannot enter a talks process, or expect others to do so, with the purpose of achieving a predetermined outcome, whether the 'ending

of partition' or anything else. It has accepted that the eventual outcome of such a process could be a united Ireland, but only on the basis of the consent of the people of Northern Ireland. Should this be the eventual outcome of a peaceful democratic process, the British Government would bring forward legislation to implement the will of the people. But unless the people of Northern Ireland come to express such a view, the British Government will continue to uphold the union, seeking to ensure the good governance of Northern Ireland, in the interests of all its people, within the totality of relationships in these islands.

The British emphasised that evidence on the ground that any group had ceased violent activity would induce a resulting reduction of Security Force activity. Were violence to end, the British Government's overall response in terms of Security Force activity on the ground would still have to take account of the overall threat – the threat posed by Republican and Loyalist groups which remained active would have to continue to be countered.[17] In a speaking note accompanying the document it was emphasised that the process was fraught with difficulties for the British Government; nevertheless they were prepared to tackle these and accept the risks they entailed: 'But it had to be recognised that all acts of violence hereafter could only enhance those difficulties and risks, quite conceivably to the point when the process would be destroyed.' If that were to occur, the British 'would consider that a potentially historic opportunity had been squandered'. The Republicans were alerted to the fact that the document had been personally approved by the Secretary of State, with all but the first sentence his own wording.[18]

Then the Warrington bombing by the IRA occurred in which two young boys were killed. The British called off MI5's planned meeting with the IRA. Brendan Duddy was devastated when the meeting was called off and told 'Fred' he simply had to come, as McGuinness and Gerry Kelly were waiting. 'If you don't come, my role as the link is over,' he said. 'I'm pulling out.' Duddy finally persuaded him, knowing how much was at stake. 'Fred' disobeyed orders. 'That's why I admire the man so much,' Duddy recalled. 'If "Fred" hadn't done what he did, we'd still be hearing bombs going off today. No Good Friday agreement. This is the kind of guy in other days you would pin medals on.' At the meeting with McGuinness and Kelly, in Duddy's house, 'Fred' said things he was never authorised to say, suggesting that Unionists would have to change and that one day the island might be united.[19]

Mayhew is now determined. He wants Sinn Fein to play a part not because he likes Sinn Fein but because it cannot work without them. Any settlement not involving all of the people North and South won't work. The final solution is union [i.e. a united Ireland]. The historical train – Europe – determines that. We are committed to Europe. Unionists will have to change. This island will be as one.[20]

Duddy, who was present, confirmed that these things were actually said. The IRA naturally assumed that 'Fred' had been authorised to say them while what the MI5 man had said never reached the British Government until the following November. And IRA violence continued. 'That's how it works,' Duddy said. 'This [IRA] department bombs. This department talks.'[21] By concocting his message about Irish unity, 'Fred' kept the dialogue going. But this appears not to have been the first massaging of messages that he was involved in: according to the Republican account the MI5 man had suggested that a limited ceasefire would be enough to begin talks. But the whole tenure of the British position delivered by 'Fred' was that there should be a permanent end to IRA violence. This misunderstanding of respective positions would dog the peace process as the IRA refused, for years, to declare their war was over and resulted in the British demand for the decommissioning of all IRA weapons as proof of this. It is also clear that the British Government did not authorise 'Fred' to suggest, orally, that Irish unity was inevitable: the written positions he delivered were clear in this. While the Sinn Fein/IRA saw the exercise of Irish national self-determination on an all-Ireland basis, the British position, as delivered by 'Fred', was based on the consent to Irish unity being based upon the self-determination of the people of Northern Ireland. To Republicans the consent of the people of Northern Ireland to Irish unity meant a 'Unionist veto' over Irish unity as the majority of people in the North were Protestant and Unionist. And they were quite good at saying 'No': as John Hume once remarked, if the word 'No' was taken out of the English language, Unionists would have nothing to say.

So, in April 1993, the message that MI5 delivered to the Prime Minister, from Republicans, stated that the route to peace in Ireland was to be found in the 'restoration to the Irish people of our right to national self-determination – in the free exercise of this right without impediment of any kind'. British sovereignty over the Six Counties, as with all of Ireland before partition, 'is the inherent cause of political instability and conflict'. This had to be addressed within the democratic context of the exercise of the right to national self-determination if the cause of instability and conflict was to be removed. Sinn Fein sought to assist the establishment of, and to support, a process, which, with due regard for the real difficulties involved, 'culminates in the exercise of that right and the end of your jurisdiction'. The Republican Movement believed that the wish of the majority of the Irish people was for Irish unity, and that an adherence to democratic principles made Irish unity inevitable. The emerging political and economic imperatives both within Ireland and the broader context of greater European political union supported the logic of Irish unity. It was their view, therefore, that the British Government 'should play a crucial and constructive role in persuading the Unionist community to reach an accommodation with the rest of the Irish people'.

The Republican Movement complained to the British Government that: 'Your disavowal of any prior objective is contradicted by commitment to uphold the unionist veto. The consequence of upholding the veto is, in effect, to set as your objective the maintenance of partition and the six-county statelet. And, consequently, the maintenance of the primary source of the conflict.' The Republicans argued that, since its creation, the Six-County statelet had been in constant crisis. Its survival had always been dependent on the existence and exercise of repressive legislation, coercion and discrimination. Its existence lay at the heart of the present conflict and divisions, both in Ireland, and between Britain and Ireland.[22]

However, the British Government reply, delivered by 'Fred', stated that the British were concerned that they had not received the necessary private assurance that organised violence had been brought to an end; they hoped that would soon receive such a message because 'without that, further progress cannot be made.'[23] The British also confirmed that any dialogue 'could only follow a halt to violent activity and receipt of a private assurance that organised violence had been brought to an end'.[24]

On 10 May 1993, the Republican Movement sent an important document to the British Government. Welcoming 'face to face exchanges with your representative', the Republicans trusted that this was only the beginning of such meetings. They were 'prepared to make a crucial move if a genuine peace process is set in place. You say that you require a private assurance in order to defend publicly your entry into dialogue with us. We have proceeded to this stage without assurance. We wish now to proceed without delay to the delegation meetings.' Despite these exchanges, the British later claimed that the reference to 'face to face exchanges with your representatives' concerned the 'unauthorised meeting between Mr McGuinness and a British official'[25] – 'Fred'.

On 17 July, the British Government acknowledged that it had understood the importance, seriousness and significance of the Republican's message of 10 May. However, the British pointed out that events on the ground, made it impossible to proceed with a response. Events on the ground were crucial: 'We cannot simply disregard them.' The British asked, 'Does the ending of the conflict remain your objective, and is there a way forward?' The British emphasised that there was one very important point which needed to be answered to remove possible misunderstandings. Recent Republican pronouncements seemed to imply that 'unless your analysis of the way forward is acceptable within a set time, the halt in violence will only be temporary. This is not acceptable.'

While the British understood the reasons for Republicans not talking about a permanent cessation, they were categorical that the 'peace process cannot be conditional on the acceptance of any particular or single analysis. The views of others involved must also be recognised as valid, though you will of course want to promote your own views.' The British asked the Republican Movement to confirm that it envisaged a peace process which was aimed at inclusive political process and that a 'lasting end to violence does not depend on your analysis being endorsed as the only way forward'. If the Republican Movement could, the British reminded them that the process of dialogue leading to an inclusive political process 'can only start after we have received the necessary assurances that organised violence had been brought to an end. In the meantime progress has to be subject to events on the ground.'[26]

On 14 August, the Republican Movement expressed its concern at the 'inflexibility of your most recent communication'. It did not reflect, in tone or content, the British position prior to 10 May. This, coupled with recent political statements, raised a serious question over the British commitment to a real peace process. The Republican Movement was perplexed that the British required a private unilateral assurance that organised violence had been brought to an end, since the purpose of a dialogue about peace was to bring all organised violence by all parties to the conflict to an end. This was implicitly recognised in the contacts which had been made in the past several years. Without any such assurance the Republican Movement were prepared to proceed to the point of a face to face meeting. In the course of that exchange, the British – in fact 'Fred' – had asserted the belief that a two week suspension to accommodate talks would result in Republicans being persuaded that there was no further need for armed struggle.[27]

The British Government now accepted that: 'Minds do not seem to be meeting at the moment.' The last communication had not dealt with a crucial point: 'It did not confirm that you envisage a peace process which is aimed at an inclusive political process and that a lasting end to violence does not depend on your analysis being endorsed as the only way forward.' On a further point, the British Government 'has not asserted' a belief that a two week suspension of violence would have the result of talks; on the contrary, 'it has been their consistent position that violence must be brought to an end before any process could begin'. Equally, the British accepted that the Republican Movement genuinely and reasonably believed it had made a serious and significant offer. If this was the case that the Republicans believed that this offer had been made with indifference, or worse, then it showed that both sides had to strive to be more clear with each other.[28] But the Government held to the position which had been publicly agreed by the British and Irish Governments, and there could be no departure from this. Dialogue would begin if 'there is an unequivocal private assurance that violence has been brought to a permanent end, and accordingly that Sinn Fein has affirmed that it is henceforth committed to political progress by peaceful and democratic means alone'.[29]

By this stage it was clear that this particular line of communication had been exhausted. When news of the contacts was revealed there was a storm of protest. However, Sir Patrick Mayhew argued that it was clear that the final message sent to the Republicans was consistent with the Government's declared policy: 'namely that if such people wanted to enter into talks or negotiations with the Government they first had genuinely to end violence. Not just temporarily, but for good. If they did, and showed sufficiently that they meant it, we would not want, for our part, to continue to exclude them from political talks. This remains our policy.'[30]

On 2 November 1993, the Government received another message via 'Fred', that again it believed had been sent by McGuinness. It said: 'Please tell us through the link as a matter of urgency when you will open dialogue' in the event of a total end to hostilities. The Government produced an encouraging reply which sent McGuinness 'ballistic'. He had never sent the message. Sinn Féin then leaked details of the secret contacts with the British. There was political meltdown. The Government retaliated by making public the 'conflict is over' message it said it had received from Martin McGuinness earlier that year. McGuinness was 'incandescent'. He had never heard about the message before and denied ever sending it. Duddy said the message should never have seen the light of day. It was the language of surrender. McGuinness didn't send it.' Suspicion fell on Duddy. 'Yes, the IRA thought I had sent it.' The consequences were potentially life-threatening. Four 'very senior Provisionals' came to Duddy's house to interrogate him. When the journalist Peter Taylor asked Duddy if they included Martin McGuinness and Gerry Adams, he replied: 'You pick out four senior republicans and you're right. They were the bosses.' Duddy was interrogated in an upstairs room. 'They questioned me for four solid hours. It was very intense but not abusive. One of them did all the questioning – and I'm not saying who.' Duddy finally convinced his interrogators that he had not sent the message. 'Let me put it this way: if I'd been guilty of anything, I wouldn't have liked to have been sitting in that room.' After that meeting, Duddy knew that his role as the LINK was over. The IRA now wanted direct talks with the British. He was more relieved than upset. 'Fred', in Duddy's words, was 'court-martialled'. As he said goodbye, 'Fred' gave Duddy a farewell present, a book inscribed with a quotation from Virgil's *Aeneid*: 'One day it will be good to remember these things.'[31]

Penetration

And so it was that the unauthorised actions of an MI5 officer helped revive ongoing contacts between the British Government and the IRA. Eventually, Martin McGuinness, the die-hard Republican, would become a minister in a power-sharing government at Stormont – and a minister of the Crown although this was not something that he would have liked attention drawn to. The IRA, after nearly three decades of war, were no nearer to a united Ireland. Strategically, the IRA had been defeated. It then became clear just how far the Provisionals had been penetrated by British Intelligence. In December 2004, it emerged that MI5 planted a sophisticated listening device at the head offices of Sinn Fein at Connolly House in Andersonstown, West Belfast. The 5ft device was found hidden in a floor joist at the headquarters of the party. Two live microphones were found, one pointed towards the upstairs office and the other at a downstairs conference room. The Connolly House bug was the latest in a series to have been found in property used by senior Sinn Fein and IRA members. Just a week earlier, a listening device had been found at the home of Paula McManus, who worked in Gerry Adams's West Belfast constituency offices. That bug consisted of a microphone, six battery packs and a transmitter. It was concealed in the beam in the loft of the flat, which could be accessed from a communal area at the front of the building. In 1999, a sophisticated listening and tracking device worth £20,000 was found built into a car owned by Martin 'Duckster' Lynch. Adams and McGuinness said the car had been used to take them to meetings with the IRA leadership.[32]

Then, in 2008, MI5 took one of Gerry Adams' personal drivers into protective custody after the man, Roy McShane, was unmasked as a British agent. The Security Service advised him to leave his West Belfast home after it emerged that an internal IRA investigation found he had been working for the British for more than a decade. McShane was part of a pool of drivers for senior Republican leaders from the time of the IRA's first ceasefire in 1994. He was one of the Sinn Féin president's drivers during the run-up to the Good Friday Agreement in 1998. McShane was understood to have worked as a pool driver for Adams at the same time as MI5 were bugging the car which transported McGuinness to and from negotiations.[33]

An MI5 assessment, in 2007, that spies who betrayed the IRA were no longer in danger of reprisal from former comrades may not have reassured McShane – nor, incidentally, did it seem to convince the Security Service itself since they pulled McShane out of Ireland a year later. At the time the Security Service had, it was claimed, received assurances from the Republican Movement's leadership that the organisation was not targeting informants. However, this same leadership also admitted that it could not guarantee individual Republicans would not seek retribution against men they regarded as traitors. One agent who has faced numerous assassination bids in England said he thought the threat would last for the rest of his life. Sean O'Callaghan was one of the most important informers operating inside the Provisional IRA: he rose to the rank of Southern Commander in the organisation while he was an agent first for the Garda Siochana and later the Royal Ulster Constabulary. Among the IRA plots he compromised was one that targeted the late Princess Diana and Prince Charles at a Duran Duran rock concert in London in the early eighties. In O'Callaghan's opinion, MI5's downgrading of the risk to him and other informants meant nothing. He cited the example of IRA man turned informant, Eamon Collins, who was stabbed to death near his home in South Armagh. No one claimed responsibility for his murder but it was widely believed to be a revenge killing by the Provisonal IRA's South Armagh Brigade. 'If something happened to me in England the republican leadership would resort to the explanation they employed at the time of Eamon

Collins' murder,' said O'Callaghan. 'They said then simply that Collins had made lots of enemies and it was nothing to do with them.'[34]

No doubt O'Callaghan also had in mind what had happened to an MI5 agent known as Dennis Donaldson. In 2002, Donaldson was arrested and accused of being a key figure in what the police claimed was a Sinn Fein spy ring at Stormont where the power-sharing Northern Ireland Executive was sitting. It caused the collapse of power sharing between Sinn Fein and the Ulster Unionists. After being warned by his handlers that he was about to be unmasked as a long-standing British agent, Donaldson confessed at a press conference in Dublin that he had been working for British intelligence and Special Branch for at least twenty years: 'My name is Denis Donaldson... I was a British agent... I was recruited in the 1980s after compromising myself during a vulnerable time in my life.' A shocked Gerry Adams admitted he had suspected that an informant was at work but that Donaldson had never occurred to him as a likely candidate. Donaldson was born in 1950 into a traditional Republican family in the nationalist enclave of Short Strand in East Belfast, an area surrounded by larger Protestant communities. He joined the IRA in the mid-1960s while he was still in his teens, before the start of the Troubles. In 1971 Donaldson was caught during an attempt to bomb a distillery and government buildings and was sentenced to four years in the Maze prison, his first and only jail term. After he was released from jail Donaldson became a key Adams ally against the previous generation of IRA leaders. He also built up links with foreign revolutionary groups which would supply the Provos with weapons and training. In August 1981, Donaldson and William 'Blue' Kelly, a leading IRA gunrunner, were arrested by French police at Orly airport in Paris. The duo, who were travelling on false passports, told the French authorities that they were returning home after spending several months in a Lebanese training camp. Donaldson continued to build Republican links with groups such as ETA and the PLO, travelling widely in Europe and South America as Sinn Fein's director of international affairs.

By 1983 he was back in Short Strand where he stood unsuccessfully as a council candidate and reorganised Sinn Fein and the IRA in the area. At one point Donaldson claimed that MI5 had tried to recruit him as an agent during a holiday abroad. As the peace process evolved, Donaldson was later moved to America, after the White House gave him a visa. He set up Sinn Fein's first office there and organised the first trips to the United States by Adams and McGuinness. He also met Larry Zaitschek, a New York chef who travelled to Ireland and who was later wanted in connection with an IRA raid on RUC Special Branch headquarters in Castlereagh. After the Good Friday Agreement, Donaldson became head of the party's administration in the Parliament Buildings in Stormont. Donaldson was believed to know about a spy-ring operating at Stormont run by Republicans. But he did not pass this information on to the British. Unfortunately for Donaldson the intelligence services already knew about it and were engaged in a three-month surveillance operation known by the codename Operation TORSION. The Police Service of Northern Ireland (the successor to the RUC) seized the mass of papers during a raid that became known as 'Stormontgate'. Donaldson and his son-in-law Ciaran Kearney were arrested. Sinn Fein claimed that the whole Stormontgate affair had been designed to collapse the power sharing executive, but this was dismissed by Nuala O'Loan, the independent Northern Ireland Police Ombudsman, who said the police operation had been fully justified. Charges against Donaldson, Kearney and a former civil servant called William Mackessy had to be withdrawn when the police were refused a public interest immunity certificate, which would have protected the identity of the agent who supplied them with the intelligence in the first place. A court hearing was told that the Director of Public Prosecutions felt that proceeding was 'no longer in the public interest'. It was suggested that Donaldson's handlers offered him protection under their 'duty of care' to informants. But Donaldson decided to admit his role to Sinn Fein in the hope that he could remain in Ireland rather resettling in Britain.[35] He was later interrogated by the IRA and made a public confession. He was given assurances he would be allowed to live, as long as he never spoke again about his actions. His decision to stay in Ireland would cost him his life. A gang tracked him down to a remote cottage in County Donegal and shot him dead. The IRA denied it had any involvement in Donaldson's murder. But it later emerged that republicans from east Tyrone and Derry, angry that the IRA had not 'executed' Donaldson, were behind the killing.[36]

Had Donaldson been outed as a British agent a decade earlier he would probably have met his death at the hands of the IRA's internal security section – also known as the 'nutting squad'. And that might have meant entering Eternity at the hands of the alleged head of that squad: Alfredo 'Freddie' Scappaticci; only he, it was claimed, was also a British agent – codename STAKEKNIFE. In 2003, Scappaticci denied the revealtions that he was a British agent. He turned up at his solicitor's office in West Belfast to read a statement denying the claims.

Martin McGuinness, like other Republicans, was astounded and said: 'I can't disbelieve his denial. Mr Scappaticci is the only person with the courage to go before the cameras and put himself before the media... All of these other stories are coming from nameless and faceless securocrats in British Intelligence.'[37] The senior Republican, Danny Morrison, also did not believe that Scappaticci was an informer. Morrison argued that such long-term, high-level infiltration of the IRA was impossible, insisting: 'I am convinced of it. It is just impossible to be of value without revealing yourself.' Those informers he had known were 'all low-level people running for four or five years... No agent can survive over a protracted length of time. If he is successful, a pattern will emerge and he will be caught. No matter who you are in the republican movement, people are going to think and talk about you. An agent would have to allow three-quarters of IRA operations he knew of to go ahead in order to survive, so that would call into question the morality of using him at all. That's why this whole picture doesn't fit.'[38]

But STAKEKNIFE was an agent of the Force Research Unit. The FRU was an Army Intelligence Corps unit which controlled undercover agents in Northern Ireland. Another British agent, Martin Ingram, was told by his handler that Scappaticci had voluntarily walked into an army base and offered to report information. An individual or group associated with the IRA had given him a beating and that prompted Scappaticci to 'turn traitor'. In conversations with handlers, it became clear to Ingram that STAKEKNIFE was also motivated by personal grudges. He hated Martin McGuinness vehemently and his reporting of the activities of McGuinness was always full and detailed. Scappaticci grew up in the Markets area of South Belfast, the son of Daniel Scappaticci, an Italian immigrant who arrived in Belfast in the 1920s. The Scappaticcis ran a number of ice-cream businesses. 'Freddie' Scappaticci was interned but released from prison in December 1974 and soon became a trusted member of the Provisional IRA. But four years later STAKEKNIFE volunteered his services to Army Intelligence. Then he worked his way up through the IRA ranks. By 1980 – the year the FRU was established – STAKEKNIFE, with guidance and help from his handlers, was firmly ensconced in the IRA's internal security department. STAKEKNIFE had a role in investigations into suspected informers, inquiring into operations suspected of being compromised, debriefings of IRA volunteers released from questioning and vetting of potential recruits.

STAKEKNIFE's internal security unit would take suspects to interrogate them in remote areas such as parts of South Armagh or across the border in the Republic. Eamon Collins – later killed by Republicans – joined the internal security unit in 1984. STAKEKNIFE, second-in-command of the unit, debriefed IRA members for hours after they had been released by the Security Forces. Collins alleged that STAKEKNIFE and another member of the squad told him how one man had confessed to being an informer after being told that he was being offered an amnesty. STAKEKNIFE promised the man that he would take him home, instead of telling him that he was going to be shot dead. STAKEKNIFE told Collins that he reassured the man that he was safe, but made him wear a blindfold as they took him on a journey by car. STAKEKNIFE opened the door and let the man step out onto the road: 'it was funny watching the bastard stumbling and falling, asking me as he felt his way along railings and walls, "Is this my house now?" And I'd say, "Not yet, walk on some more." STAKEKNIFE's colleague finished the story saying, 'and then you shot the f***ker in the back of the head'.[39] The STAKEKNIFE case raised fundamental questions concerning the role of long-term penetration agents in the IRA – as well as Loyalist terrorist organisations: had their handlers, for example, allowed their high value agents to commit crimes, inlcuding murder, in order to protect their positions?

In 1992, Colleen McMurray, a police officer, was killed by a mortar set off by a photographic flash. Kevin Fulton, a former British agent in the IRA, subsequently claimed that he tipped off Jonathan Evans – then his MI5 handler – that an attack was likely. The Handler, whom Fulton said he knew as 'Bob', helped him to organise a trip to New York in 1993 to buy infrared transmitters for use in IRA bombs. The idea was that MI5 would have the equipment sabotaged so that the bombs failed to explode. Security sources strongly deny all Fulton's allegations.[40] Fulton, described how British intelligence co-operated with the FBI to ensure his trip to New York in the 1990s went ahead without incident so that his cover would not be blown. He claimed the technology he obtained had been used in Northern Ireland and copied by terrorists in Iraq in roadside bombs that later killed British troops. To be convincing, explained Fulton, 'You cannot pretend to be a terrorist... I had to be able to do the exact same thing as the IRA man next to me. Otherwise I wouldn't be there.' Fulton, a Catholic, was serving in the British Army when he was recruited by Military Intelligence to infiltrate the IRA. He later worked for the Force Research Unit. For thirteen years Fulton was an IRA Volunteer, involved first in courier runs, later as a driver and enforcer, and finally as a master bomb-maker in a unit in Newry, County Down, credited with numerous advances in explosive technologies. 'I was recruited as a serving British soldier,' he said. 'I was in the Royal Irish Rangers. I agreed to go into the IRA as a soldier.' He also claimed that his handlers knew the nature of his role but ignored his warnings of forthcoming bomb attacks, including the Omagh atrocity, which killed twenty-nine people in 1998.

Fulton and four other members of his unit in Newry pioneered the use of flash guns to detonate bombs. This technology was used in the bomb that killed Colleen McMurray in 1992. Her colleague Paul Slaine lost both his legs in the attack. He was later awarded the George Cross for his bravery. Fulton claimed he tipped off his handlers about this attack but they allowed it to go ahead to protect agents. 'Two days before the attack on Slaine and McMurray I knew my [IRA] officer commanding was using what we called a doodlebug, a horizontal mortar.' According to Fulton, 'I told my MI5 handlers and they took me to London for two days. The day I came back the bomb went off. The police were taken off the streets to allow the bomber to get in, set the device and get out.' The trip to America came after the killing of McMurray, when the IRA had built sufficient trust in Fulton for commanders to send him abroad to buy remote control infrared devices that would allow IRA teams to refine the flash technique and detonate explosives from up to a mile away. When he told his MI5 handlers about the mission, they arranged with the FBI to procure the detonators for Fulton. An MI5 agent was sent ahead of him by Concorde to make preparations. In New York he attended a meeting with FBI agents and British Intelligence Officers. There he agreed to expose IRA operatives in America to the FBI. However, the same terrorists, who were arrested months later, were first allowed to procure and send the infrared technology to the IRA.[41] 'Bob', it was claimed, went on to become Director General of MI5.

A New World Disorder:
9/11 to 7/7 & Beyond

One of the major events, constitutionally, in the history of MI5 was when, for the first time, it was put on a statutory basis in 1989. The Security Service Act enabled MI5 to take certain actions on the authority of warrants issued by the Secretary of State, with provision for the issue of such warrants to be kept under review by a Commissioner; to establish a procedure for the investigation by a Tribunal or, in some cases, by the Commissioner of complaints about the Service; and for connected purposes. The function of the Service 'shall be the protection of national security and, in particular, its protection against threats from espionage, terrorism and sabotage, from the activities of agents of foreign powers and from actions intended to overthrow or undermine parliamentary democracy by political, industrial or violent means'. It was also to be the function of the Service to 'safeguard the economic well-being of the United Kingdom against threats posed by the actions or intentions of persons outside the British Islands'. The Director General, appointed by the Secretary of State, was to be responsible for the efficiency of the Service 'and it shall be his duty' to ensure: '1. that there are arrangements for securing that no information is obtained by the Service except so far as necessary for the proper discharge of its functions or disclosed by it except so far as necessary for that purpose or for the purpose of preventing or detecting serious crime; and 2. that the Service does not take any action to further the interests of any political party.'[1]

In addition, the Intelligence and Security Committee established a degree of accountability beyond the Home Secretary. The ISC was established by the Intelligence Services Act 1994 to examine the policy, administration and expenditure of the Security Service, Secret Intelligence Service and the Government Communications Headquarters. The Committee had developed its oversight remit, with the Government's agreement, to include examination of the work of the Joint Intelligence Committee and the Intelligence and Security Secretariat, which included the Assessments Staff in the Cabinet Office. The Committee also took evidence from the Defence Intelligence Staff (DIS), part of the Ministry of Defence (MOD), which assisted the Committee in respect of work within the Committee's remit. The Prime

Minister, in consultation with the leaders of the two main opposition parties, appointed the ISC members. The Committee reported directly to the Prime Minister, and through him to Parliament, by the publication of the Committee's reports. The ISC members were subject to the Official Secrets Act 1989 and had access to highly classified material in carrying out their duties. The Committee took evidence from Cabinet Ministers and senior officials – all of which was used to formulate its reports.[2]

On the ground, MI5's assumption of the primary role in fighting the Provisional IRA after the end of the Cold War appeared to suggest that the threat to British national security would be more localised than global. In 1992 the Security Service reconsidered its files policy in the light of the changing nature of the threat with the decline in the threat from subversion i.e. actions intended to overthrow or undermine Parliamentary democracy by political, industrial or violent means. Since that time, MI5 had been reviewing and destroying files on a case-by-case basis but the Service switched to reviewing files systematically by category, and routine reviewing was suspended. By 1997–1998, around 110,000 files had been destroyed or 'marked for destruction'. The vast majority of these related to subversion, on which the Service was no longer conducting any investigations. Reviewing in this respect was restricted to files on individuals who were over fifty-five years old. This meant that there might be files on individuals under the age of fifty-five because they joined an organisation that was categorised as subversive possibly twenty years ago, and that these files might still be used for vetting and other purposes. However, 'no such files would be opened on somebody who joined the same organisation today'.

When reviewing files, a number of considerations were taken into account, including whether the information was of continuing relevance to the Security Service's functions, and MI5's responsibilities under the Public Records Act 1958. The former was left entirely to the judgement of the Service alone; the criteria for the retention of files on historical grounds were the subject of discussion with the Public Record Office and a number of historians. The latter were announced by the Home Secretary in the House of Commons in February 1998, and included files relating to: major investigations; important subversive figures, terrorists or spies; individuals involved in historical events; causes célèbres in a security context; major changes in the Service's policy, organisation or procedures, and milestones in the Service's history; and cases in which the Service had a public profile.

A further factor was that MI5 was required to retain copies of all files where inquiries had been made since 1989 or where vetting disclosures had been made, to meet the requirements of the Security Service Tribunal under the Security Service Act 1989 in relation to the investigation of complaints. There might also be occasions, for example, when an investigation of an individual turned out to have been mistaken or where a particular recording category was deleted or assessed in retrospect to have been invalid since its inception, where a file could be destroyed by the Service prior to its normal review date.[3]

Security Service policy on the creation, use and retention or destruction of files was set out in a Service Manual of Recording Policy, whose fundamental purpose was to ensure that MI5 complied with its statutory duty to collect and disclose only such information as was necessary for the discharge of its functions under the Security Service Acts 1989 and 1996. Service papers were collected into permanent and temporary files; there were also computerised indices for recording basic details about individuals or organisations which had come to notice in the course of investigations but where there was as yet insufficient information to make a judgement about their significance. Permanent files included personal records, containing security information on individuals, as well as other records covering, for example, organisations of interest, particular subjects of study, major Service projects, and policy and administrative issues. At that time, the Service held around 250,000 hard copy personal records on individuals who might, at some time during the Service's history, have been the subject of inquiry or investigation; a further 40,000 were archived on microfiche.

The function of opening a file was performed by the Central Registry, acting on a request by a desk officer with management approval where necessary. The Registry was responsible for ensuring that the request complied with Service policy that no file was opened unless the subject fell within a current 'recording category'. For the most part, the categories reflected the nature of the threats which the Service was engaged in countering, and specified types of behaviour which indicated that an individual might pose or contribute to a threat. They were defined by the branches within the Service, in consultation with the Registry and the Service's legal advisers, and were regularly reviewed. Once a file was opened it was initially coded green, the first stage in a 'traffic-lighting' process first described in the Security Service Commissioner's 1991 Annual Report:

GREEN: 17,500 hard copy files (7% of total) Open for inquiries; papers may be added to file. Individual/organisation falls within current recording category, and is or may be subject of current investigation. We were told, however, that at any one time only a very small proportion of GREEN files are the subject of active investigation, and that most such records will never be the subject of intrusive investigation.

Of all GREEN files... roughly two-thirds – around 13,000 files – relate to British citizens.

File remains GREEN for up to five years, depending on recording category, and is then reviewed for transfer to.

AMBER: 97,000 hard copy files (39%) Closed for active inquiries, but may have relevant new papers added.

AMBER period depends on recording category, but in most cases until subject is 75 years old or until five years after investigation ceases, whichever is later.

RED: 135,500 hard copy files (54%) File closed, and retained for research purposes only, or destroyed.

There were, in addition, some 3,000 temporary (GREEN) files opened to house papers for active investigation pending a decision on whether or not to open a permanent file. These had to be converted into a permanent file or destroyed after a maximum of three years, subject to the requirements of the Security Service Tribunal. This amounted 'to a substantial body of information containing a great deal of sensitive and personal information'. According to the Director General and others within the Service, some files required and were given special protection because of the particularly sensitive nature of the material they contained, for example, on agents of the Service or on espionage or other especially sensitive investigations. In the majority of cases though, there was potentially much broader access to current files, whether it be by line managers and colleagues working in the same general area or by officers in other branches when, for example, a subject might fall within two separate recording categories. Beyond this, whenever an individual came to the attention of a desk officer, a check must be made with the Service file indices to see whether any record already existed on that individual; the desk officer might need to examine all the files on a resultant list to ascertain whether any of them referred to the particular individual of interest. This was a process which was repeated 'hundreds of times every day across the Service'.

The Service made available to an incoming Prime Minister, in relation to the formation of a Government, any relevant national security information (concerning, for example, contacts with a foreign intelligence service, or a relationship with a terrorist organisation) held on candidates for election. A similar service had been provided to the Leader of the Opposition, in forming a shadow cabinet, since 1992. Individuals' files were sifted by the Service's central secretariat, before summaries were prepared for the Director General for a decision on whether to pass on the information to the Prime Minister. There was a 'heavy responsibility' on the Director General, in putting forward any such file, to ensure that the information on it had been properly checked and related solely to national security.[4]

For the Security Service, the renewed ceasefires in Northern Ireland led directly to a drop of over 5 per cent in the Service allocation of resources to Irish and domestic counter-terrorism work, from 24.8 per cent to an anticipated 19.5 per cent during the course of the year. MI5 played a key role in operations AIRLINES and TINNITUS which resulted in the convictions of some of the most important terrorists in the Provisional IRA. In the first case, forty Security Service staff gave witness statements, in the second, around 200 – though, in the event, none were called to give evidence.

There were also some increases in resources devoted to work against the other threats from international terrorism, at 16.4 per cent and proliferation, espionage and serious organised crime, which together comprised 19.1 per cent. The Service had taken on twenty-four taskings – from the Regional Crime Squads, the Metropolitan Police, provincial forces and HM Customs and Excise – since October 1996, when the new arrangements came into effect. Six of these taskings had been successfully completed, and the Service had issued around 1,000 reports in respect of the investigations in which it was involved.[5]

By 1999–2000, MI5 was devoting over 50 per cent of its effort to the fight against terrorism. A significant proportion of this was still linked to Irish related terrorism, with work against state sponsored, separatist and Islamist terrorist groups covering the remainder. Just over 20 per cent of the Service's work was directed against hostile activity by foreign intelligence services. A 'significant' amount of this was against Russian activity in the UK.[6] But MI5's priorities changed radically after two commercial aircraft, hijacked by Al Qaeda operatives, flew into the twin towers of the World Trade Center in New York on 11 September 2001.

At the national level the Security Agencies' Heads were brought into the centre of the UK decision-making process immediately, not only as members of the War Cabinet but as members of smaller decision-making groups. The day after the attacks the Director GCHQ, Chief of the SIS and the Deputy Director General of the Security Service were in the USA, to co-ordinate the intelligence picture with their US counterparts. For the Agencies themselves the main change after the 11 September attacks was that the volume of reporting increased and the threshold of intelligence that was circulated decreased both internationally and within the UK. MI5 continued to acquire intelligence from UK and overseas agencies about threats to UK interests, analysing the reports and transferring them into threat assessments. The Service thus re-examined the threat and stepped up its investigative and intelligence collection effort against Islamist extremists in the UK. It provided relevant protective security advice and took part in the Government's response in consequence management. SIS re-deployed some of its staff to the London-based counter-terrorism team and the focus of many stations and teams was redirected. The contacts that had been developed through the Agencies' counter-drugs and international terrorism work were now directed exclusively at Al Qaeda and the Taliban in Afghanistan. In addition, GCHQ doubled the size of its counter-terrorism team.[7]

After the attacks, the Treasury approved £54 million for use by the Agencies in the financial year 2001–2002 and a further £54 million was allocated for the year 2002–2003. These amounts were judged necessary to avoid reducing work against other high-priority targets to unacceptably low levels. In MI5 the increase in capability arising from the extra funding involved the recruitment of some 130 extra staff by March 2003. They were to be directed towards more collection (including surveillance, interception and agent-running), investigation and dissemination of intelligence.[8] The tasking of the Security Service reflected its functions under the Security Service Acts 1989 and 1996 and the UK's Requirements and Priorities for Secret Intelligence. Overall, and for the longer-term tasking, MI5's annual Plans and Priorities paper was put to the Joint Intelligence Committee and consolidated with papers from SIS and GCHQ for Ministerial consideration and approval. In the period 2001–2002 the Service was devoting 33 per cent of its effort to Irish Counter Terrorism, a result of which was the successful conviction of three Real IRA (a splinter group from the Provos) terrorists for attempting to buy arms and explosives overseas. Work on International Counter Terrorism accounted for 23 per cent of the Service's effort while counter-espionage accounted for 16 per cent. Rafael Bravo, a security guard at a BAe Systems site, was convicted for espionage and jailed. Even in the post-Cold War era individuals were willing to sell secret information for financial gain.

In addition to these commitments, 11 per cent of the Service's effort was directed at providing Protective Security advice. MI5 worked with the Civil Contingencies Secretariat, the Home Office and other departments to reduce the vulnerability of key parts in the Critical National Infrastructure (CNI). This meant MI5 making arrangements to ensure that those in Government, industry and among the public who had assets to protect had access to expert advice and training on physical protective security measures. There was a framework of standards and access to specialist help as well as standardised, public information on counter terrorism contingency planning and business contingency plans produced by the Home Office. By now MI5 was playing a leading role in identifying new areas for counter terrorism advice, given the recognition of attacks, possibly suicide attacks, aimed at causing mass casualties. Additionally the Security Service managed a research and development programme to develop counter terrorism protection technologies for the future.[9]

A position of Security and Intelligence Co-ordinator was created in the summer of 2002. It was designed to allow the Cabinet Secretary to hand over his responsibility for security and intelligence functions, and for the new task of developing resilience and crisis management capability within the Civil Service, to an experienced Permanent Secretary. Sir David Omand, was appointed as the first Security and Intelligence Co-ordinator. The main reason for the creation of the position was the need to have an individual in place who could devote significant time to security, intelligence and resilience matters in an evolving threat environment. Sir Andrew Turnbull, the Cabinet Secretary, explained, how, in the past, intelligence and security had also been one of those areas that the Cabinet Secretary had had some responsibility for: 'The decision we took... was that post-9/11 there was a major change. The whole demands of security had changed, in that we had gone away from a world where you kind of knew your enemy; in the Cold War or Republican terrorism, you knew kind of what they intended to do and the degree of violence they could inflict upon you. We are not in that world any more – we haven't the faintest idea what are the limits. In the last week [the terrorist siege and massacre at a school in Beslan, Russia] there are no limits any more... it is a much more difficult world to cope with. So we had a growing requirement, but also three very high-class Agencies, a well-regarded co-ordination mechanism, but a gap around what the Americans call "homeland security".' Sir David Omand, as Security and Intelligence Co-ordinator, performed the necessary leadership role within the intelligence community by achieving consensus and workable solutions to the challenges that he faced. He also spent a considerable amount of his time developing and implementing the UK's counter-terrorism strategy as well as developing the Government's civil contingencies and resilience programmes and links with allies.[10]

And what dominated MI5's agenda was the threat from Al Qaeda. What Dame Manningham-Buller, Director General of MI5 from 2002–2007, noticed about the post 9/11 language of counter terrorism was that it was dominated by the word 'new': 'new groups, new threats and the need for new types of response'. She agreed with some of those sentiments but disagreed with others. As she pointed out, for practitioners, the threat from international terrorism 'is not a "new" phenomenon. It is a development of a threat that has been with us for many years.' During her own career she had seen significant changes in the international terrorist threat. In the late 1980s, Manningham-Buller was head of one of the Service's international counter terrorist sections. 'Our pre-occupations then were the state sponsors of terrorism and terrorism linked to nationalism.' She could remember that too was a period when international terrorism dominated the headlines. Some of the language used to describe the impact of 9/11 was used much earlier in 1988 to describe the terrorist bombing of PA103 over Lockerbie. That attack was the single biggest terrorist outrage on UK soil which led to the most intensive, lengthy and complex investigation (and subsequent prosecution) in UK history.

Nevertheless, Manningham-Buller accepted that the 'the events of September 11 were a watershed in the history of terrorism. These were dramatic and devastating attacks, resulting in major loss of life, destruction of property and economic damage across the globe. From Al Qaeda's perspective the attacks were their most audacious and ambitious; representing an impressive demonstration of the organisation's capability to plan, co-ordinate and execute simultaneous attacks against the United States.' Sixty-seven British citizens died in the 9/11 attacks: 'the single greatest loss of British lives in a terrorist attack – a fact that sometimes gets overlooked as the events of that dreadful day begin to recede into memory'. The Director General described Al Qaeda as 'the first truly global terrorist threat'. Manningham-Buller was quick to clarify that: 'I am not talking about a threat from Islam. It is true that terrorists use Islamic doctrine to provide a justification for terrorist attacks. We do not see the Muslim community as a threat. In the same way that we do not see the Irish community as a threat. Our focus is the terrorists. But international terrorism, compared with our experience of Irish terrorism, poses new challenges for us. Challenges of scale, geography, culture and language; it represents a complex and diverse target, capable of real harm to our way of life.' Al Qaeda members, and others, had demonstrated their willingness to take part in suicide or martyrdom operations. This was an important consideration in planning MI5's response to terrorism. If the terrorist planned no escape or did not worry about the possibility of detection then his planning for the attack would be quite different. A bomber intent on suicide was difficult to deter through conventional means. The response to that type of attack must therefore be different. Terrorist attacks by Al Qaeda had inflicted large-scale civilian casualties and they had deliberately attacked 'soft' targets to inflict widespread civilian casualties. This was not just a war against the State and its representations in Britain and abroad. 'In the front line, alongside military forces, diplomats and government targets are tourists, and people going about their normal business.' Al Qaeda's targeting demonstrated, she concluded, the vulnerability of sophisticated Western societies.

Manningham-Buller also warned that Al Qaeda had the ambition to carry out unconventional attacks against the West. The Al Qaeda leadership had said so: 'The question we must ask is do they have the capability to carry out such an attack? We know that renegade scientists have co-operated with Al Qaeda and provided them with some of the knowledge they need to develop these weapons. My conclusion, based on the intelligence we have uncovered, is that we are faced with the realistic possibility of some form of unconventional attack.' That could include a chemical, biological, radiological or nuclear attack. Sadly, she warned, given the widespread proliferation of the technical knowledge to construct these weapons, 'it will be only a matter of time before a crude version of a CBRN attack is launched at a major Western city.' The discovery of traces of ricin in the UK demonstrated that interest in unconventional weapons. The unconventional threat posed significant new challenges for government and society in general.

The organisational structure of Al Qaeda also differed 'significantly from many of the terrorist groups that my Service and its partners have studied'. At the centre, and to some extent directing global operations, rested Usama bin Laden and his close lieutenants. They were surrounded by a relatively small group of hardcore terrorists and facilitators who formed the backbone of the terrorist organisation. Their responsibilities included planning and financing terrorist attacks. Beyond them were looser networks of terrorists and their sympathisers whose connections to Al Qaeda and its leadership were less strong. They shared many of the goals of Al Qaeda but they might have stronger ties to more nationalistic or regional Islamist terrorist groups. Al Qaeda's success had been to forge alliances and partnerships with a range of separate and seemingly disparate groups. Al Qaeda did not have the rigid structures of other terrorist groups, instead their strength was drawn from alliances, affiliations and networks forged in the terrorist training camps of Afghanistan and the conflicts of Algeria, Bosnia and Chechnya. This type of structure made the collection of pre-emptive intelligence even more difficult for security and intelligence services.

Manningham-Buller, recalled how she was head of one of MI5's international counter terrorist sections in the late 1980s, had been 'working actively to deal with the problem of the Islamist terrorism then, so it certainly would not be true to say that we woke up to the threat on 12 September 2001.' From the mid-1990s MI5 were 'working closely' with their French counterparts who were dealing with a deadly threat from the Algerian extremist groups inside France. During the summer of 2001, the UK Agencies knew that attacks, probably against US interests, were imminent but their nature and target were unknown. 'What shocked us all was the scale and devastation of the attacks.' The response to the terror threat, emphasised the Director General, was not just a responsibility of the security and intelligence agencies and the police. This was a much wider problem 'and our work forms part of broader Government strategy. That strategy extends beyond the security response to many other parts of Government. All of this work must rest upon vigorous efforts to maintain the confidence of the Muslim population both here and overseas.' In the immediate aftermath of the attacks, MI5 stepped up its investigative and intelligence collection efforts against Islamist extremists in the UK. The Security Service's work could be divided into three parts: 'first – to reduce the threat of terrorism by stopping it and disrupting it; second – to reduce our vulnerability to terrorist attack; and finally – to support others to manage the consequences of any attacks.'

As Manningham-Buller pointed out, the UK had unrivalled expertise in dealing with terrorism – thirty years of Irish terrorism had given the UK a robust and well-established system of handling the terror threat with wide-ranging counter terrorist legislation in place to deal with the terrorists, including the Anti-Terrorism Crime and Security Act introduced in the aftermath of September 11. Part of the legislation was designed to deal with terrorism before it took place. Indeed: 'Our systems for terrorist protection and advice are the envy of the world.' Having said that, the Director General was savy enough to realise that 'of course things occasionally go wrong, but the system does work and in our rush to deal with the Al Qaeda threat we risk discarding those elements of the system that work well. We are not complacent about the threat or in our response to it. We have had some successes in stopping terrorism and, working with the police, in arresting and prosecuting terrorists. But no matter how successful we are, there is no such thing as complete security. There are no guarantees in the counter terrorism business.'[11]

That this was so was demonstrated just a year after 9/11 when MI5 suffered its first major intelligence failure relating to Islamist terrorism. On Saturday 12 October 2002 a number of explosive devices were detonated on the Indonesian Island of Bali. One of these exploded outside a packed nightclub and more than 190 people were killed, including 24 Britons, and many more injured. The majority of those killed were Australians although nationals from some twenty countries died.[12] It was the task of Britain's Intelligence and Security Agencies to collect secret intelligence of any potential threats to the United Kingdom and the security of its citizens. So far as the collection of secret intelligence overseas was concerned, Ministers approved the requirements and priorities. These requirements were then met by SIS and GCHQ operating under authorisations and warrants, which were approved by Ministers. It was the responsibility of the Counter-Terrorism Analysis Centre in MI5 to collate this secret intelligence, together with any other intelligence and open source material they had collected, and produce threat assessments. These assessments were classified and known as Security Service Threat Reports or Security Service Reports. They were distributed to the relevant government departments including the Ministry of Defence and the Foreign Office, as well as diplomatic missions overseas. Such reports were issued whenever significant and important intelligence was received. These Reports assessed the level of threat to British interests, both diplomatic and general, in a given country or region. The level of threat was based on a ranking system, ranging from IMMINENT to NEGLIGIBLE, depending on the severity of the threat and likelihood of attack. MI5 did not consult Ministers when threat assessments were produced nor when the level of threat to British interests rose. The Security Service Threat Levels were as follows:

Level 1: IMMINENT

Specific Intelligence shows that the target is at a VERY HIGH level of threat, and that an attack is IMMINENT.

Level 2: HIGH

Specific intelligence, recent events or a target's particular circumstances indicate that it is a HIGH priority target, and is at a HIGH level of threat.

Level 3: SIGNIFICANT

Recent general intelligence on terrorist activity, the overall security and political climate, or the target's individual circumstances, indicate that it is likely to be a priority target, and that there is a SIGNIFICANT level of threat.

Level 4: MODERATE

A target's circumstances indicate that there is the potential for it to be singled out for attack, and there is a MODERATE level of threat.

Level 5: LOW

There is nothing to indicate that a target would be singled out for attack. There is a LOW level of threat.

Level 6: NEGLIGIBLE

A target would be unlikely to be attacked. There is a NEGLIGIBLE level of threat.[13]

On 1 February 2002, MI5 assessed the threat, in Indonesia, to diplomatic interests to be HIGH and the threat to general British interests to be SIGNIFICANT. The Joint Intelligence Committee reported in May 2002 that there was an Al Qaeda presence in Indonesia, along with many other terrorist groups, which was likely to develop a local terrorist capability. The intelligence from September 2002 reported that attacks on US and UK interests, including tourists in nightclubs, were being discussed by terrorists. There was also a failed grenade attack on 23 September on an American diplomatic residence; however, as the Intelligence and Security Committee stated: 'None of these developments caused the Security Service to revise the threat level to general British interests in Indonesia.' The fact that the Security Service took over two weeks after the failed grenade attack on an American diplomatic property to issue a Security Service Report on Indonesia was 'also a matter of concern'. The Committee believed that MI5's system, with its six levels, did not provide sufficiently clear, differentiated definitions of the threat level. They needed to be of greater use to 'customer departments' and quoted the words of a Foreign Office official to make its point: 'Threat levels are imperfect but they are not useless.'[14]

The Committee, which had access to all the intelligence, found no evidence of intelligence that described or directly related to any form of terrorist attack on Bali on or around 12 October 2002 despite the fact that the UK, Australia and the USA shared intelligence on terrorism in South-East Asia. The Committee therefore concluded that, on the available intelligence, 'there was no action that the UK or its allies could have taken to prevent the attacks'. The Committee, though, did not let MI5 off the hook completely. During the period in question, the security and intelligence agencies received at least 150 separate reports a day relating to terrorist activity in more than twenty different countries, including Indonesia and the UK itself. This intelligence came from a range of sources of 'varying reliability, and difficult judgements about follow up action have to be made in each case.' However, none of the developments or intelligence caused MI5 to revise the threat level to general British interests in Indonesia. These, 'when considered together with both the public reluctance of the Indonesian authorities to deal with terrorism and the target displacement effect' lead the ISC to conclude that the threat assessments to general British interests ought to have been raised to HIGH: 'This was a serious misjudgement and meant that the Security Service did not assess the threat correctly and, therefore, raise the level of threat to HIGH. However, we repeat that, on the available intelligence, we do not believe that the attack could have been prevented.'[15]

In MI5's – general – defence, Manningham-Buller explained: 'In the intelligence world it is a truism, and also something that we just have to put up with, that out failures are apparent to all, our successes usually known only to a few. Like the best administration, you never notice it. It is only when things go wrong that you do.' Intelligence was key to any successful counter terrorist strategy but she asked: 'what is the nature of intelligence that we are dealing with? Where do we get it and what are the limits to its use? Why can't we provide the complete assurance to keep the UK free from attacks?' Counter-terrorist intelligence, she explained, could include intercepted communications between terrorists and their supporters and reports from agents inside the terrorist cells or networks. MI5 received reports from other Services, in Britain and overseas. It also obtained intelligence by the physical surveillance of terrorists and by gathering information on the movements of terrorist suspects at ports and airports. Reports from the public about suspicious activity could be valuable and volunteers to the intelligence services from among the terrorists themselves could provide unique insights to the activities of the terrorist groups. Not all the material MI5 used was from secret sources. For example, the public communiqués and statements of the terrorists themselves formed part of this matrix of intelligence, providing clues to their intentions and plans.

Much of this raw intelligence, pointed out the Director General, was of variable quality and was incomplete. 'Some of it is of exceptionally high quality but some is dubious.' With many agencies across the world operating in this field, there were unscrupulous individuals who would fabricate material, 'exploiting the laws of supply and demand in an effort to offer a product that someone, somewhere, will pay for'. Furthermore, nearly all of MI5's investigations in this field had an international dimension, and simple enquiries were rendered complex by the need to liaise with several different countries. MI5 had links to intelligence services in over 100 countries. Thus: 'The volume of material from all these different intelligence sources can threaten to overwhelm. Now clearly, it is the job of the Intelligence officer to separate the important from the unimportant, but rarely is the whole picture visible at the start of an investigation, and leads to possible terrorist activity are usually fragmentary and unclear. One element of the conspiracy may be visible, others, perhaps overseas, are hidden. Rigorous prioritisation is demanded and risks evaluated.' This required expertise and judgement to decide where finite resources had to be allocated. Leads to plots to carry out terrorist attacks 'must be pursued until (a) they are resolved or (b) new information shows that the original lead was not worth pursuing or (c) until nothing more can be done. Then there is the matter of "interpretation". Some intelligence is aspirational, not substantial, some designed to mislead, some accurate in parts but wrong in others. Analysing it rarely leads to certainty. Often the accumulated intelligence is vague, conflicting and raises more questions than it answers.' Intelligence Officers were 'always asking questions through the process of evaluating the material. Is there an attack at the end of this and in what timescale? What sort of activity has been uncovered and how concerned should we be about it? Difficult professional judgements have to be made every day – that's what we are paid for.'[16]

Partly as a result of some of the concerns highlighted by the Bali failures, the Government created the Joint Terrorism Analysis Centre, together with the introduction of a new threat assessment system, that brought together cross-community expertise on terrorism, with members from MI5, SIS, GCHQ, DIS, the police, the Security Division of the Department for Transport (TRANSEC) and others.[17] The importance of JTAC was its reports and assessments filled the gap in detailed intelligence for short-term decision-making that Ministers found useful at the operational level. It produced assessments that informed Ministers who had to make decisions based on threat intelligence.[18] The Director General of MI5 occupied the key position of chair.

Following Bali a new threat level system was introduced on 4 June 2003. The main change from the old to the new system was the introduction of a more detailed assessment of the threat at the higher end – the four levels from SUBSTANTIAL to CRITICAL all reflected a significant threat. The seven threat levels and their definitions were as follows:

NEGLIGIBLE (Level 6) – available intelligence and recent events indicate that terrorists currently have no capability and/or no intent to mount an attack on the target. It is assessed that an attack is very unlikely to be mounted.

LOW (Level 5) – available intelligence and recent events indicate that terrorists currently have little capability and/or intent to mount an attack on the target. It is assessed that, although it cannot be ruled out, an attack is unlikely to be mounted.

MODERATE (Level 4) – available intelligence and recent events indicate that terrorists have some capability to mount an attack on the target and such an attack would be consistent with the group's general intent; or that they have the capability but their intent is qualified by current circumstances. It is assessed that an attack is possible.

SUBSTANTIAL (Level 3) – available intelligence and recent events indicate that terrorists have the capability to mount an attack on the target and that such an attack is within the group's current intent. It is assessed that an attack is likely to be a priority for the terrorists and might well be mounted.

SEVERE (GENERAL) (Level 2(G)) – available intelligence and recent events indicate that terrorists have an established capability and current intent to mount an attack on the target or targets of this nature. It is assessed that an attack is a priority for the terrorists and is likely to be mounted.

SEVERE (DEFINED) (Level 2(D)) – available intelligence and recent events indicate that terrorists have an established capability and current intent to mount an attack on the target and there is some additional information on the nature of the threat. It is assessed that an attack on the target is a priority for the terrorists and is likely to be mounted.

CRITICAL (Level 1) – available intelligence and recent events indicate that terrorists with an established capability are actively planning to attack the target within a matter of days (up to two weeks). An attack is expected imminently.[19]

By 2004, terrorism was clearly the biggest threat to the national security of the UK and its interests. The Prime Minister, Tony Blair, stated in a speech on 5 March: 'the [security] threat we face is not conventional. It is a challenge of a different nature from anything the world has faced before.' Manningham-Buller added, on 16 October: '…the scale of the problem… has become more apparent as the amount of intelligence collected and shared has increased. The absence of an attack on the UK… may lead some to conclude that the threat has been reduced or been confined to parts of the world that have little impact on the UK. This is not so. The initiative generally rests with the terrorists. The timing of any attack is of their choosing and for them patience is part of the struggle.'[20]

As a result of recognising that the scale of the threat had been underestimated, the Agencies reassessed the challenge presented by international terrorism to the national security of the UK and its interests. The result of this reassessment process in 2003 was to increase dramatically the size of the Security Service.[21] MI5 now allocated 66 per cent of its resources in 2003–2004 to counter-terrorism (41 per cent to international and 25 per cent to Irish). In 2004–05 the allocation was 67 per cent. As a result of this, the allocation of resources to counter-espionage and 'providing external assistance' fell, from 10.7 per cent to 10.2 per cent and 2.7 per cent to 1.9 per cent respectively, while the allocation to counter-proliferation and serious crime rose slightly to 2.7 per cent and 6.4 per cent respectively.[22] Manningham-Buller described the UK's work on this subject in the post 11 September environment as a 'continuum with expansion, rather than a kick-start'. The DG stressed that the main developments after the 11 September attacks were a key change in American attitudes.[23] In November 2004, she reflected on how: 'I am often asked why there have been no attacks in the UK since 9/11, an entirely reasonable question.' Part of the answer was the effectiveness of the UK's counter-terrorist response and the great increase in international co-operation and exchange of intelligence. Following operations involving MI5, the police and many other partners, plots had been disrupted and terrorist suspects arrested in the UK. A significant number of those arrested have been charged with serious terrorist offences. They would appear before the courts in due course.[24]

By 2005, MI5 had started its expansion programme, which would increase its 2004 operational capability to 50 per cent by March 2008. The Service set about establishing a number of regional stations around Britain to work closely with police forces and establishing a Northern Operating Centre outside London.[25] With 67 per cent of its Net Resource Requirement devoted to counter-terrorism work, of which 23 per cent was allocated to Irish-related terrorism and 44 per cent to international terrorism these allocations were due to change in 2005–2006, when the total Net Resource Requirement was due to increase by 14 per cent above the 2004–2005 amount. The plans involved the counter-terrorism allocation rising to 69 per cent of the Net Resource Requirement, which was made up of 48 per cent for international and 21 per cent for Irish-related terrorism. The Irish-related allocation would increase further once the Security Service had been given the additional funding necessary to conduct the national security role in Northern Ireland.[26]

Alongside this there were a number of notable successes in the counter-terrorism field during this period. Between 11 September 2001 and 31 March 2007, forty-one individuals were convicted under the Terrorism Act and another 183 convicted of terrorist-related offences, including murder, illegal possession of firearms and explosives offences. In February 2002, Moinul Abedin was sentenced to twenty years' imprisonment after being convicted of making large amounts of detonators and the explosive HMTD in a Birmingham house; in April 2003, Leicester residents Brahim Benmerzouga and Baghdad Merziane were each sentenced to eleven years' imprisonment for their roles in fundraising for Al Qaeda and other extremist groups; in the same month 'Ricin plotter' Kamel Bourgass was convicted of the murder of PC Stephen Oake in Manchester and conspiracy to cause a public nuisance using explosives and the deadly poison ricin; and Saajit Badat was imprisoned for thirteen years following his admission that he had plotted with jailed shoe-bomber Richard Reid to destroy an airliner over the Atlantic.[27]

A Hindu convert to Islam, Dhiren Barot plotted to build a radioactive 'dirty bomb' and carry out a series of attacks in Britain. Barot's key plan, which he called the Gas Limos Project, was to commit mass murder by packing three limousines with propane gas cylinders and explosives and detonating the giant bombs in underground car parks beneath crowded buildings. He intended to follow those attacks with a 'synchronised' dirty bomb explosion designed to contaminate hundreds of people with radiation sickness and cause nationwide panic. Barot, aged thirty-four, from Willesden, north-west London, also admitted to planning a wave of 'no warning' attacks against buildings in the United States, including the headquarters of the World Bank and the New York Stock Exchange. Barot was arrested during a series of anti-terrorist raids in August 2004. Many of Barot's plans for attacks in Britain were written down in notebooks. In one he outlined a 'Rough Presentation for Gas Limos Project' which, he wrote, was 'the main cornerstone of a series of planned attacks'. Evidence from experts concluded that the dirty bomb would not have caused death but, if constructed to Barot's plan, would have spread enough radioactive material to make 500 people sick. There was no evidence that Barot had obtained money to finance his plot nor acquired any bombmaking materials or vehicles.[28]

Barot had written a book in 1999, about Kashmir, where he was believed to have had terrorist training, in which he advocated bringing 'interfering' Western countries to their knees through strategies including germ and chemical warfare. With the cover picture of an AK-47 rifle placed over a copy of the Koran, the 150-page *The Army of Madinah In Kashmir* was written by Barot under the alias Esa Al-Hindi. The book was published by an Islamic bookstore in Birmingham. Immediately below a quote from the Koran, Barot wrote: 'Great stealth is required. To attempt to bring any one of these interfering nations to its knees is a major task which undoubtedly takes a great deal of carefully coerced interaction. At the same time, do not be disheartened by those who would dare to brand you as terrorists, for perhaps you may even be proactive only as a show of power, minus civilian casualties.' He added: 'The Irish Republican Army (IRA) is a good example of what can be achieved through commitment, sacrifice and constancy – even if the means employed are a little outdated.' Describing his strategy of targeting Western countries on their home ground as 'Flank Protection', he believed that only Muslims living in those nations would succeed: 'For it is they, the locals, and not foreigners, who understand the language, culture, area and common practices of the enemy whom they coexist amongst'. Barot suggested creating 'a big enough problem on their home front, one that is destabilising enough to force them to sway their glances away from the Eastern Muslim world. For this, it would seem that the most favourable target would be the national economy of the western block.'

In Barot's opinion some Muslims were 'frightened to advance and take the initiative, afraid of being branded as terrorists'. After he quoted from the Koran he wrote: 'Terror works and that is why the believers are commanded to enforce it by Allah.' And: 'Whatever one does, it should be synchronised with other activities for more effective results.' Later in the book Barot hinted at some methods that might be used against the West, with a list of possible strategies: 'For the benefit of the reader, to end we outline some of the "stealthy" modern-day war stratagems, which are commonly used by the western world to bring others to their knees. An exploration of some of these avenues could well be long overdue.Ideological warfare, Psychological warfare, Economical warfare, Colonial warfare, Physical warfare, Drug warfare, Germ warfare, Chemical warfare, Sabotage warfare'.[29]

Barot's terrorist 'tradecraft' was so expert that police and intelligence surveillance teams lost him on a number of occasions as they tried to track his movements. When Barot was identified as a terror suspect in June 2004 it was not known that he was an Al Qaeda operative with nine years' training. But it soon became clear to those watching him that he was an experienced terrorist. Surveillance officers described Barot as being 'very aware'. He walked into a *cul de sac*, hid behind bins, checked behind himself and at a station did not commit himself to any train platform until the very last minute. Rarely did he spend more than one night at an address and when driving he used a number of different vehicles. Barot travelled extensively using false passports and bogus identities. Though Barot and his associates all had mobile phones they never used them to speak with each other. Instead they met in parks or by reservoirs, in shops or on street corners and carried on conversations in places where it was difficult to eavesdrop on or monitor them. They also set up Yahoo! e-mail accounts and used them to leave coded messages for one another. Barot used the logon 'kewl n kini' and two of his associates had the addresses 'nightwithkylie' and 'bridget jones diaries'. From these addresses coded messages were sent. The messages were written in the style of teenagers discussing music and television and using language and employing sexual references. On one occasion two alleged members of the terror cell drove from London to Swansea just to spend fifty minutes in an internet café. Among the messages intercepted was one that said: 'make sure u don't bring your friend, the one who loves listening 2 red hit chillie. u know i don't like her at all'. This was a reminder to the recipient to make sure that he was not followed to an arranged meeting point. While in cars there were instances when they drove around roundabouts more than once, drove 'illogical' routes to their destinations, sometimes turning back on themselves. They left junctions on motorways suddenly and vehicles used were, on occasions, parked some distance from their home addresses. When Barot was lost to his watchers the authorities decided to arrest him when he next appeared because they feared that whatever attack he was planning might be close to execution.[30] Barot was sentenced to life and told by a judge that he would serve a minimum of forty years before he would be considered for release.[31]

Another two Islamist extremists discussed crashing a British Airways flight with thirty suicide bombers on board. In a conversation bugged by MI5 officers during Operation CREVICE, one of them described an aircraft suicide attack as a 'good idea'. Omar Khyam, twenty-four, and Jawad Akbar, twenty-two, were arrested in March 2004 after surveillance by MI5. The pair talked about infiltrating utility companies and launching attacks on water, gas and power cables simultaneously, and also referred to a friend who had access to all areas at Gatwick airport. On one discussion, covertly recorded by the Security Service, at Akbar's flat in Uxbridge, West London, Khyam was heard to say: 'It's just ideas coming out. Like the last idea to hijack the plane, it's just an idea, we could have done it. Imagine you've got a plane, 300 people in it, you buy tickets for thirty brothers in there. They're massive brothers, you just crash the plane. You could do it easy, it's just an idea.' Akbar, a student at Brunel University, interrupted to say: 'Thirty brothers, to find thirty brothers willing to commit suicide is a big thing.' Khyam replied: 'If you spoke to some serious brothers, to the right people, you'd probably get it, bro.' In an apparent reference to the September 11 attacks, he continued: 'Thirty brothers on a British Airways flight got up – nineteen were split up in four planes. Thirty brothers on a plane, the beauty of it is they don't have to fly into a building, just crash the flipping thing.' Khyam was recorded as saying: 'If you do something in this country you are getting caught, trust me 100 per cent, don't even think about it that you will get away with it.' He added: 'If anything happens here all you lot are going down... It's a matter of time, something will get through.' At the end of the hour long conversation, Khyam asked: 'Do you think your room is monitored?' Akbar replied: 'Nah, do you think that? Do you know, I think we give them too much credit bruv.' In an earlier conversation Khyam refered to another man, Waheed Mahmood, who worked for a subcontractor of the power firm Transco, saying: 'I've got a rough idea what he wants to do.' Akbar replied: 'It's a lot more complicated and it's a beautiful plan.' Talking about simultaneous strikes, Akbar told Khyam that any operation would have to be 'big... destructive... and combined with something to make proper, proper effect and terror'. The pair also discussed poisoning water supplies, but this was dismissed by Akbar as a 'weak idea'.[32]

Omar Khyam, the ringleader of the so-called fertiliser bomb plot, was the grandson of a British Army colonel and the son of a wealthy businessman. He grew up in a comfortable middle class childhood in a secular household in the West Sussex commuter town of Crawley. Like many British schoolboys, 'he loved those twin pillars of English life – Manchester United and fish and chips.' Although his parents divorced, he was still part of a close family, studied hard at school and was 'mad about cricket' – a sport at which he excelled. According to some, he dreamed of playing for Sussex, or even England. Khyam's family claimed he had been 'brainwashed' at an impressionable age by religious extremists. Khyam became interested in radical Islam at a young age – several years before the conflicts in Afghanistan and Iraq. He was twenty-two at the time of his arrest in March 2004, and was already in the final stages of preparing a major Al Qaeda-inspired attack and had risen to become the leader of a terror plot designed to kill British civilians in nightclubs and shopping centres.

It was thought this transformation began when he was aged about fifteen when Khyam was becoming more and more interested in religion, particularly in 'the freedom of Muslim lands from occupation', as he would later put it. As a teenager, he attended a largely white secondary school, as opposed to the local school where there were many Asians. There he played football, was captain of the cricket team, had many non-Muslim friends and performed well in his GCSEs. After school, he went to study A-levels at East Surrey College apparently with the aim of going on to study for a university degree. But it was about this time that Khyam began to take a keen interest in the trouble between India and Pakistan and, on a 1999 visit to the family homeland of Pakistan, he spoke to members of groups active in the disputed Kashmir territory about the independence movement. Khyam had also been regularly worshipping at his local mosque and – without his family and friends being aware – he was attending meetings of the radical Islamic group al-Muhajiroun, led by the extremist cleric Omar Bakri Mohammed.

At the age of seventeen, while still at college, Khyam convinced his mother he was moving to France to continue his studies and left the family home. He even persuaded a friend to post a letter to her from France to keep up the pretence. But in reality, he had run away to the hills of Pakistan to join a militant training camp. The first the family knew was when he called them from Pakistan. Khyam told his trial that, while at the camp, he learnt 'everything I needed for guerrilla warfare in Kashmir', including weapons training in AK47s, pistols, rocket-propelled grenades (RPGs), and sniper rifles, climbing and crawling techniques and reconnaissance. In March 2000, after three months there, members of his family – some of whom were in Pakistani military intelligence – managed to trace him. He travelled back down from the mountains and was reunited with his grandfather.[33]

To provide the material for their explosives, the cell needed fertiliser. Anthony Garcia was chosen to buy fertiliser because he had paler skin than the others. He arrived at Bodle Brothers agricultural merchants in a customised Audi, rap music blaring, and asked for 600 kg of ammonium nitrate fertiliser for his allotment. John Stone, a salesman, was surprised by the request. It was winter, thought Stone, and the order was enough to cover five football pitches. Stone asked, sardonically, 'What do you want all that for?... Are you planning a bomb attack?' The unspoken answer was yes. The group had discussed attacking the Ministry of Sound nightclub, Bluewater shopping centre, a train, a pub and a list of synagogues. Months earlier, Garcia had also been among a group learning about weapons and explosives in Pakistan. Two accomplices learnt how to prepare ricin. Another arrived with digital scales for weighing ratios of ammonium nitrate to aluminium powder. Garcia had taught the others how to dismantle and reassemble weapons. The fertiliser was taken to Access Storage near Heathrow. When Khyam refused to answer questions about why he was paying £207 a month to store £90 worth of fertiliser, staff contacted police in February 2004, on the same day that Khyam collected an expert on detonators from Heathrow. The pair were heard talking about remote-controlled devices. They went to a key meeting the next day in Crawley. Five weeks passed before the gang were arrested. During this time they seemed 'surveillance sensitive' – executing U-turns en route to meetings, using multiple names and code words, disposing of laptop computers and changing mobile phones. Instead of sending e-mails, they saved draft messages and logged on with the same user names. They discussed targets, praised the Madrid train bombings that killed 200 people and mentioned wanting to do something 'sooner rather than later'. One suspect was recorded asking whether something was 'ready to go'.

On 30 March, officers from five forces arrested seven men and other alleged accomplices. Khyam, twenty-five, his brother Shujah Mahmood, twenty, their neighbours Jawad Akbar, twenty-three, and Waheed Mahmood, thirty-five, all from Crawley, Garcia, twenty-five, from Ilford, East London and Nabeel Hussain, twenty, a student from Horley, Surrey, were charged with conspiring to cause an explosion likely to endanger life. Khawaja was arrested in Canada. Detectives found aluminium powder in a biscuit tin behind the shed at Khyam's family home. He and Shujah Mahmood were charged with possessing the substance for the purposes of terrorism. Khyam, Garcia and Hussain were charged with possessing the fertiliser for the same intent. Both Shujah Mahmood and Nabeel Hussain were found not guilty of the conspiracy charge. Shujah was also found not guilty of possession of aluminium powder for terrorism and Hussain was cleared of possession of 600 kg of ammonium nitrate fertiliser for terrorism.

A week after the arrests, Mohammed Babar, an American Al Qaeda operative who trained with Khyam in Pakistan, was arrested in New York. He immediately 'crumbled', pleaded guilty to terrorist offences and agreed to give evidence in return for immunity from prosecution for the fertiliser plot. British officers flew to New York to interview Babar, who said he spent time in Pakistan preparing for jihad with fifteen to twenty 'brothers', mostly from Britain. He organised the training camp and visited Khyam in Britain. Babar told police that the fertiliser gang had experimented with ammonium nitrate explosions in Pakistan. He made police aware that dozens of British Muslim men were involved in jihad. The intelligence services struggled to keep track of the names uncovered by their investigations. They compiled a huge list of friends, relatives and contacts, many with multiple identities.

Accomplices included 'AD', who was sectioned under the Mental Health Act but escaped from hospital. He had been on the run since October. He attended a training camp in Pakistan alongside Khyam, turning up at the airport in his London Underground uniform. He was asked to carry out a suicide attack on the Tube but refused because he thought it would come to nothing. Two men from Luton – one who identified only as Q and the other who used the name Abu Munthir – played key roles in recruiting the Khyam cell. Both reported directly to Al Qaeda figures in Pakistan. Q, forty, worked as a taxi driver and was monitored. The surveillance operation on him led the authorities to Khyam. In 2003 Amin was asked by Q to help transmit money and equipment to Al Qaeda fighters in Pakistan. Q's home was searched but he was never arrested. Abu Munthir, arrested in Pakistan, received vital supplies and wanted to meet everyone involved in the fertiliser plot. Khyam sought his advice. He recommended multiple bombings on one day and provided vital details of how to make explosives. Some of the defendants and associates worked at Gatwick and discussed its levels of security, leading surveillance officers to fear that the airport could be attacked.[34] CREVICE was an outstanding success for the Security Service.

On 26 May 2005, JTAC reduced the UK threat level from SEVERE GENERAL to SUBSTANTIAL. The main reason given in the JTAC report for the reduction in the UK threat level was that there was no intelligence of a current credible plot to attack the UK at that time (i.e. a group with established capability and current intent). The report noted that the threat level had been maintained since August 2004 on the back of concerns, arising from intelligence and investigations, that attack planning 'might' be going on. At this time, however, there was no firm intelligence of attack planning. By May 2005 the investigative leads that had previously been a cause for concern had been followed up and discounted. JTAC concluded that the SEVERE GENERAL threat level could not be maintained in the absence of any suggestion (from credible intelligence or current investigations) of possible attack planning. According to the Director General there was also a belief, 'it turned out wrongly', that terrorist capability had been dented by the disruptions in 2004. The threat level was accordingly reduced to SUBSTANTIAL: 'We judge that at present there is not a group with both the current intent and the capability to attack the UK.'[35] However, JTAC also cautioned that 'SUBSTANTIAL indicates a continued high level of threat and that an attack might well be mounted without warning'. The JTAC report explained that intelligence continued to show activity in the UK which was of concern and noted that these networks could very quickly evolve from support to operational activity:

> The UK threat picture is not currently dominated by one particular network or threat. The threat from Al Qaeda (AQ) leadership directed plots has not gone away and events in Iraq are continuing to act as motivation and a focus of a range of terrorist related activity in the UK. However, many of our current concerns focus on the wide range and large number of extremist networks and individuals in the UK and individuals and groups that are inspired by, but only loosely affiliated to AQ, or are entirely autonomous. Some of these have the potential to plan UK attacks and it is also possible that

lone extremists or small groups could attempt lower-level attacks. While there remain many areas of concern, we judge that at present there is not a group with both the current intent AND the capability to attack the UK. We are therefore reducing the overall threat level for the UK to SUBSTANTIAL (Level 3). Readers are reminded that SUBSTANTIAL indicates a continued high level of threat and that an attack might well be mounted without warning.[36]

The complex nature of the threat from international terrorism, including from core Al Qaeda at one end and unaffiliated groups and individuals at the other, had been assessed. A three-tier model was introduced into JTAC assessments in early 2005 to describe the varying degrees of connection between targets and the Al Qaeda leadership: 'Tier 1' describing individuals or networks considered to have direct links with core Al Qaeda; 'Tier 2', individuals or networks more loosely affiliated with Al Qaeda; and 'Tier 3', those without any links to Al Qaeda who might be inspired by their ideology. In May 2005 JTAC judged that the majority of its concerns focused on individuals and groups from Tiers 2 and 3, who were only loosely affiliated to Al Qaeda or entirely separate (albeit with shared ideological beliefs). In the aftermath of 9/11, Agency concerns were focused on Al Qaeda networks, or 'Tier 1', and the possibility of attacks similar to those against the World Trade Center. This focus shifted, however, as more was learned and understood about the threat and its development within the UK. The group responsible for the Madrid bombings were assessed as belonging to 'Tier 3'. The majority of extremists in the UK were also currently assessed as belonging to 'Tier 3'.[37]

The possibility of British nationals becoming involved in Islamist terrorist activity against the UK, had been recognised prior to 7/7. In 2004 the JIC judged that over the next five years the UK would continue to face a threat from 'home-grown' as well as foreign terrorists. An understanding of the potential threat from British citizens, including those born and brought up in the UK, appeared to have developed over the period 2001–2005. The attempt by Richard Reid, the British shoe-bomber, to blow up a transatlantic flight in 2001 demonstrated this. But the judgements of the JIC in 2002 suggested attacks against the UK were felt more likely, at that time, to be conducted by terrorists entering from abroad than by British nationals resident in the UK. By early 2004 perceptions of the threat, and the threat itself, had changed. The possibility of attacks against the transport network had been recognised prior to 7/7. The London Underground was specifically recognised by the JIC as a potential target as far back as April 2003. 'Soft' targets (including transport networks and shopping centres) became identified as the most likely targets for Islamist terrorist groups in the UK from around April 2004, following the Madrid attacks and continued investigation of terrorist activity in the UK. This represented a shift in focus from 'hard' (i.e. well protected) targets such as Government and iconic buildings. The intelligence community had initially focused on these after the 9/11 attacks because of Al Qaeda's known aspirations to commit 'spectacular' attacks against high-profile or symbolic targets. JTAC, in May 2005, concluded that attacks on UK rail networks were high on the list of possible target options for terrorists and were likely to remain so. The report emphasised that terrorists were more likely to attack high-profile or iconic rail targets. It stated, however, that there was no intelligence to suggest that attacks on the rail infrastructure, the London Underground, or any part of the UK public transport infrastructure, were currently being planned.

MI5 and the other security forces were well aware that British citizens were capable of engaging in suicide attacks. In April 2005, a second shoe-bomber – Saajid Badat – was sentenced to thirteen years in jail for planning to blow up a passenger aircraft travelling from Europe to the United States in 2001. He was also a British national and was born and raised in the UK. Omar Sharif and Asif Hanif were two British citizens who attempted to conduct suicide attacks on a Tel Aviv bar in 2003. In June 2002 the JIC judged that loose networks of Islamist extremists capable of conducting suicide attacks were present in the UK and, in June 2005, that suicide techniques could become the preferred technique for extremist attacks elsewhere, following their impact in Iraq. The overall JIC assessment, however, was that suicide attacks were not likely and that they would not become the norm in Europe.[38]

But, on 7 July 2005, four British suicide bombers struck. Khan, Tanweer and Hussain left Leeds at 4 a.m. in a silver Nissan Micra. Lindsay, meanwhile, arrived at Luton rail station at 5 a.m.; the other three joined him at 6.51 a.m. All four then took a 7:48 a.m. Thameslink train to King's Cross, arriving around 8:30 a.m. before dispersing into the London Underground system. Khan and Tanweer took Circle Line trains, one heading east the other west. Lindsay boarded a southbound Piccadilly Line train. Hussain, it was believed, intended to bomb a Northern Line train but found the service suspended. Khan, Tanweer and Lindsay all set off their bombs around 8.50 a.m., while Hussain panicked and was evacuated from King's Cross station with thousands of other commuters. After making a series of frantic phone calls, Hussain boarded a No 30 bus and blew it up at 9.47 a.m., killing thirteen people. More than fifty people were killed by the attacks. The bombers had used a peroxide-based explosive to carry out the bombings. Two bottles of peroxide explosive encased in nails were found in a bag under the front passenger seat of a red Nissan Micra which three of the bombers had used to travel to Luton on the day of the attacks. In a video, Ayman al-Zawahri, second in command of Al Qaeda, said that it had been 'honoured to launch' the 'blessed' London attacks. He said the bombings were a response to British aggression against the Islamic world: 'The blessed London attack was one which Al Qaeda was honoured to launch against the British Crusader's arrogance and against the American Crusader aggression on the Islamic nation for 100 years'. It later emerged that three of the 7/7 suicide bombers visited London for a dummy run nine days before carrying out the attacks. The bombers, two of whom were carrying rucksacks, scouted the Underground system for three hours on June 28. CCTV pictures, found among 80,000 tapes collected by police, showed Khan, Tanweer and Lindsay travelling to London during the morning rush hour following the same route they used on 7 July.[39]

Mohammad Sidique Khan was born at St James's hospital in Leeds on 20th October 1974 to Tika Khan and his first wife, Mamida Begum. He was the youngest of four children, three boys and a girl. Tika was a foundry worker, already in his fifties, and one of the first Pakistanis to settle in Yorkshire. Soon after Sidique was born, the Khans moved to Tempest Road in Beeston. During the mid-1990s, he became interested in Wahhabi fundamentalism; 'this pitted him against his family's traditional approach to Islam'. The first time his brother, Gultasab, noticed his brother had become a Wahhabi was when he started praying differently – Wahhabis add extra hand gestures between prostrations. Sidique found that the traditional, community-run mosque on Hardy Street had nothing to offer him. They spoke and wrote in Urdu, and the only time they interacted with the younger Muslims was when they taught them to recite the Koran by rote – in Arabic. The Wahhabis, on the other hand, delivered sermons and printed publications in English. Sidique's Urdu was poor, so the only things on Islam he could read were Wahhabi-approved publications. 'A second source of friction between Sidique and his family was his determination to marry for love.' He met his future wife, Hasina Patel, at Leeds Metropolitan

University in 1997; Sidique was taking a one-year course to convert a business diploma from a local college into a degree, while Hasina was studying for a three year sociology degree. Her family was from India, and she was a Deobandi Muslim – a South Asian Wahhabi-linked movement directly opposed to the Khan family's traditionalist Barelvi convictions. Wahhabis 'reject all theological innovation since the life of Muhammad and his closest companions. Muslims, they say, should pay attention only to the holy book and the collected sayings and doings of Muhammad' while 'traditionalists will not hesitate to draw upon centuries of scholarly argument, evolution in Sharia law and changes in accepted Islamic practice'.

Sidique began his first efforts to recruit for jihad training in Afghanistan when he was in Manchester – there he worked with Omar Sharif and Asif Hanif. Sidique Khan was 'plugged into a wider Islamist network well before the Iraq war, and even before 9/11.' Back in Beeston he developed 'a solid reputation' as a youth worker among local young Pakistanis. Khan 'would spend three hours a night as a "detached worker... going out and talking to kids and gaining their trust so you can help them through various problems. Like a mentor"'. But, by late 2004, some youth workers began taking unregistered leave to Pakistan – among them Sidique.

Of the four bombers, Khan and Tanweer, the Aldgate bomber, were the closest. They were thought to have known each other since childhood. The brother of the eighteen-year-old Hasib Hussain, the bus bomber, played cricket with Tanweer when they were children. It was not known how Hussain met Khan, but from 2001 onwards Hussain was involved in local youth work projects. By late 2004, Khan was a regular visitor to the family home. Jermaine Lindsay, the one 7/7 bomber not from Beeston, (he was born in Jamaica and brought up in Huddersfield) was believed to have been introduced to Khan through his associations with the radical preacher Abdullah Al-Faisal, who twice preached in Beeston before being jailed in 2003 for inciting racial hatred. Lindsay, who was nineteen when he blew himself up, was in regular contact with Khan from late 2004.

Hassan Butt, a former recruiter for the British jihadi network explained that the reason radical Islamic movements in Britain were able to recruit thousands of young Muslims was that they have managed to exploit their identity problem. As a recruiter, Butt's 'most important job was to discover what his potential recruit identified with, and then to pick holes in it'. For example, if the potential recruit felt Pakistani, then Butt would focus upon the difficulty of being both

British and Pakistani. Butt and many other recruiters 'find this easy because they know what it is like.' Having lived in Britain all his life within a strongly Pakistani household, Butt felt neither British nor Pakistani:

> When I went to Pakistan... I was rejected. And when I came back to Britain, I never felt like I fitted in to the wider white British community. And you've got to remember that a lot of our parents didn't want us to fit into the British community... the Islamists they give you an identity... you don't need Pakistan or Britain. You can be anywhere in the world and this identity will stick with you and give you a sense of belonging... When you're cut off from your family... the jihadi network then becomes your family. It becomes your backbone and support... the moment he leaves his house in the morning, they're there until he returns to his house in the evening... If the network see a drug dealer or someone from a gang, they will not condemn him like the traditionalists and say 'oh brother haram, haram [forbidden].' What they'll try to do is to utilise his energy.

As Shiv Malik pointed out in a study of Khan's radicalisation, his Al Qaeda-produced video suicide note was only the first – about British foreign policy – that ever got played in the mainstream media. Part two, which made up three quarters of Khan's speech, was addressed to Muslims in Britain:

> Our so-called scholars today are content with their Toyotas and semi-detached houses. They seem to think that their responsibilities lie in pleasing the kufr instead of Allah. So they tell us ludicrous things, like you must obey the law of the land. Praise be God! How did we ever conquer lands in the past if we were to obey this law? By Allah these scholars will be brought to account, and if they fear the British government more than they fear Allah then they must desist in giving talks, lectures and passing fatwas, and they need to sit at home and leave the job to the real men, the true inheritors of the prophets.

Khan, in Malik's opinion, 'may have felt indignant about Western foreign policy, as many anti-war campaigners do, but that wasn't the reason he led a cell of young men to kill themselves and fifty-two London commuters. At the heart of this tragedy is a conflict between the first and subsequent generations of British Pakistanis – with many young people using Islamism as a kind of liberation theology to assert their right to choose how to live. It is a conflict between tradition and individuality, culture and religion, tribalism and universalism, passivity and action.'[40]

In the aftermath of the bombings, London was gripped by the fear that another attack was imminent. Two weeks later this fear became a reality when four more Islamists mounted an attempted copycat bombing on 21 July. This time the explosive devices failed to explode. The type of hydrogen peroxide explosive used on 7/7 and 21/7 had not been seen before in Britain. The concentration of the chapatti flour, hydrogen peroxide, nail polish remover and metal shrapnel failed to detonate because the consistency was wrong. A combination of poor scientific calculation, extremely warm weather and 'sheer good luck' meant the bombs failed to go off. The bombs had a series of flaws: the hydrogen peroxide concentration was not strong enough and the detonator was not powerful enough. After a nationwide manhunt, three of the bombers were captured; the fourth surfaced in Italy from whence he was extradited. Unlike the 7/7 bombers, the four would be martyrs had came to Britain as refugees from war-torn African nations and were turned by extremist clerics into suicide terrorists. Muktar Said Ibrahim, 29, Yassin Omar, 26, Ramzi Mohammed, 25, and Hussein Osman, 28, were found guilty by a jury of conspiracy to murder by detonating rucksack bombs on Tube trains at Oval, Warren Street and Shepherds Bush and on the top deck of a No 26 bus at Shoreditch. Their suicide mission failed only because of a single error by Ibrahim in making the hydrogen peroxide explosives. All four were young refugees from Somalia, Eritrea and Ethiopia who had sought safety in Britain. But they turned for religious guidance to a radical cleric Abu Hamza al-Masri.[41]

Ibrahim, the cell's leader, had arrived in Britain with his family in November 1990 as refugees from civil war in Eritrea. He left school in 1994 with two GCSEs, went to college in Harrow to study leisure and tourism but dropped out after less than a year, taking jobs as a waiter. He had fallen out with his family, was smoking cannabis heavily and sleeping on friends' floors and had already been in trouble with the police. In June 1993 he pleaded guilty to an indecent assault on a fifteen-year-old girl whom he had lured into an alleyway. Less than a year later Ibrahim and an accomplice robbed a seventy-seven-year-old woman late at night outside Southgate Underground station in North London. Their victim was pushed to the ground and had her bag snatched. Ibrahim was also part of a gang of North London youths who travelled to Hertfordshire to carry out a series of street robberies.

In one incident, in May 1995, five youths threatened two local men with a knife and a broken bottle and robbed them of a watch and an airgun. In January 1996, Ibrahim pleaded guilty at Wood Green Crown Court to the robbery of the elderly woman. He was jailed for three years. The following month he received a further two-year jail term for his involvement in the spate of street robberies. But, despite his criminal record, Ibrahim applied successfully for British citizenship in 2004 and was issued with a British passport. Between May 1995 and September 1998 Ibrahim was detained in various young offender institutions and prisons.

Ibrahim later claimed that he did not become a strict Muslim until 2003. He had studied the Koran, become reasonably proficient in Arabic and began to attend the mosque. In 2000, through mutual friends, he first met Yassin Hassan Omar, who was already espousing radical religious ideas. After a period in a probation hostel, Ibrahim got a housing association flat in Stoke Newington, North London, and was working on market stalls while claiming income support and housing benefit. He sublet his flat. The proceeds of a three-month let at the beginning of 2003 funded a trip to Sudan. When he returned, he told of having had jihad training and being taught how to fire rocket-propelled grenades. He and Omar often went to the mosque at Finsbury Park, in London, where Abu Hamza was based. Ibrahim met another of the July 21 plotters, Hussein Osman, at the mosque and at 'study circles' in East London, or Speakers' Corner at Hyde Park. In May 2004 they attended 'Islamic camps' in the Lake District – although they apparently believed they were in Scotland. Ibrahim, Osman, Ramzi Mohammed and Omar were, along with others, in fact training for jihad[42] and had been photographed by a covert police surveillance team in May 2004 – fourteen months before the attack. Omar, Mohammed and Osman were also present. In August that year, police cameras captured Ibrahim during disturbances outside the Finsbury Park mosque in North London. In February 2005 – five months before the bombing attempts – an arrest warrant was issued for Ibrahim when he failed to answer the assault charge. Police wrote to him twice saying: 'Come to us before we come to you.' He was not arrested, however, and Ibrahim returned from Pakistan in March 2005 and remained free to plan the 21/7 attacks.[43]

In the weeks and months after the 7/7 attacks MI5 were still in the dark over the background to the 7/7 bombing. An MI5 report, entitled 'London Attacks: the Emerging Picture', delivered in October, stated that some 'AQ (Al Qaeda) associations' were 'emerging'; but it also said 'there is no evidence yet of Al Qaeda involvement'. On the possible role of the Al Qaeda leadership, the report stated: 'We still have no insight into the degree... of command and control of the operation... How long the 7/7 attack had been planned remains unknown... We do not have any conclusive findings from forensic examinations of the group's bomb-making expertise.' The report concluded that 'we know little' about how the suspects operated. It emerged that some of the bombers had been to Pakistan but: 'We know little about what... the bombers did in Pakistan, when attack planning began, how and when the attackers were recruited, the extent of any external direction or assistance and the extent and role of any wider network.' JTAC reported: 'The last few weeks have seen few significant developments... and we are not that much further on in our assessment.' Referring to the MI5 codenames for both terror plots, the report stated: 'There is still no intelligence to link the Stepford (7 July) and Hat (21 July) attacks; we still do not know whether we are dealing with an orchestrated campaign or coincidental/copycat attacks. We do not know how, when and with whom the attack planning originated. And we still do not know what degree of external assistance either group had. While investigations are progressing, there remain significant gaps in our knowledge.'

The report stated that certain links between terrorist groups were 'plausible' and 'probably the most likely scenario'; and that it 'strongly suspects' one man's visit to Pakistan was relevant to one plot. Among the findings the report claimed that a network of 'Iraqi jihadis' was attempting to bring a terrorist campaign to Britain. MI5 was investigating a group of 'Al Qaeda facilitators' in the West Midlands. The men, led by a British citizen of Syrian origin, were believed to be trying to extend the insurgency in Iraq to Britain. The main West Midlands suspect had recruited at least one man to lead a terrorist cell and sent him to a terror camp in Pakistan for training. The suspect was connected to a number of extremist groups and networks, including Al Qaeda, as well as militant Kashmiri and North African groups: 'He has played a major role in facilitating support for the Iraq jihad.' The Security Service believed that he directed a second man, an Iraqi, who arranged a trip to a Pakistan training camp for the leader of a separate British terrorist cell. The camp, which the cell leader visited over three months in early 2005, might have been the same one where Mohammad Sidique Khan was trained. The report 'speculates' that both men may have been trained by Al Qaeda at the same time. The second member of the group was said to have arrived in Britain in autumn 2004. He worked on 'jihad support' until his arrest in January 2006 after intelligence suggested that he 'may have acquired weapons in support of some unspecified action in the UK'. He had been detained by immigration authorities pending his deportation to Iraq. MI5 believed the two men might have been working ultimately for another West Midlands-based suspect who had links to Al Qaeda in Pakistan.

MI5 originally concluded that the 7/7 gang had acted alone. The report suggested this view had changed, but with no certainty: 'There is a distinct possibility that the Stepford Four were not acting alone and that fellow accomplices are still at large.' The attacks were 'likely' to have been supported by Al Qaeda operatives in Pakistan, revealing that in May and June 2005, 'there were repeated phone calls from public telephone boxes in Pakistan to mobile telephones recovered at a "bomb factory" in Leeds' where the July 7 rucksack bombs were made. The gang's Pakistani contact 'is likely to have been providing support, advice and/or direction'. MI5 was investigating the significance of a training camp in northern Pakistan set up shortly after Tony Blair ordered British troops to join America in the invasion of Iraq. Khan – known to MI5 as MSK – went there along with other British terrorists in July 2003 for training: '(The camp) may have had a role in Stepford, encouraging MSK to turn his sights away from Afghanistan (his original intent) towards the UK.'[44]

In a separate report, John Scarlett, head of SIS, reported that one of the 21 July suspects was tracked on a trip to Pakistan just months before the attempted bombings. MI5 allowed the 21 July suspect to travel to Pakistan after he was detained and interviewed at a British airport. Once in Pakistan he was monitored by SIS. It stated: 'On the events of July itself, and the question of whether intelligence was missed, C [Scarlett] noted that SIS had previously been involved in an earlier investigation of one of the 21 July (suspects) in Pakistan. This had been at the Security Service (MI5)'s behest and should be discussed with MI5.' Scarlett conceded that his agency had reacted too slowly: 'Summing up the position before July 2005, C noted SIS were conscious of the size of the target, but equally conscious of what we did not know; we were thinly spread in North and East Africa; we were looking at new ways of increasing our reach; and we had sought funding to grow as fast as we thought feasible. Turning to the lessons learnt, C noted that SIS had understood the nature of the threat and that there was a great deal that we did not know. SIS had developed strategies to meet this threat. The attacks had shown that our strategies were correct, but needed to be implemented more extensively and more quickly.' Scarlett explained that even before the attacks, SIS had planned to expand overseas. 'C concluded by explaining how post-July SIS were speeding up implementation of the pre-July strategy.' He said the agency did not want more money for staff.[45]

Slowly a picture began to emerge of the bombers. It seemed that Ibrahim, had been in Pakistan in 2004–2005 at the same time as the 7/7 bombers Mohammad Sidique Khan and Shehzad Tanweer. In March 2005, Ibrahim returned from Pakistan, where he had been taught how to make hydrogen peroxide bombs. In Pakistan it appeared that Ibrahim was trained by the same men who had trained Mohammad Sidique Khan. Khan and Ibrahim were both in Pakistan in late 2004 to early 2005. Ibrahim returned to Britain with a mission statement that had been dictated to him by his trainers. Written in Arabic, it was found in a notebook with his fingerprints on it, and laid out the principles of his operation. This included 'a clear and defined goal' and 'realistic ambition' and were designed to achieve 'martyrdom in the path of God'.[46] The Al Qaeda connection was clear.

In the aftermath of the attacks, the intelligence apparatus – and MI5 in particular – came under scrutiny. There had obviously been a massive intelligence failure and the result was more than fifty people had lost their lives. A post-July assessment by JTAC explained that extremists in the UK had been thought less likely to carry out suicide attacks because long-term indoctrination in the UK was 'more difficult than in countries with larger extremist communities and a more pervasive Islamic culture'. Manningham-Buller admitted it was a 'surprise that the first big attack in the UK for ten years was a suicide attack'. On the earlier JIC judgement she said: 'I think it is a reasonable judgement that still stands. I do not think we expect these to be the norm.'[47] The speed of radicalisation of some of those involved in the attacks was also unexpected. According to Manningham-Buller, July showed that extremists could be created at any time through a very quick process. This meant that the window of opportunity for identifying and disrupting potential threats could be very small. Following the disruptions in 2004, a lot of work was undertaken on radicalisation in the UK by Government. This included detailed work by the Security Service which identified that 'there is no simple Islamist extremist profile in the UK and that the threat is as likely to come from those who appear well assimilated into mainstream UK society, with jobs and young families, as from those within socially or economically deprived sections of the community'. The July attacks emphasised that there was no clear profile of a British Islamist terrorist. The Chief of the Assessments Staff said there was a tendency prior to July to think in terms of ethnic groups and to describe, for example, South Asian or North African groupings as the source of the majority of extremist activity and the greatest cause for concern. The July attacks showed that it was probably wrong to think and describe the threat in such terms as the picture that emerged was diverse, including individuals of Pakistani and Jamaican origin among others.[48]

For Manningham-Buller the main lesson learned from the July attacks was the need to get into 'the unknowns' – to find ways of broadening coverage to pick up currently unknown terrorist activity or plots. MI5 and police efforts, prior to July, were focused on following up known intelligence leads in the UK, arising either out of other terrorist investigations, from GCHQ or the SIS, or from foreign intelligence reporting. Resources were fully consumed with the pursuit of existing leads and there was little capacity to look beyond to see where other threats might be developing. A crucial element in this was the relationship between MI5 and Special Branches throughout the country. While Special Branches remained an integral part of local police forces in the UK, they also recruited and ran agents in support of Security Service work and operations, and acted as a major extension to the Security Service intelligence collection capability. Their primary function as set out in the guidelines on Special Branches was 'covert intelligence work in relation to national security'. One of the problems, historically, in terms of MI5–police co-operation was that the vast majority of Special Branch work depends on the resources allocated by individual Chief Constables and the variation in resources available meant that not all Special Branches were able to provide an optimum level of support to the Security Service. The appointment of a National Co-ordinator of Special Branches in early 2004 to co-ordinate and promulgate Special Branch policy and to promote higher standards was an improvement. Despite this, there remained a lack of detail – in relation to targets and objectives – regarding police Counter-Terrorism work. Crucial, therefore, would be the role of the pre-7/7 planned MI5 regional offices in developing links with local Special Branches to enable the police and the Security Service together to build what was referred to as a 'rich picture' of extremist activity at the local level. Their goal was 'to become more proactive at identifying those who may be being groomed for terrorism, and those doing the grooming, and so to spot where terrorism may next occur'.[49]

By 2006 the Security Service had a presence in the Midlands, North East, North West, South, East and Scotland, which grew in 2006/07, while new offices were opened in the South East and Wales during this period. By 2008, regional stations housed three times the number of staff originally planned. Nine arrests in Birmingham, at the beginning of February 2007, were an example of where the regional capability of MI5 had helped police to carry out counter-terrorism operations. Manningham-Buller said during the case: 'It is clear to me that having an established station in [the West Midlands] that is able to work very closely with both the Special Branch and the CT (Counter Terror) unit in [the West Midlands] on this case is extremely helpful for co-ordination which involves also the Met. So having that sort of coordinating function... is of real value.'[50] On 10 October 2007, MI5 also assumed the lead role for national security in Northern Ireland (as part of the process of normalisation of policing and security with the rest of the UK). The Service's new headquarters in Belfast, known as Loughside, was part of the Service's regionalisation strategy and also provided an important contingency capability in the form of a back-up for MI5's HQ at Thames House.[51]

By March 2006, MI5 was allocating 53 per cent of its operational effort to international counter-terrorism (an increase of 11 per cent on the previous year), and 14 per cent to protective security (largely related to international counter-terrorism work). Subsequently, the Director General updated this, saying: 'We have agreed a package of measures that will increase [international counterterrorism investigator] to around 80 per cent of our total (currently 70 per cent) effort through the reallocation of over 100 existing and newly recruited staff. This will be achieved through a reduction in [other areas of] work... [which is not] welcome, but... its [terrorism's] strategic significance compels us to make hard choices...' The scale of the challenge MI5 was facing was summed up by the fact that the Service currently had around 200 networks – some 2,000 individuals – under investigation;[52] but as Manningham-Buller pointed out, 'there will be many we don't know' – who were actively engaged in plotting, or facilitating, terrorist acts in the UK and overseas.

The Director General recognised that the extremists were 'motivated by a sense of grievance and injustice driven by their interpretation of the history between the West and the Muslim world. This view is shared, in some degree, by a far wider constituency.' If the opinion polls conducted in the UK since July 2005 were only broadly accurate, 'over 100,000 of our citizens consider that the July 2005 attacks in London were justified'. What MI5 saw at the extreme end of the spectrum were resilient networks, some directed from Al Qaeda in

Pakistan, some more loosely inspired by it, planning attacks including mass casualty suicide attacks in the UK: 'Today we see the use of home-made improvised explosive devices; tomorrow's threat may include the use of chemicals, bacteriological agents, radioactive materials and even nuclear technology.' More and more people were moving from passive sympathy towards active terrorism through being radicalised or indoctrinated by friends, families, in organised training events in Britain and overseas, by images on television, through chat rooms and websites on the Internet. As in most terrorist campaigns, propaganda was a key element with Al Qaeda itself saying that 50 per cent of its war was conducted through the media. In Iraq, attacks were regularly videoed and the footage downloaded onto the internet within thirty minutes. Virtual media teams then edited the result, translated it into English and many other languages, and packaged it for a worldwide audience. 'And, chillingly, we see the results here, young teenagers being groomed to be suicide bombers.' MI5 were aware of numerous plots to kill people and to damage the British economy: 'What do I mean by numerous? Five? Ten? No, nearer thirty – that we know of.' These plots often had links back to Al Qaeda in Pakistan and through those links Al Qaeda gave guidance and training to its 'largely British foot soldiers' in the UK on an extensive and growing scale. Manningham-Buller also addressed the perception, held by many, that:

> My Service and the police have occasionally been accused of hype and lack of perspective or worse, of deliberately stirring up fear. It is difficult to argue that there are not worse problems facing us, for example climate change, and of course far more people are killed each year on the roads than die through terrorism. It is understandable that people are reluctant to accept assertions that do not always appear to be substantiated. It is right to be sceptical about intelligence... But just consider this. A terrorist spectacular would cost potentially thousands of lives and do major damage to the world economy. Imagine if a plot to bring down several passenger aircraft succeeded, thousands dead, major economic damage, disruption across the globe. And Al Qaeda is an organisation without restraint. There has been much speculation about what motivates young men and women to carry out acts of terrorism in the UK. My Service needs to understand the motivations behind terrorism to succeed in countering it, as far as that is possible. Al Qaeda has developed an ideology which claims that Islam is under attack, and needs to be defended. This is a powerful narrative that weaves together conflicts

from across the globe, presenting the West's response to varied and complex issues, from long-standing disputes such as Israel/Palestine and Kashmir to more recent events as evidence of an across-the-board determination to undermine and humiliate Islam worldwide. Afghanistan, the Balkans, Chechnya, Iraq, Israel/Palestine, Kashmir and Lebanon are regularly cited by those who advocate terrorist violence as illustrating what they allege is Western hostility to Islam. The video wills of British suicide bombers make it clear that they are motivated by perceived worldwide and long-standing injustices against Muslims; an extreme and minority interpretation of Islam promoted by some preachers and people of influence; and their interpretation as anti-Muslim of UK foreign policy, in particular the UK's involvement in Iraq and Afghanistan. Killing oneself and others in response is an attractive option for some citizens of this country and others around the world.

At the same time as she recognised these grievances, the Director General pointed out that that the first Al Qaeda-related plot against the UK was the one discovered and disrupted in November 2000 in Birmingham: 'Let there be no doubt about this: the international terrorist threat to this country is not new. It began before Iraq, before Afghanistan, and before 9/11.'

Manningham-Buller lamented that intelligence gathering and execution was not like that on the popular television series about MI5, 'Spooks', 'where everything is (a) knowable, and (b) soluble by six people'. But those whose plans that MI5 wished to detect in advance were determined to conceal from the Service what they intended to do. 'And every day they learn, from the mistakes of others, from what they discover of our capabilities from evidence presented in court and from leaks to the media.' MI5 was faced by acute and very difficult choices of prioritisation. 'We cannot focus on everything so we have to decide on a daily basis with the police and others where to focus our energies, whom to follow, whose telephone lines need listening to, which seized media needs to go to the top of the analytic pile. Because of the sheer scale of what we face (80 per cent increase in casework since January), the task is daunting. We won't always make the right choices. And we recognise we shall have scarce sympathy if we are unable to prevent one of our targets committing an atrocity.' This was despite an increase in staff, roughly 2,800 of them, (an increase of almost 50 per cent since 9/11, 25 per cent under thirty, over 6 per cent from ethnic minorities, with fifty-two languages and with links to well over 100 services worldwide), were working very hard, at some cost to their private lives and in some cases their safety, to do their utmost to collect the intelligence MI5 needed. The first challenge was to find those who would cause Britons harm, among the 60 million or so people who lived in the UK and the hundreds of thousands who visited each year. That was no easy task, particularly given the scale and speed of radicalisation and the age of some being radicalised. The next stage was to decide what action to take in response to that intelligence. 'Who are merely talking big, and who have real ambitions? Who have genuine aspirations to commit terrorism, but lack the know-how or materials? Who are the skilled and trained ones, who the amateurs? Where should we and the police focus our finite resources?'[53]

And MI5 proved itself once more when a Islamist cell, led by Parviz Khan, thirty-seven, who planned an Iraq-style kidnap and beheading of a British soldier taken from a Birmingham street, was broken up. Khan was the leader of a Birmingham-based cell which, for three years, had shipped equipment to insurgents in Afghanistan. In 2006 he developed a plan to kidnap a Muslim soldier serving in British Forces, video his beheading and broadcast it over the internet. MI5 placed a bug in his home, recording him speaking of cutting the soldier's head off 'like a pig', before burning the body and sending the video to Al Qaeda leaders based in Pakistan. Khan wanted to fight, but Al Qaeda leaders thought he was more useful to their cause buying equipment in Birmingham and sending it to fighters in and around the Afghanistan and Pakistan border. The cell bought gloves, video cameras, electronic equipment and laser rangefinders from shops in the West Midlands, and shipped them out to Pakistan where they would be used by those fighting British troops. Basiru Gassama, thirty, Mohammed Irfan, thirty-one, Hamid Elasmar, forty-four and Zahoor Iqbal, thirty, were also part of the group. Khan was sentenced to a minimum of fourteen years in jail.[54] The conversation recorded by MI5, between Parviz Khan (PK) and Basiru Gassama (BG), concerning the plot to behead a soldier was as follows:

PK: You have to, you want to go to Islamic countries, with, fight with kuffar [non-believers] against Muslims? OK, I have some brothers there. Maybe you, maybe some other brothers speak Arabic. We give like a (Bis), we give the judgment, well then cut it out/off like you cut a pig, man

BG: Would you wear this, man?

PK: Like that, I think you cut it out/off like you cut a pig. Then you put it on a stick and we say, this is to all Muslimee, man, we likes to, we want to join the kuffar army, this is what will happen to you. Then we throw the body, burn it, send the video to the chacha, the chacha can release it there. These people gonna go crazy. Didn't say the chacha, he do this in the other country he release it there. Where is the chacha? He could be next door, he could be upstairs, he could be downstairs. These people will go crazy, man.

BG: So what happens? True man.

PK: These people will go mad. This is what they call you will terrorise them, they will go crazy. They will start searching. Are they London, Birmingham, Newcastle, where are these people? They killed one of our soldiers in country. They've gone into countries, they're in our countries. They'll go crazy, Achi.

BG: True man.

PK: Then all these other people who slowly joining the British army, these Pakistani, these Afghan, these Gambia. They gonna say, no man, I don't want that. Look like, chop him up, man! We don't to join this army. At least we can stop them from doing the haram. We, first, we give them da'wa. Don't join the army, it is haram. Wait til you go into kuffar. They're not listening. So now we have to use force. Obviously, if they were insa'an they would listen to our word and listen to the.

BG: Well you know that's true man, brother, brother, man brother, this is please man, not.

PK: Achi, all I say to you is set it up. Even you don't have to do it yourself. How about that drug dealer, brothers. Not brothers, donkeys, I call them, because they're drug dealers, they will go with him, one day, they do deal, if you bring anything back. Then the next time you'll take him Broad Street, wine and dine and girl and things. After that they don't get friendly. Third time, I'm gonna say, Achi let's go for a meal, man. When they for a meal, they're sitting, they sit him down. And when they come out, or when they're eating the meal, that's when me and three, four brothers come in and say when you come out we, we, we give you a lift. But we don't give 'em a lift, we give him a lift to jahannama [hell]. Game over.

PK: That way nobody know. Then we don't, we've got enough places man. We just hang him up. We've got enough brothers own garages man. Night time, they're got a big shutters. Hang him up, man. Just bring the thing. The chef style, say bismillah, and let's do it, man.

BG: Inshallah.

PK: The first thing we need is his cards.

BG: His card.

PK: We need his card, and especially this card, we need his picture.

BG: What you need is, you know, his, his badge.

PK: They know these people, they have, eh, the link. Then they gonna go even more crazy.

BG: True man and that could, and that could make come and release the brother.[55]

By the time Jonathan Evans replaced Manningham-Buller as Director General, in 2007, the number of extremists that MI5 had to contend with had risen partly because the Security Service's coverage of the extremist networks was now more thorough; but it was also because there remained a steady flow of new recruits to the extremist cause. Terrorists, warned Evans, were methodically and intentionally targeting young people and children in the UK. They were radicalising, indoctrinating and grooming young, vulnerable people to carry out acts of terrorism – the Security Service had seen individuals as young as fifteen and sixteen implicated in terrorist-related activity. Another development from 2006 to 2007 had been the extent to which the conspiracies in Britain were being driven from an increasing range of overseas countries. Since 2003 much of the command, control and inspiration for attack planning in the UK had derived from Al Qaeda's remaining core leadership in the tribal areas of Pakistan; but worryingly, MI5 had seen similar processes emerging elsewhere: Al Qaeda in Iraq aspired to promote terrorist attacks outside Iraq; there was training activity and terrorist planning in East Africa – particularly in Somalia – which was focused on the UK; and the extension of what Evans called called the 'Al Qaeda franchise' to other groups in other countries – notably in Algeria – had created a significant upsurge in terrorist violence in these countries. It was no coincidence that the first suicide bombing in Algeria followed the creation of the new 'Al Qaeda in the Lands of the Islamic Maghreb'. This sort of extension of the Al Qaeda brand to new parts of the Middle East and beyond posed a further threat to the UK because it provided Al Qaeda with access to new centres of support which it could motivate and exploit. Faced with a generation-long threat, Evans – as someone with experience in the Long War in Ireland – pointed out that:

the work of the intelligence and security agencies will not be enough. We will do our utmost to hold back the physical threat of attacks, but alone, this is merely containment. Long-term resolution requires identifying and addressing the root causes of the problem. This is not a job only for the intelligence agencies and police. It requires a collective effort in which Government, faith communities and wider civil society have an important part to play. And it starts with rejection of the violent extremist ideology across society – although issues of identity, relative deprivation and social integration also form important parts of the backdrop.

This will not, however, happen overnight. I have been directly engaged in work against this violent extremist threat for most of the last decade, and I believe that terrorism inspired by it is likely to dominate the work of my Service well into the future.

And here is an important point. We know that the strategic thinking of our enemies is long-term. But public discourse in the UK works to a much shorter timescale whether the electoral cycle or the media deadline. We cannot view this challenge in such timescales. If we only react tactically while our enemies plan strategically, we shall be hard put to win this. A key part of our strategy must be perseverance.

Again, as with his predecessor, Evans warned that intelligence 'will rarely provide a complete picture. It gives us pieces of a whole, which then require assessment and interpretation. It helps improve our chances of success. And as we have seen in more than 200 terrorist convictions in the UK since 9/11, it does save lives. But it will not in itself provide certainty.' There was, however, a further difficulty in relation to intelligence work against the current threat, and it was one that Evans thought had led to a degree of misunderstanding about MI5's work. The networks the Security Service investigated were not the hard-edged cells typical of some other terrorist groups. Even though it might only be a handful of people who actually carried out a violent attack, it was now rare to see extremist groups acting entirely in isolation:

So the deeper we investigate, the more we know about the networks. And the more we know, the greater the likelihood that, when an attack or attempted attack does occur, my Service will have some information on at least one of the perpetrators. And in a sense this is a benefit. Why? First, because it means we can move more swiftly from intelligence to arrests. It means we can provide an informed assessment for the police, emergency services and Government, of the context of an attack, the likely depth of the conspiracy, and most importantly, the potential leads to follow to ensure that culprits can be arrested. And second, it demonstrates how the counter-terrorist net that the British intelligence community and our liaison partners have strung across the globe is working.

But we cannot know everything. There will be instances when individuals come to the notice of the Security Service or the police but then subsequently carry out acts of terrorism. This is inevitable. Every decision to investigate someone entails a decision not to investigate someone else. Knowing of somebody is not the same as knowing all about somebody. And it would be perverse for my Service to avoid knowing of somebody for fear of being held to blame if they later become involved in an attack. I think we should be very careful to bear this in mind when talking about so-called 'intelligence failures'.[56]

But with success came the uncomfortable reality of gaps in the intelligence picture: in the summer of 2007 two men drove a Cherokee Jeep into Glasgow Airport attempting to cause an explosion and kill civilians. Witnesses said that, after the Jeep was stopped by security bollards, Kafeel Ahmed appeared to smile as he doused himself with petrol before setting himself alight while crying 'Allah'. With 90 per cent burns Ahmed later died in the Royal Infirmary in Glasgow. The attack came just two days after the discovery of two Mercedes packed with propane and nails in London's West End – the two incidents were believed to be connected. Ahmed was a doctor of technology who studied at the Anglia Ruskin University with interests in aerodynamic design, electronic maps and inkjet cartridges, producing a seminal paper on the latter subject. Ahmed was thought to be an associate of Abbas Boutrab, an Al Qaeda explosives expert in Maghaberry prison, County Antrim. Boutrab lived in Northern Ireland between 2001 and 2004 while studying at Queen's University for an M.Phil. in aeronautical engineering. The Algerian-born terrorist was convicted at Belfast Crown Court in 2004 for possessing information likely to be of use to terrorists. These included instructions on how to build bombs that could destroy airliners. In 2006 Boutrab built a home-made bomb while in prison.[57] Ahmed was the latest in a succession of well-educated men drawn into Islamist terrorism. This seemed to mystify observers. Few it seemed, noticed that none of these educated terrorists appeared to have a schooling background in humanities.

However it was the failures rather than the successes that continued to cast a shadow over the Security Service: it was on Evans's patch that, following the conviction of the CREVICE terrorists in court, in 2007, it was revealed that MI5 actually had two of the 7/7 bombers under watch – but decided they were not priority targets. This was devastating news for the families who had loved ones killed or injured in the attacks. In addition to the men charged in connection with the fertiliser plot, fifty-five people had been identified as worthy of follow-up investigations. They were divided into 'essential targets' and 'desirable targets'. Mohammad Sidique Khan and Shehzad Tanweer were placed in the lower category. This decision was taken despite the intelligence agenices being aware that the two men had met Omar Khyam, the leader of the fertiliser plot, on five occasions in the weeks when he was engaged in the final stages of planning. Khan and Tanweer were followed driving with the bomb plotters and observed taking anti-surveillance precautions. Their car was followed from the South East to West Yorkshire where Khan, who was driving, stopped in Beeston, and then drove to his own home in Dewsbury.

Several of Khan's conversations with Omar Khyam were recorded by MI5. One transcript comprised two pages of discussion of financial crime, but eight pages about terrorist training and travelling overseas to pursue jihad. In one extract Khan asked Khyam: 'Are you really a terrorist, eh?' Khyam: 'They're working with us.' Khan: 'You're serious, you are basically.' Khyam: 'No, I'm not a terrorist but they are working through us.' Khan: 'Who are? There's no one higher than you.' Later, Khyam offered Khan some advice about obeying the Al Qaeda leaders at training camps. Khyam: 'The only thing, one thing I will advise you, yeah, is total obedience to whoever your emir [leader] is... up there you can get your head cut off.'

Khan and Tanweer were also captured on surveillance talking to Khyam and on their own at an M1 service station. During 2004 a number of surveillance pictures was sent to the US to be shown to terrorist detainees. One of those was Mohammed Junaid Babar, who had met Khan (whom he knew as Ibrahim) in Pakistan in 2003. Babar had pleaded guilty to terrorist offences but agreed to become a supergrass witness to avoid a seventy-year prison term. Initially, during the CREVICE trial, it was suggested that the pictures were of such poor quality that they were not sent to the United States and thus never shown to Babar. As the trial progressed the suggestion was that Scotland Yard, not MI5, had sent the pictures to the FBI. Babar had not recognised Khan/Ibrahim. Scotland Yard, on the other hand, were suggesting that it was MI5 that continued investigations into 'peripheral' targets.[58]

As a result of the fallout from the CREVICE trial revelations, Jonathan Evans was forced to take the unusual step of defending his officers who had monitored Khan and Tanweer. He claimed that the Service 'has never been complacent... The attack on 7 July in London was a terrible event... The sense of disappointment, felt across the service, at not being able to prevent the attack, despite our efforts to prevent all such atrocities, will always be with us.'[59] MI5 also argued that 'even with the benefit of hindsight, it would have been impossible from the available intelligence to conclude that either Khan or Tanweer posed a terrorist threat to the British public'. Khan and Tanweer were 'never identified during the fertiliser plot investigation because they were not involved in the planned attacks'. Rather, they appeared as petty fraudsters in loose contact with members of the plot. 'There was no indication that they were involved in planning any kind of terrorist attack in the UK.' The key point here was the emphasis on the lack of evidence relating to a forthcoming UK attack. The intelligence leads generated by the investigation into the July 7 bombings enabled MI5 and police to go back over the fertiliser plot records and put names to voices and faces. MI5 argued that it was the scale of intelligence gathering involved in CREVICE that 'meant switching resources from other less urgent investigations. It also meant making judgements on a daily basis about where to concentrate resources based on who presented the greatest threat to the UK public.' It was in the investigation of this conspiracy that Khan and Tanweer first came to the Security Service's attention as unidentified individuals on the periphery of the plot. 'To give an idea of scale, the links between the fertiliser plot bombers and Khan and Tanweer represent less than 0.1 per cent of all the links on record in relation to the fertiliser plot investigation.'

It was during February and March 2004, stated MI5, that 'an unknown man subsequently identified as Khan' met with members of the fertiliser plot on five occasions. He was accompanied by another unknown man, subsequently identified as Tanweer, on three of these occasions. The meetings took place in Crawley, the home of several of the fertiliser plot conspirators. There was 'no indication as a result of the intelligence available at the time on these meetings that either Khan or Tanweer were involved in terrorist plotting'. These meetings appeared to centre on the raising of money. Conversations recorded Khan and Tanweer discussing how to raise cash through a variety of fraud scams, such as purchasing building equipment on credit, defaulting on payment and selling the goods on for cash. There was no record of Khan and Tanweer discussing terrorist activity or bomb building. MI5 did record another conversation involving an individual identified after 7 July as Khan. From the context of the recorded conversation it was possible 'that Khan was talking about going to fight with militia groups in the Pakistani border areas.'

Follow-up investigations in 2004 into the unidentified men on the periphery of the fertiliser plot included the circulation of photographs to foreign intelligence services in an attempt to identify these individuals. Photographs of Khan were shown to two detainees who had provided the earlier information, but without a positive result. If Khan had been recognised, the Security Service 'might have allocated more resources to investigating him. However, given the operational priorities at the time, there is no guarantee that Khan would have been seen as a high priority target even then. In the event, the investigation was put on hold due to the need to focus on far more urgent cases posing potential large-scale threats to life.'

Following the atrocities of 7/7, MI5 and police undertook a large-scale investigation into the perpetrators of the attacks. It was only at this point that the identities of Khan and Tanweer 'became clear'. Painstaking analysis of surveillance records following the attacks, in order to determine what – if anything – of the bombers was known to the Security Service and police prior to 7/7, revealed their presence on the periphery of the fertiliser plot. Examination of Khan's telephone records showed his contact with Omar Khyam. This, along with a subsequent review of surveillance photographs taken during the fertiliser plot investigations, confirmed his presence in meetings with Khyam and others during February/March 2004.[60]

In reality it is likely that MI5's claim that the sheer pressure on resources was the key reason the Sercuity Service failed to focus on Khan and Tanweer. But this merely masks the fact the MI5 – and all the Agencies involved in counter-terrorism, including the police – were playing catch up because they fundamentally misunderstood the nature of the threat posed by Islamists. Whatever the circumstances of the tactical decisions taken during CREVICE, more revealing was the fact that a strategic error was committed, by MI5 and Special Branch, years before. At the centre of this mistake was the almost comical figure of Abu Hamza al-Masri. But Abu Hamza was far from the comic figure many of the tabloids protrayed him as. Born Mostafa Kamel Mostafa in Alexandria, Egypt, on 15 April, 1958, Abu Hamza was the son of a naval officer and a primary school headmistress. After studying civil engineering, he left for Britain in 1979, where he initially found work as a nightclub bouncer in Soho. In 1980, he met and married an Englishwoman, Valerie Traverso, who complained later that he had become increasingly radicalised during their marriage. When the couple divorced in 1984, Abu Hamza kept custody of their son, Muhammed. He remarried the following year, eventually fathering seven more children, and was granted British citizenship in 1986, on the basis of his previous marriage. His radicalisation appears to have been influenced by world events: the Iranian revolution and the Soviet invasion of Afghanistan. The 'apparent turning point' for Abu Hamza came in 1987 when he met Abdullah Azzam, the founder of the mujahidin resistance against the Soviets, on a pilgrimage to Mecca. He emigrated to Afghanistan in 1991, where, he claimed, he lost his arms and an eye in a landmine explosion in 1993, after which he returned to Britain. Hamza journeyed to Bosnia towards the end of the Balkan wars to joint the Arab mujahidin there. He first came to prominence in the British Muslim community when he started preaching at a mosque in Luton in 1996, moving to Finsbury Park mosque the following year. He was arrested in 1999 over alleged bomb plots in Yemen, for which his son received a three-year sentence in Yemen. But Abu Hamza was never charged. He was suspended from the mosque in 2002 after a Charity Commission investigation, but carried on preaching there until it was closed down after the police raid in January 2003. After that, he took his sermons to the streets outside. He was arrested on a American extradition warrant in 2004 with the United States stating that it wanted to charge him for facilitating terrorism and trying to set up a terrorist training camp in Oregon.[61]

In the meantime it was alleged that MI5 judged Abu Hamza a 'clown' who had the right to express himself, according to Reda Hassaine, an Algerian who claimed he was paid by MI5 to spy inside the Finsbury Park mosque in North London. Hassaine's handler, whom he knew only as 'Steve', told him that Hamza and other militants had the right to a roof over their heads in Britain, even if they had carried out murders in other countries. Hassaine was an agent for MI5 and Special Branch for sixteen months from July 1999 to November 2000, a period when Hamza was in control of the mosque. Hassaine alleged MI5 told him that it was 'not interested' in prosecuting Hamza for such offences: 'I told them Abu Hamza was brainwashing people and sending them to terrorist training camps in Afghanistan, that he was preaching jihad and murder and that he was involved in the provision of false passports. I told them he was a chief terrorist... The MI5 officer told me Abu Hamza was harmless and that MI5 thought he was a clown.' Hassaine said he even offered to wear a small camera and recording device while he was inside the mosque talking to Hamza and fellow militants. 'They told me not to bother, that they weren't interested.'[62] Hassaine, who certainly had a grievance against MI5, signed no contract with the Security Service but claimed that he was promised that the authorities would provide him with the safety and protection of British citizenship.[63] The irony that Abu Hamza successfully secured British citzenship while Hassaine did not was not lost on the Algerian.

Scotland Yard had investigated Abu Hamza's activities on a number of occasions and had sent files of evidence to the Crown Prosecution Service in March 1999 and June 2003. Both files related to allegations that Hamza was connected to the kidnapping in the Yemen in 1998 of sixteen Western tourists, during which three Britons died. However, the evidence was judged to be 'clearly insufficient' to support a successful prosecution. Only when Scotland Yard submitted a third file, in June 2004, did the CPS decide it had sufficient evidence to prosecute. This had only occurred following a police raid on Abu Hamza's home in west London the previous May after the United States applied for his extradition. It was the 'overwhelming bulk' of material seized in May 2004 that was used in evidence at Hamza's Old Bailey trial. By then Mohammad Sidique Khan, Shehzad Tanweer and Jermaine Lindsay had, personally, heard Abu Hamza call on Muslims to kill unbelievers in the name of Islam. Khan and Tanweer heard the sermons inside the North London mosque while they and Lindsay were also among crowds that heard Abu Hamza preach on the street after the building was closed in a police raid in 2003.[64] When police raided the mosque in January 2003, they found an array of terrorist paraphernalia, including nuclear, biological and chemical protective suits, blank firing weapons, a stun gun and a CS canister. Abu Hamza argued that police had first arrested him in 1999 and taken away hundreds of tapes including an eleven-volume encyclopaedia. He said that the tapes' contents were very similar to those which formed the bulk of the prosecution's case seven years later.[65]

Hamza contended, in court, that suicide bombing was a legitimate tool of war, regarded by religious scholars as 'the highest form of martyrdom'. He condoned suicide attacks if they were the only way that Muslims had of defending themselves: 'If it is the only way of preventing the enemies of Islam or resisting oppression, then that would be your only tactic of war. It is as if a woman was being raped – are you telling her, don't use the scissors? Use what is available to you.' An example of when suicide attacks would be appropriate, said Abu Hamza, was when Palestinian villagers were faced with Israeli tanks and bulldozers and could legitimately use such tactics: 'You cannot condemn the suicide bombing if you allow the Apache [helicopter] bombing at the same time.' Respected authorities had ruled that suicide bombs were a lawful and elevated form of martyrdom, he claimed. But he denied that when he spoke about suicide bombings he was encouraging his audience to take part in such actions. He said that none of his sermons was intended to exhort his followers to commit acts of violence in Britain. Nor, he claimed, had he read the alleged terrorist manual that was found in a raid on his West London home and he had no idea that it referred to Big Ben and the Eiffel Tower as potential targets. *The Encyclopaedia of the Afghani Jihad* had been a gift from the mujahidin when he was working as a civil engineer in Afghanistan. 'I am not a military man,' he said, explaining why he had not read the 11-volume publication. 'Look at it, it is in very good condition. It is not used, it has not been opened.' In fact it had been 'seized from me in 1999, returned nine months later and seized again in 2004. The condition of it suggests that it has only been opened by the security services. The first I heard that Big Ben was mentioned in it was in this court. I have many books, I kept it as a piece of history.' Hamza also pointed out that the book was produced by veterans of the Afghan war against the Soviet Union, which had been encouraged by America and the West, reviving for Muslims the notion of physical jihad.[66]

Abu Hamza also claimed that Special Branch officers once told him that he could say what he liked so long as there was no blood on the streets. Asked if he had urged listeners to kill abroad, he said: 'In the concept of murder, no. In the concept of fighting, yes.' He described lengthy meetings with MI5 officers and police between 1997 and 2000, in which he was warned that his sermons were taking him close to the edge of the law. 'They said, "We think you are walking on a tightrope"… They said: "You say things sometimes we don't like".' During another meeting with Special Branch officers, however, Hamza said that they had appeared unconcerned by his preachings. 'They said: "You have freedom of speech, we don't have to worry as long as we don't see blood on the streets".' He said that police had seized the documents when they searched his house in 1999, but later returned them. When they searched his property again in May 2004 they did not remove the documents, the court heard.[67] The jury, however, did not believe him: in 2006, Abu Hamza al-Masri was jailed for seven years after being found guilty of inciting his followers to kill non-believers. He was convicted of eleven of fifteen charges of using his influence as a spiritual leader of the Muslim community in North London to become, in the words of the prosecution, 'a recruiting sergeant for terrorism'. He was also convicted on a final charge, under section 58 of the Terrorism Act, of possessing a document, the *Encyclopaedia Of Afghani Jihad*, which was described as a manual for terrorism. It included a dedication to Usama bin Laden and a passage suggesting a list of potential targets including skyscrapers, the Eiffel Tower and Big Ben.[68] But, by then, the damage had been done. The failure to take action against the cleric allowed him to preach his message of jihad to three of the suicide bombers. This may not, of course, been the decisive experience in their road to 7/7 but it did appear to illustrate MI5's failure – indeed the entire security apparatus's failure – to understand what they were dealing with. Having said this, the Security Service produced an effective response. But the unpalatable truth is that no counter-espionage or Counter-Terrorism service is infallible. As Dame Eliza Manningham-Buller reflected in the wake of the 7/7 bombings:

Could we, could others, could the police have done better? Could we with greater effort, greater imagination, have stopped it? We knew there were risks we were running. We were trying very hard and very fast to enhance our capacity, but even with the wisdom of hindsight I think it is unlikely that we would have done so, with the resources available to us at the time and the other demands placed upon us. I think that position will remain in the foreseeable future. We will continue to stop most of them, but we will not stop all of them.[69]

9

Reflections

In the century since its creation, MI5 has had to adapt to a number of different opponents. Its successes and failures have been down to the men and women who have constituted that organisation; for at heart MI5 is a human organisation vulnerable to the inspirations, genius and failings of the relatively small number of men and even smaller number of (senior) women, who shaped and created its policies. In its first three decades one man, Sir Vernon Kell, impressed his personality and prejudices upon the Service. The organisation was shaped in his own image. He exaggerated its success during the First World War and completely overestimated the German threat before that war. Yet his misjudgement of the haphazard German espionage campaign against the United Kingdom was as much a justification for the SSB he headed as a criticism of him, for there was a German threat (however limited) and the fact that Kell was unaware of the true nature of that threat suggests that a counter-espionage service was long overdue. Kell and the British were playing catch-up with other countries. He established a reliable system for co-operating with the police, compiling a vital registry and pushing for competent legislation. The fundamental principles he established remained the same.

Kell was, however economical with the truth about the 'one powerful blow' MI5 supposedly delivered to Germany at the beginning of 1914; a 'lie' repeated when the very survival of MI5 was an issue. This remained the situation until 1931 when the Security Service, as it became, succeeded in taking over all anti-subversion activities from the police. It should be remembered however, that 'proof in intelligence terms is not necessarily the same level of proof accepted by a court or commissioner'. At the heart of Kell's fight to see his Service survive was the crippling factor of finance, or lack of it. MI5 was chronically under-financed. Only in time of war did the Service enjoy the full extent of resources required, the rest of the time it struggled along, acutely short of both money and personnel. Considering the task it faced in confronting Soviet Communism, MI5 did reasonably well in the inter-war period. No counter-espionage service will catch every spy; and given the lack of resources MI5 experienced, any decision, such as the political decision to raid Arcos in 1927 and the consequent loss of British Intelligence's opening into the heart of Soviet espionage in Britain, could prove catastrophic in the long-term. And this one did.

The Soviets changed tack and it was very difficult to achieve anything like the same penetration of an enemy that had learned from its mistakes. In this, partly, lay the disasters of the 1950s; and, partly, it was the blind spot of class.

It was said that Kell did not recruit Roman Catholics (apart, it seems, from William Melville): this may, or may not, have had something to do with his marriage to the Anglo-Irish Constance. However, it is more likely that he already had an aversion to the influence of the Roman Church, an institution that was considered by many Protestants in Great Britain, during the Home Rule era, to be a temporal as well as a spiritual organisation that claimed from its flock an allegiance that transcended the allegiances of nation state and class. It is, therefore, somewhat ironic that it was precisely such a temporal and spiritual manifestation that transcended national and class loyalty which exposed Kell's policy of recruiting from a particular class of men. The appeal of Communism with its offer of a New Jerusalem on earth, had the exterior visage of a secular religion. This was what appealed to traitors, such as Blunt, who had been drawn from the very class and background that Kell perceived as the most independent and patriotic. This failure to understand the pan-class appeal of Communism extended to other, brilliant, MI5 officers such as Guy Liddell and Dick White too.

It can also be said that the most difficult opponents that MI5 has faced over a century have had similar characteristics to Communism. It is merely that MI5 has forgotten this: in the present century Islamist terrorism again demonstrates the appeal of an ideology that, like Communism, appeals across national, state and class boundaries. Similarly, if MI5 was more institutionally aware of its past, it may not have so badly misjudged Islamist preachers and fundraisers in Britain prior to 9/11 and 7/7 if it had referred to how it had previously dealt with religious fanaticism in the form of Zionist terrorism. While foreign policy is undoubtedly a factor in religious terrorism, whether in 1948 or 2009, religious belief as a key underlying factor is crucial. Without this potent ingredient there would be no Zionists and no Islamists.

However, by the time the modern Security Service faced the new variety, it had long forgotten how dangerous religion as a rallying cause could be: in Northern Ireland, although compromising two religiously ethnic groups, one of those (the *de facto* Catholic IRA) focused on its war against the British state in Ireland and saw this campaign in territorial nationalist, not religious terms. The battle against Irish terrorism had more in common with the fight against

German espionage than Islamist terrorism. Both German espionage and Irish terrorism were rooted in a comparatively easy conceptual framework: that of loyalty to the idea of the nation.

MI5's record in World War Two was simply outstanding. It more than justified its existence in the XX deception plans; rarely has deception worked so well since the Trojan Horse. However, at the outbreak of war the Service had been teetering at the point of collapse. In 1940 no one could have predicted the dramatic turn around in MI5's fortunes. The key point of counter-espionage is that it is a slow burner. When considering how, in contrast, MI5's record in the Cold War was a mixed one, perhaps it should be remembered that the ebb and flow of espionage and counter-espionage is what should be expected in a conflict with a sophisticated enemy. The Service faced a determined enemy whose greatest successes were the result of decisions made before the Cold War emerged. MI5's record after the damage of the Cambridge spy ring was revealed holds comparison with other intelligence agencies. What was most damaging, however, was the paranoia in some quarters that the Soviets had penetrated even deeper into the Establishment. Despite all of this, surely the most important fact is that MI5 finished on the winning side without damaging the liberties of the individual in any significant manner and helped preserve Parliamentary democracy.

To do this the Security Service actively targeted Marxists or Trotskyists who were committed to overthrowing the sovereignty of Parliament through extra-Parliamentary action. The extent of MI5's monitoring of groups, such as CND or trade unionist activitsts, remains controversial. However it was in Ireland that the whole question of how far MI5, alongside other British Intelligence agencies, should go in combating subversion and terrorism, is raised.

The British victory against the IRA was a long time coming – and despite many concerns relating to the appeasement of terrorists it is clear that the Republican Movement suffered a significant strategic defeat. The British state contained the IRA militarily and it was the intelligence aspect of the campaign that was absolutely critical in achieving this. But this took decades to emerge. Again this was because British Intelligence – and MI5 – failed to learn the lessons of the past: the greatest handicap that the British faced during the Anglo-Irish War of 1919–1921 was the absence of a single intelligence machine to confront the enemy. The same thing happened all over again with the Long War from 1970. But with the Long War came the Dirty War and the question of just how far should an intelligence service go to protect its long-term penetration agents? To be effective they have to burrow deep into terrorist organisations. And if blown too early no great value could be derived from them. But what, then, does an MI5 financed or run agent have to do to maintain that cover? Must it be inevitable that the law must be broken? All states have the capacity to engage in repression. The key point is whether the checks and balances of a liberal democracy – the rule of law, the conscience of individuals and even institutional intolerance of abuse is enough. British state collusion with Loyalist targeting of Republicans in Northern Ireland is balanced with state investigations that exposed it. Sometimes it is not always so – but in the end it was covert intelligence that was key in winning the Irish war.

MI5 will continue to make errors of judgement. That is inevitable. And this may cost lives. But it will continue to have successes that only a select few will know about until some future historian reveals them. And MI5 will continue to be embroiled in controversy between the rights of the individual and the security of the state, for that, as its motto states, is its very reason for existing: *Regnum Defende* – Defend the Realm.

Select Bibliography

The National Archives

CAB – Cabinet Office
DEFE – Ministry of Defence
FO – Foreign Office
KV – Security Service
WO – War Office

Imperial War Museum
Lady Constance Kell Memoir
Sir Vernon Kell Diary

Bloody Sunday Inquiry
Witness Statements

Northern Ireland Political Collection
British Government–IRA exchanges

Secondary Sources
Christopher Andrew, *Her Majesty's Secret Service: The Making of the British Intelligence Community* (Viking 1987).
Christopher Andrew & Oleg Gordievsky, *KGB: The Inside Story* (Harper 1991).
Christopher Andrew Vasili Mitrokhin, *The Mitrokhin Archive: The KGB in Europe and the West* (Penguin 1999).
Christopher Andrew Vasili Mitrokhin, *The Mitrokhin Archive II: The KGB and the World* (Penguin 2005).
Tom Bower, *The Perfect English Spy: Sir Dick White and the Secret War 1935–90*.
John Bulloch, *The Origin and History of the British Counter-espionage Service MI5* (Corgi 1963).
Jason Burke, *Al Qaeda: The True Story of Radical Islam* (Penguin 2007).
Bryan Clough, *State Secrets: the Kent-Wolkoff Affair* (Hideaway Publications Ltd 2005).
Eamon Collins & Mick McGovern, *Killing Rage* (Granta Books 1998).
Andrew Cook, *M: MI5's First Spymaster* (Tempus 2006).
Philip Davies, *MI6 and the Machinery of Spying* (Routledge 2004).
Richard Deacon, *'C'. A Biography of Sir Maurice Oldfield* (London 1985).
Kevin Fulton, *Unsung Hero* (John Blake 2008).
Peter Hennessy, *The Secret State: Whitehall and the Cold War* (Penguin 2003).
Mark Hollingsworth and Nick Fielding, *Defending the Realm: Inside MI5 and the War on Terrorism* (Andre Deutsch 2003).
Oliver Hoare (ed), *Camp 020: MI5 and the Nazi Spies* (The National Archives 2000).
Ed Husain, *The Islamist: Why I joined radical Islam in Britain, what I saw inside and why I left* (Penguin 2007).
Martin Ingram & Greg Harkin, *Stakeknife: Britain's Secret Agents in Ireland* (O'Brien Press 2004).
Alan Judd, *The Quest for 'C': Mansfield Cumming and the Founding of the Secret Service* (Harper Collins 1999.
David Leigh, *The Wilson Plot: How the Spycatchers and Their American Allies Tried to Overthrow the British Government* (Pantheon 1988).
Ben Macintyre, *Agent Zigzag: The True Wartime Story of Eddie Chapman: Lover,*

Traitor, Hero, Spy (Bloomsbury 2007).

J.C.Masterman, *On the Chariot Wheel: An Autobiography.*

J.C.Masterman, *The Double-Cross System.*

Anthony Masters, *The Man Who Was 'M': The Life of Maxwell Knight* (Basil Blackwell 1984).

Joan Miller, *One Girl's War: Personal Exploits in MI5's Most Secret Station* (Brandon 1986).

Sean O'Callaghan, *The Informer* (Corgi 1999).

Sean O'Neill & Daniel McGrory, *The Suicide Factory: Abu Hamza and the Finsbury Park Mosque* (Harper 2006).

Melanie Philips, *Londonistan: How How Britain Is Creating a Terror State Within* (Gibson Square 2006).

Juan Pujol & Nigel West, *Garbo: The Personal Story of the Most Successful Double Agent Ever* (Grafton 1986).

James Rennie, *The Operators: On the Streets with Britain's Most Secret Service* (Leo Cooper Ltd 2004).

Stella Rimington, *Open Secret: The Autobiography of the Former Director General of MI5* (Arrow 2002).

Michael Smith, *The Spying Game. The Secret history of British Espionage* (Simon & Schuster 2002).

Peter Taylor, *The Guardian*, March 18 2008

Mark Urban, *Big Boys' Rules: SAS and the Secret Struggle Against the IRA* (Faber and Faber 2001).

Nigel West, *MI5: British Security Service Operations, 1909–45* (Triad 1983).

Nigel West, *A Matter of Trust: MI5, 1945–72* (Coronet 1987).

Nigel West, *MI6: British Secret Intelligence Service Operations, 1909–45* (Grafton 1985).

Nigel West, *The Crown Jewels: The British Secrets at the Heart of the KGB's Archives.*

Nigel West, *Mask: MI5's Penetration of the Communist Party of Great Britain.*

Lawrence Wright, *The Looming Tower: Al Qaeda's Road to 9/11 (Penguin 2007).*

Peter Wright with Paul Greengrass, *Spycatcher: The Candid Autobiography of a Senior Intelligence Officer* (Viking 1987).

Notes

Chapter 1
1. KV 4/2.
2. KV 4/197, Report on "CHEESE" alias "LAMBERT" alias "EMILE" alias "ROBERTO".
3. KV 4/197 Notes on Special Section Cases
4. KV 4/197, Summary CHEESE by Captain C.H. Roberts Special Section SIME, 19 February 1943.
5. KV 4/197, Notes on Special Section Cases.

Chapter 2
1. KV 3/67, The Zionist Problem Today, 13 August 1943.
2. KV 3/41, Present Trends in Zionism.
3. KV 3/67, The Zionist Problem Today, 13 August 1943.
4. KV 5/29, GOC Palestine and Transjordan to War Office, 12 February 1942.
5. KV 3/67, The Zionist Problem Today, 13 August 1943.
6. KV 5/29, Extract made... on 23 /2/42.
7. KV 5/29, Palestine Jewish Illegal Forces, 18 March 1942.
8. KV 5/29, Extract from *The Times*, 24 April 1942.
9. KV 5/29, Copy of letter to the Colonial Office from Chief Secretary's Office, Jerusalem, 23 September 1943.
10. KV 5/29, Defence Security Office, Palestine and Transjordan SIME GHQ Middle East, 19 July 1944.
11. KV 5/29, Extract from Security Summary Middle East, no. 181.
12. KV 5/29, Extract from Fortnightly Intelligence Summary no. 86, Defence Security Office... Palestine, dated 27/8/44.
13, KV 5/29, The Stern Gang and the IZL. Views held in the Jewish Agency. Harrington to the Colonial Office, 28 January 1945.
14. KV 5/29, Petrie to Maxwell, nd.
15. KV 5/29, Stern Group, 15 February 1946.
16. KV 5/29, Liddell to Cannering, 14 February 1946.
17. KV 5/29, General Sir A Cunningham to Secretary of State for the Colonies, 26th April 1946.
18. KV 5/29, Extract from DSO Palestine and Transjordan report re HAGANA.
19. KV 3/67, The Zionist Problem Today, 13 August 1943.
20. KV 3/41, Notes on the Security Situation in Palestine with particular reference to counter-terrorism and illegal immigration, 27 March 1947.
21. KV 3/41, Zionist subversive activities, 16 March 1948.

Chapter 3
1. Bower, op.cit. p.75.
2. DNB, Anthony Simkins, rev. Sept.2004.
3. Bower, op.cit. p.76.
4. Ibid. p.138.
5. Ibid. p.77.
6. Ibid. p.76.
7. Ibid. p.77.
8. DNB, Anthony Simkins, rev. Sept.2004.

9. Bower, op.cit. p.78.

10. *The Times*, 23 March 1946.

11. KV.2/2212, Extract from the Report of the Royal Commission on Allan Nunn MAY, February 5 1946.

12. KV.2/2212, Statement by Igor GOUZENKO, 14th March, 1946.

13. KV.2/2212, Extract from the Report of the Royal Commission on Allan Nunn MAY, February 5 1946.

14. KV.2/2212, Statement by Igor GOUZENKO, 14th March, 1946.

15. KV.2/2209, MacDonald to Cadogan, 10 September 1945.

16. KV.2/2209, Second Telegram MacDonald to Cadogan, 10 September 1945

17. KV.2/2209 Extract from RCMP report on the CORBY Case, 13 September 1945.

18. Bower, op.cit. pp.79-80.

19. KV.2/2209, CXG.288, 12 September 1945.

20. KV.2/2209, CXG. B24, 14 September 1945.

21. KV.2/2209, CXG. 310, 14 September 1945.

22. KV.2/2210, Agenda re May.

23. KV.2/2210, Marriott note, 4 October 1945.

24. KV.2/2210, Telegram CXG 908, 4 October 1945.

25. KV.2/2210, Telegram CXG 909.

26. KV.2/2210, CXG 910.

27. KV.2/2210, Note, 6 October 1945.

28. KV.2/2210, Re: Dr Allan Nunn May, and possible "Meet" with another. 8 October 1945.

29. KV.2/2212, Special Branch statement.

30. KV.2/2212, Extract from the Report of the Royal Commission on Allan Nunn May, February 5 1946.

31. Bower, op.cit. pp.86-88.

32. KV 4/204, The Civil Service 'Purge' Procedure.

33. KV 4/204, Lea to Hollis, 21 May 1948.

34. Bower, op.cit. pp.89-91.

35. Ibid. p.85.

Chapter 4

1. KV 2/1264, The Case of Dr Klaus Fuchs, 2 March 1950.

2. KV 2/1245, Chief Constable to Kell, 5 November 1934.

3. KV 2/1264, The Case of Dr Klaus Fuchs, 2 March 1950.

4. KV 2/1245, Minute, 8 October 1941.

5. KV 2/1245, Minute, 18 October 1941.

6. KV 2/1245, Minute, 28 May 1942.

7. KV 2/1245, Minute, 6 May 1942.

8. KV 2 1245, Minute, 30 May 1942.

9. KV 2/1264, The Case of Dr Klaus Fuchs, 2 March 1950.

10. KV 2/1245, Minute, 30 August 1943.

11. KV 2/1245, Chief Constable to Petrie.

12. KV 2/1245, Minute, 22 November 1943.

13. KV 2/1245, Minute, 30 August 1943.

14. KV 2/1264, The Case of Dr Klaus Fuchs, 2 March 1950.

15. KV 2/1245, Minute, 10 October 1946.

16. KV 2/1263, Statement of Henry Arnold, Wing Commander RAF (retired).

17. KV 2/1263, Statement of Henry

Arnold, Wing Commander, RAF (Retired).

18. KV 2/1245, Minute, 15 October 1946.

19. KV 2/1245, Minute, 13 November 1946.

20. KV 2/1245, Minute, 19 November 1946.

21. KV 2/1245, Minute, 26 November 1946.

22. KV 2/1245, Minute, 27 November 1946.

23. KV 2/1245, Minute, 12 December 1946.

24. KV 2/1245, Minute, 20 December 1946.

25. KV 2/1245, Minute, 2 April 1947.

26. KV 2/1245, Minute, 24 November 1947.

27. KV 2/1245, Minute, 10 December 1947.

28. KV 2/1245, Report of Visit to AERE Harwell on 18th March 1948, by Lt. Col. J.A. Collard.

29. KV 2/1246, Appendix 'C', Difficulties presented by the investigation into the case of Emil Julius Klaus FUCHS.

30. KV 2/1246, J.C. Robertson minute, 7 September 1949.

31. KV 2/1246, Klaus Fuchs Further Investigation Plan.

32. KV 2/1246, Investigation into the Activities of Emil Julius Klaus FUCHS.

33. KV 2/1245, Visit to Harwell on 14/15.9.49.

34. KV 2/1245, Fuchs Investigation Progress Report, 16.9.49.

35. KV 2/1246, Visit of W/Cdr. Arnold, 26.9.49.

36. KV 2/1246, Investigation into the

Activities of Emil Julius Klaus FUCHS.

37. KV 2/1246, Visit of W/Cdr. Arnold, 26.9.49.

38. KV 2/1264, The Case of Dr Klaus Fuchs, 2 March 1950.

39. KV 2/1263, Statement of Henry Arnold, Wing Commander, RAF (Retired).

40. KV 2/1264, The Case of Dr Klaus Fuchs, 2 March 1950.

41. KV 2/1263, Fuchs First Interview, 22 December 1949.

42. KV 2/1263, Statement of William James Skardon, 4 February 1950.

43. KV 2/1263, Fuchs First Interview, 22 December 1949.

44. KV 2/1263, Fuchs Second Interview, 2 January 1950.

45. Bower, op.cit. pp.95-96.

46. KV 2/1263, Statement of Sir John Douglas Cockcroft, CBE., FRS, 30 January 1950.

47. KV 2/1250, J.H. Marriott minute, 13 January 1950.

48. KV 2/1263, Fuchs Third Interview, 18 January 1950.

49. KV 2/1250, Sillitoe to Rowlands, 19 January 1950.

50. KV 2/1250, Robertson note, 23 January 1950.

51. KV 2/1263, Statement of Henry Arnold, Wing Commander, RAF (Retired).

52. KV 2/1263, Fourth, Fifth, Sixth and Seventh Interviews, 31 January 1950.

53. KV 2/1263, Statement of Henry Arnold, Wing Commander, RAF (Retired).

54. KV 2/1263, Fourth, Fifth, Sixth and Seventh Interviews, 31 January 1950.

55. KV 2/1263, Emil Julius Klaus Fuchs,

27 January 1950.

56. KV2/1263, Fourth, Fifth, Sixth and Seventh Interviews, 31 January 1950.

57. KV2/1263, Statement of Michael Willcox Perrin. Deputy Controller Atomic Energy (Technical Policy) Ministry of Supply, 31 January 1963.

58. Bower, op.cit. p.96.

59. KV 2/1263, MI5 Report on Emil Julius Klaus FUCHS.

60. KV 2/1263, Note, 31 January 1950.

61. KV 2/1263, Metropolitan Police Special Branch, 13 February 1950.

62. KV 2/1264, 7 March 1950.

Chapter 5

1. Bower, op.cit. p.98.

2. Ibid. p.97.

3. Ibid. p.101.

4. KV 2/1888, Note, nd.

5. KV 2/1888, Note on the DDG's interview with the Prime Minister, 23 October 1950.

6. KV 2/1888, Letter to Hollis, 13 November 1950.

7. KV 2/1888, Note, nd.

8. KV 2/1888, Note of meeting between Sillitoe and Prime Minister, 1 November 1950.

9. Bower, op.cit. pp.102-103.

10. DNB, Robert Cecil. rev.

11. Bower, op.cit. pp.104-107.

12. DNB, Sheila Kerr.

13. DNB, Nigel Clive.

14. Bower, op.cit. pp.133-135.

15. The Times, 4 May 1961.

16. The Times, 26 April 1963.

17. Peter Wright with Paul Greengrass, Spycatcher, (hereafter Wright), pp.214-215.

18. DNB, Sheila Kerr.

19. Peter Hennessy, 'Professor Blunt describes double life as MI5 man and Soviet agent', The Times, November 21, 1979.

20. DNB, Michael Kitson, rev. Miranda Carter.

21. Peter Hennessy, 'Professor Blunt describes double life as MI5 man and Soviet agent', The Times 21 November 1979.

22. Bower, op.cit. pp.107-108.

23. Ibid. pp.1.

Chapter 6

1. Stella Rimington, Open Secret. The Autobiography of the Former Director General of MI5, pp.92-93.

2. Ibid. pp.101-103.

3. Ibid. op.cit. pp.116-118.

4. DNB, Peter Martland, Sept 2004.

5. Wright, op.cit. pp.187-189.

6. Ibid, pp.280-283.

7. DNB, Eunan O'Halpin, Sept 2004.

8. Bower, op.cit. p.146.

9. The Times, 6 November 1973.

10. Wright, op.cit. pp.286-291.

11. DNB, Marc B. Davis, Sept 2004.

12. Wright, op.cit. pp.298-299.

13. Ibid. p.302.

14. Ibid, pp.338-341.

15. Wright, op.cit. pp.362-368.

16. Christopher Warman, The Times, 5 November 1968.

17. A.M. Rendel, The Times, 25 September 1971.

18. Rimington, op.cit. pp.120-121.

19. DNB, Michael Kitson, rev.Miranda Carter.

20. DNB, Peter Martland.

21. The Times, 18 July 1984.

22. The Times, 19 July 1984

23. Rimington, op.cit. pp.160-161.

24. Ibid. p.163.

25. Ibid, pp.189-190.

26. MI5., Website.

27. DNB, Peter Martland.

28. Rimington, op.cit. p.180.

29. *Daily Telegraph*, 23 August 2001.

30. Rimington, op.cit. pp.180-181.

Chapter 7

1. Kevin Fulton with Jim Nally and Ian Gallagher, *Unsung Hero*.

2. Operation BANNER, para.101.

3. Ibid. paras.105-107.

4. DEFE 25/304, Northern Ireland – Ministerial Meeting, 27 April 1971.

5. DEFE 25/304, Northern Ireland Intelligence Arrangements, April 1971, JIC (A) 23.

6. Peter Taylor, *The Guardian*, 18 March 2008.

7. Powell, op.cit.

8. Taylor, *The Guardian*, op.cit.

9. *Irish Times*, 17 February 1992.

10. Gerry Adams, *Free Ireland: Towards a Lasting Peace (Dublin 1995)*, p.209.

11. *Irish News*, 27 July 1992.

12. Eamon Mallies and David McKittrick, *The Fight for Peace: The Secret Story Behind the Irish Peace Process* (London 1996), pp.246-248.

13. LHLNIPC Messages Between the IRA and the Government, 29 November 1993.

14. LHLNIPC Messages Between the IRA and the Government. British Message sent 26 February 1993.

15. LHLNIPC Messages Between the IRA and the Government. Message from the leadership of the Provisional Movement, 5 March 1993.

16. LHLNIPC Messages Between the IRA and the Government: British message sent 11 March 1993

17. LHLNIPC Messages Between the IRA and the Government British. 9-paragraph note, sent on 19 March 1993.

18. LHLNIPC Messages Between the IRA and the Government. Speaking note accompanying the 9-paragraph British side sent on 19 March 1993.

19. Peter Taylor, *The Guardian*, op.cit.

20. LHLNIPC Messages Between the IRA and the Government.Message from the leadership of the Republican Movement, 22 March 1993.

21. Peter Taylor, *The Guardian*, op.cit.

22. LHLNIPC Setting the Record Straight. Sinn Fein's 'April' document: Sinn Fein's basis for entering dialogue.

23. LHLNIPC Messages Between the IRA and the Government. British message sent on 5 May 1993.

24. LHLNIPC Messages Between the IRA and the Government. British message of 7 May 1993.

25. LHLNIPC Messages Between the IRA and the Government. Message from the leadership of the Provisional Movement of 10 May 1993.

26. LHLNIPC Setting the Record Straight. July 17 1993. British Government message to Sinn Fein.

27. LHLNIPC Setting the Record Straight. August 14 1993. Sinn Fein message to British Government.

28. LHLNIPC Setting the Record Straight. September 1 1993. British Government message to Sinn Fein.

29. LHLNIPC Setting the Record Straight. November 5 1993. British

government message to Sinn Fein.

30. LHLNIPC Messages Between the IRA and the Government, 29 November 1993.

31. Peter Taylor, *The Guardian*, op.cit.

32. David Leppard, *The Sunday Times*, 16 January 2005. MI5 boss admits bugging Adams.

33. Henry McDonald, *The Guardian*, 9 Febraury 2008.

34. Henry McDonald, *The Observer*, 9 September 2007.

35. Liam Clarke, *The Sunday Times*, 18 December 2005. Focus: The spy at the heart of the IRA.

36. Henry McDonald, *The Observer*, 9 September 2007.

37. David Lister and Ian Cobain, *The Times*, 16 May 2003. 'Stakeknife' gets benefit of doubt from Sinn Fein.

38. *The Sunday Times*, 18 May, 2003. All the bluff and counter-bluff in fingering Freddie.

39. Greg Harkin and Martin Ingram, *Stakeknife: Britain's Secret Agents in Ireland*, (O'Brien Press).

40. Liam Clarke, *The Sunday Times*, 18 March, 2007. New MI5 chief named in probe over murder of policewoman.

41. Edna Leahy, *The Sunday Times*, 19 March 2006. MI5 'helped IRA buy bomb parts in US'.

Chapter 8

1. Security Service Act, 1989.

2. Intelligence and Security Committee Annual Report 1997–1998, Cm 4073 preface.

3. Ibid. paras.47-49.

4. Ibid. paras.41-46.

5. Ibid. Cm 4073, paras.16-17.

6. Intelligence and Security Committee Annual Report 1999–2000, Cm 4897 para.16.

7. Intelligence and Security Committee Annual Report 2001–2002, Cm 5542 paras.66-69.

8. Ibid. paras.71-72.

9. Ibid. paras.18-21.

10. Intelligence and Security Committee Annual Report 2004–2005, Cm 6510 paras.10-12.

11. Transcript of the Lecture by the Director General of the Security Service, Eliza Manningham-Buller, at the Royal United Services Institute (Rusi) Conference, "The Oversight of Intelligence and Security", 17 June 2003.

12. Intelligence and Security Committee Inquiry into Intelligence, Assessments and Advice prior to the Terrorist Bombings on Bali, 12 October 2002, Cm 5724 para.1.

13. Ibid. paras.7-9.

14, Ibid. 18-21.

15. Ibid. paras.42-44.

16. Transcript of the James Smart Lecture by the Director General of the Security Service, Eliza Manningham-Buller, City Of London Police Headquarters, 16 October 2003.

17. Intelligence and Security Committee Annual Report 2003–2004, Cm 6240 paras.92-93.

18. Ibid. paras.97-98.

19. Intelligence and Security Committee Report into the London Terrorist Attacks on 7 July 2005, para.65.

20. Intelligence and Security Committee Annual Report 2003–2004, Cm 6240 paras.8-9.

21. Ibid. para.15.

22. Ibid. para.38.

23. Ibid. paras.73-74.

24. Speech by the Director General of the Security Service, Dame Eliza Manningham-Buller, at the CBI Annual Conference 2004, Birmingham, 8 November 2004.

25. Intelligence and Security Committee Annual Report 2004–2005, Cm 6510 para.23.

26. Ibid. Cm 6510 para.28.

27. MI5 website.

28. Sean O'Neill, The Times, October 13, 2006 'Dirty bomb' mastermind plotted wave of atrocities across Britain.

29. The Times, 7 November 2006, Barot's guide to terrorism.

30. Sean O'Neill and Adam Fresco, The Times, 7 November 2006. He switched trains and cars to throw secret agents off his tail.

31. Adam Fresco, The Times, 7 November 2006, Al Qaeda plotter sentenced to life.

32. Nicola Woolcock, The Times, 'Suicide plan to crash BA flight' was heard by MI5, 17 June 2006.

33. The Times, 30 April 2007.

34. Nicola Woolcock, The Times, 30 April 2007. How police and MI5 foiled 'Britain's 9/11'.

35. Intelligence and Security Committee Report into the London Terrorist Attacks on 7 July 2005, para.68-69.

36. Ibid. para.82.

37. Ibid. para.98-101.

38. Ibid. paras.91-95.

39. Sam Knight, The Times, 20 September 2005, July 7 bombers rehearsed suicide attacks.

40. Shiv Malik, Prospect, June 2007.

41. David Brown, The Times, 19 April 2008. 'I told FBI about ringleader before 7/7 bombings says Al Qaeda man.'

42. Sean O'Neill, The Times. 10 July 2007. Muktar Said Ibrahim: From robbery and indecent assault to bomb plot leader'

43. David Brown, The Times, 19 April 2008. 'I told FBI about ringleader before 7/7 bombings, says Al Qaeda man.'

44. David Leppard, The Sunday Times, 29 January 2006. MI5 admits: 'We've run out of leads on bombers.'

45. David Leppard, The Sunday Times, 26 February 2006. 'MI5 rebels expose Tube bomb cover-up.'

46. David Brown, The Times, 19 April 2008. 'I told FBI about ringleader before 7/7 bombings, says Al Qaeda man.'

47. Intelligence and Security Committee Report into the London Terrorist Attacks on 7 July 2005, para.100.

48. Ibid. paras.104-106.

49. Ibid. paras.129-134.

50. Intelligence and Security Committee Annual Report 2006–2007, Cm 7299 para.28.

51. Ibid. Cm 7299, para.26.

52. Ibid. 2006–2007, Cm 7299, para.18.

53. Speech by the Director General of the Security Service, Dame Eliza Manningham-Buller, at Queen Marys College, London, 9 November 2006.

54. Vikram Dodd, The Guardian, 19 February 2008, 'Life sentence for the extremist who plotted to murder soldier.'

55. Vikram Dodd, The Guardian, 18 February 2008, 'They'll say they killed

one of our soldiers. These people will go crazy.'

56. Address to the Society of Editors by the Director General of the Security Service, Jonathan Evans, The Society of Editors' 'A Matter of Trust' conference, Radisson Edwardian Hotel, Manchester, 5 November 2007.

57. Jamie Doward, Mark Townsend and Henry McDonald, The Observer, 8 July 2007. The making of a new terror.

58. Sean O'Neill, The Times, 2 May 2007, 'MI5 still might have case to answer.'

59. David Batty, The Guardian, 30 April 2007. 'MI5 chief denies complacency over July 7 bombers.'

60. MI5 Website.

61. Philippe Naughton, The Times, 7 February 2006. Profile: Abu Hamza.

62. David Leppard, The Sunday Times, 12 February 2006. 'Agent says MI5 dismissed Hamza as "harmless clown".'

63. Sean O'Neill, The Times, 29 November 2007. 'Informant who risked his life to fight extremists "betrayed by MI5".'

64. Sam Knight, The Times, 8 February 2006. 'Police defend Hamza inquiry as blame game begins.'

65. Simon Freeman, The Times, 7 February 2006. 'Abu Hamza jailed for seven years for inciting murder.'

66. Sean O'Neill, The Times, 21 January 2006. 'Suicide bombing is a legitimate tactic, Abu Hamza tells court.'

67 Jenny Booth, 'Abu Hamza: "Special Branch said I had freedom of speech".'

68. Simon Freeman, The Times, 7 February 2006. 'Abu Hamza jailed for seven years for inciting murder.'

69. Intelligence and Security Committee Report into the London Terrorist Attacks on 7 July 2005, para.144.

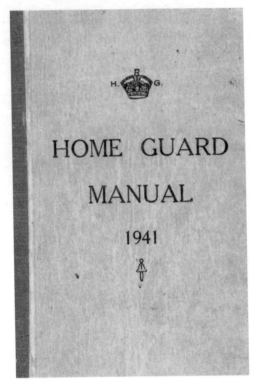

Also available from Amberley Publishing

A fabulous slice of wartime nostalgia, a facsimile edition of the propaganda booklet issued following victory in the Battle of Britain

First published in 1941, *The Battle of Britain* was a propaganda booklet issued by the Ministry of Information to capitalise on the success of the RAF in defeating the Luftwaffe. An amazing period piece, hundreds of thousands of copies were printed and sold for 6d and it became one of the year's best selling books. It is the first book to embed in the public imagination the heroics of 'The Few'.

£4.99 Paperback
25 illustrations
36 pages
978-1-4456-0048-2

Available from all good bookshops or to order direct
Please call **01285-760-030**
www.amberleybooks.com

Also available from Amberley Publishing

'A poignant and evocative account of what it felt like to be a young fighter pilot in the Battle of Britain'
JULIA GREGSON, *bestselling author & daughter of Barry Sutton*

Fighter Boy

Life as a Battle of Britain Pilot

BARRY SUTTON

The Battle of Britain memoir of Hurricane pilot Barry Sutton, DFC

At 23 years of age, Barry Sutton had experienced more than the average person experiences in a lifetime. This book, based on a diary he kept during the war, covers September 1939 to September 1940 when he was shot down and badly burned.

£20 Hardback
20 illustrations
224 pages
978-1-84868-849-0

Available from all good bookshops or to order direct
Please call **01285-760-030**
www.amberleybooks.com

Also available from Amberley Publishing

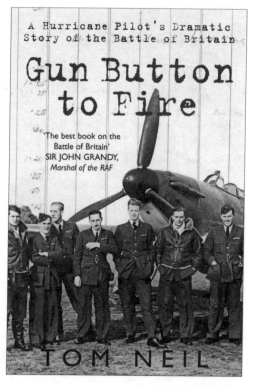

The amazing story of one of the 'Few', fighter ace Tom Neil who shot down 13 enemy aircraft during the Battle of Britain

'A thrilling new book... Tom Neil is one of the last surviving heroes who fought the Luftwaffe'
THE DAILY EXPRESS

'The best book on the Battle of Britain' SIR JOHN GRANDY, Marshal of the RAF

This is a fighter pilot's story of eight memorable months from May to December 1940. By the end of the year he had shot down 13 enemy aircraft, seen many of his friends killed, injured or burned, and was himself a wary and accomplished fighter pilot.

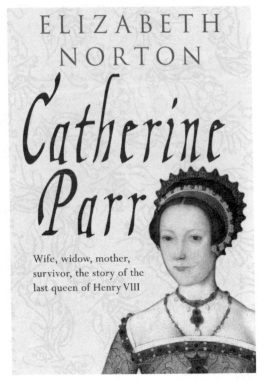

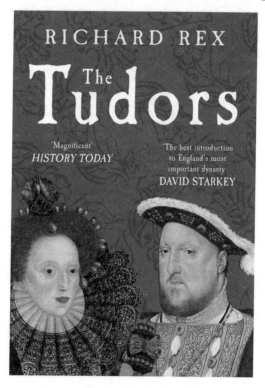

Also available from Amberley Publishing

'Impeccably researched and highly original... David Baldwin is a brilliant historical detective'
PHILIPPA GREGORY

ROBIN HOOD

DAVID BALDWIN

The English Outlaw Unmasked

The identity of Robin Hood is one of the great historical mysteries of English history – until now

'Impeccably researched and highly original... David Baldwin is a brilliant historical detective'
PHILIPPA GREGORY

David Baldwin sets out to find the real Robin Hood, looking for clues in the earliest ballads and in official and legal documents of the thirteenth and fourteenth centuries. His search takes him to the troubled reign of King Henry III, his conclusions turn history on it's head and David Baldwin reveals the name of the man who inspired the tales of Robin Hood.

£20 Hardback
40 illustrations (20 colour)
320 pages
978-1-84868-378-5

Available from all good bookshops or to order direct
Please call **01285-760-030**
www.amberleybooks.com

Also available from Amberley Publishing

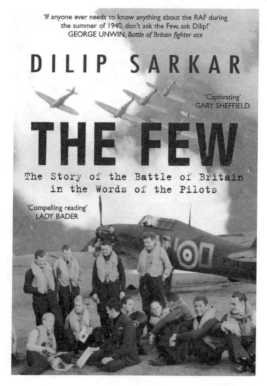

The history of the Battle of Britain in the words of the pilots

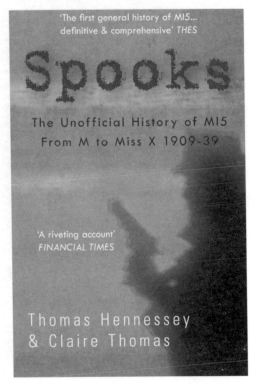

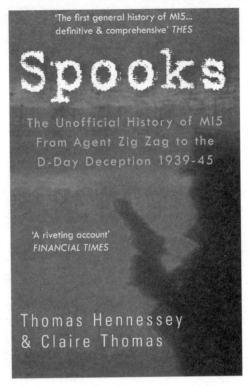

About the Authors

Thomas Hennessey is Reader in History at Canterbury Christ Church University. His other books include *A History of Northern Ireland, 1920-96*; *Dividing Ireland: World War One & Partition*; *The Evolution of the Troubles 1970-72*; *The Northern Ireland Peace Process: Ending the Troubles?* and *Northern Ireland: The Origins of the Troubles*. He lives in London and Canterbury.

Claire Thomas is a historian who specialises in the early years of the Cold War. She is currently working on a history of Britain's involvement in the Korean War. She lives in Folkestone.